F Minus

THIS CAN'T BE LEGAL

F Minus

THIS CAN'T BE LEGAL

BY TONY CARRILLO

**Andrews McMeel
Publishing, LLC**

Kansas City

F Minus is distributed internationally by United Feature Syndicate, Inc.

 For information, write Andrews McMeel Publishing, LLC, an Andrews McMeel Universal company, 1130 Walnut Street, Kansas City, Missouri 64106.

09 10 11 12 13 WKT 10 9 8 7 6 5 4 3 2 1

ISBN-13: 978-0-7407-8136-0
ISBN-10: 0-7407-8136-7

Library of Congress Control Number: 2008938041

www.andrewsmcmeel.com

To Lindsay. She gets all of them.

Introduction

In 1981, my wife Cindy and I became parents for the very first time with the birth of our son Tony. As new parents, we didn't realize how much our lives were about to change. We began to see the world differently. Our world, which until then had seemed relatively safe, was now fraught with peril. Although we remained safe, danger for our child was everywhere. This was especially true when our child became ambulatory. We had to protect him from falls, from poison, from chemicals, from burns, from bugs, from the little brat two doors down who used bad language, and always played with matches; it was endless.

In addition to all the potential physical dangers, we wanted to protect his tender, little psyche from all the ugliness in the world. Modern media is absolutely no help. All we see is story after story about war, crime, torture, disease, and pestilence, and that is just a single episode of *24*. It wasn't like that growing up in the 50s and 60s. Television watched out for us. We had *Leave It to Beaver* and *My Three Sons*. As for sex, married couples on television slept in separate beds. Even when we watched nature shows about predators and prey, the camera always tastefully cut away just before "the kill."

Television in the 80s offered no such protection. We watched as the shark violently ripped the flesh from the unsuspecting seal. We saw the terror in the eyes of the baby wildebeest as a pride of lions ate it alive. We were spared nothing.

I was quite naturally concerned when I walked into our living room one Saturday afternoon and found three-year-old Tony totally engrossed in one of these nature shows.

On the screen, I could see a large predatory cat slowly creeping toward an unsuspecting gazelle. I wanted to try to distract Tony, but just as I opened my mouth to speak, the gazelle spotted the big cat and the chase was on. Both animals sprinted with amazing speed and agility, but it was clear that the cat was gaining on its prey. Tony watched unblinkingly as the chase unfolded. Just as the cat was about to make its final lunge, the gazelle made one last desperate cut across a small shallow stream. Although the water was not deep, it slowed the predator just enough to allow the gazelle to widen the gap and ultimately make good his escape. The frustrated cat broke off the chase and walked slowly in the opposite direction.

Tony glanced up at me, then looked back at the screen and asked, "Did he get away?"

"Yes," I was relieved to say.

Tony pointed at the cat as it walked away and said, "So he's not going to eat him?"

"No," I replied, "he's not."

Tony was quiet for a while then said hopefully, "Well . . . maybe he can find another one."

It is from that mind, a mind that sees the world not as most of us do, but with a twist, that now gives rise to my favorite comic strip: *F Minus*.

Andy Carrillo

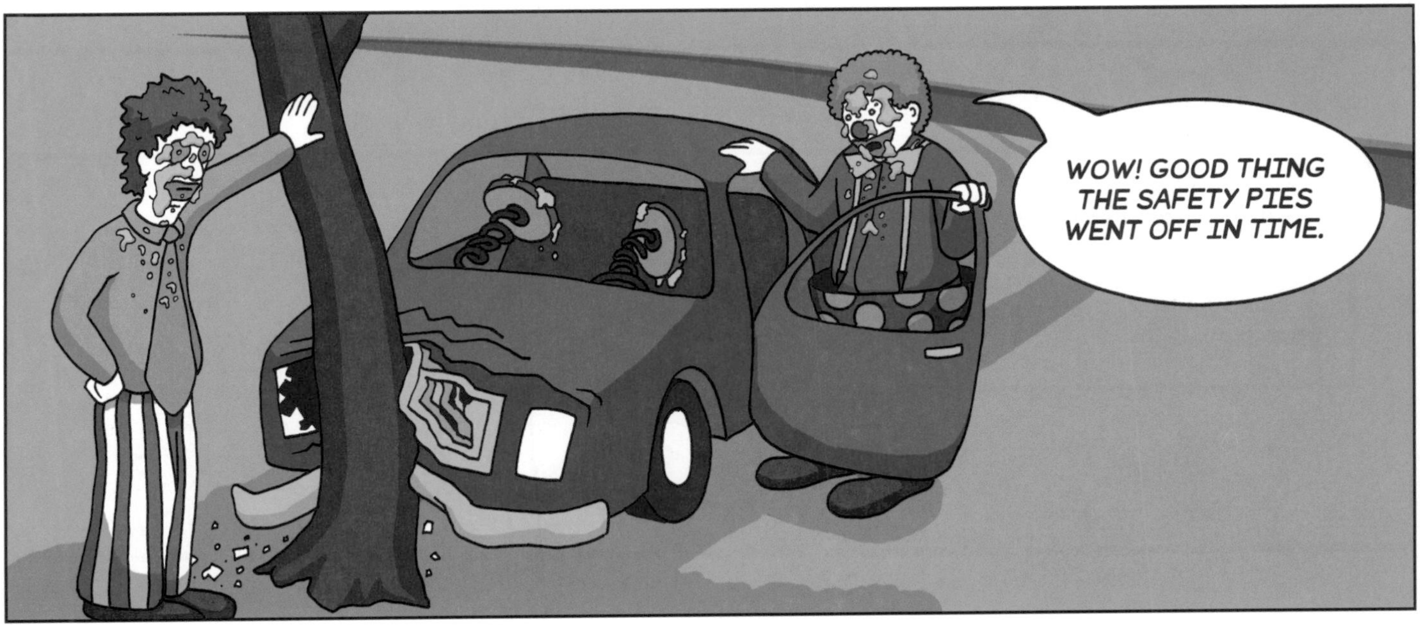
WOW! GOOD THING THE SAFETY PIES WENT OFF IN TIME.

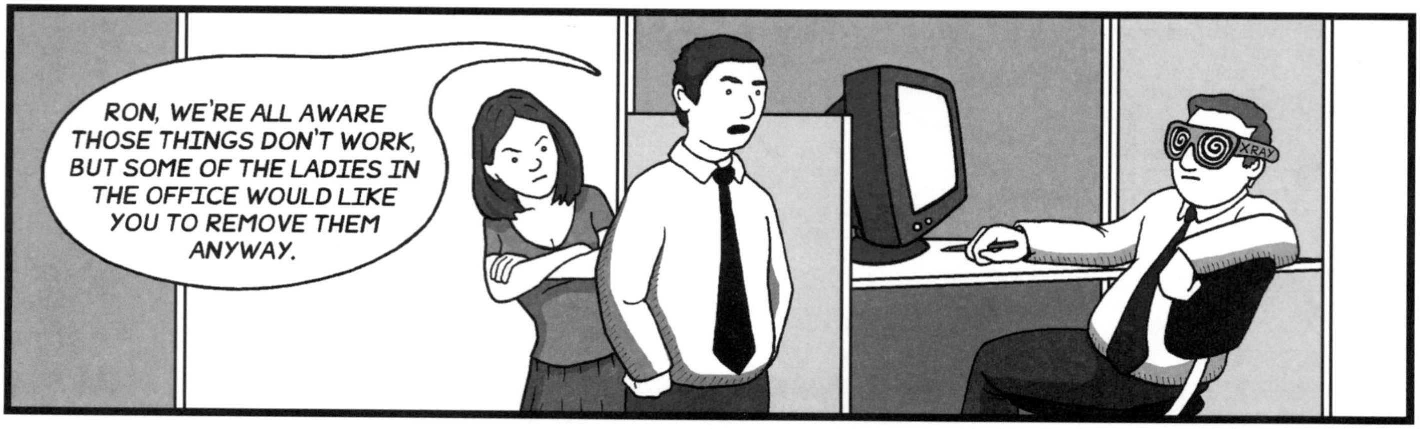
RON, WE'RE ALL AWARE THOSE THINGS DON'T WORK, BUT SOME OF THE LADIES IN THE OFFICE WOULD LIKE YOU TO REMOVE THEM ANYWAY.
XRAY

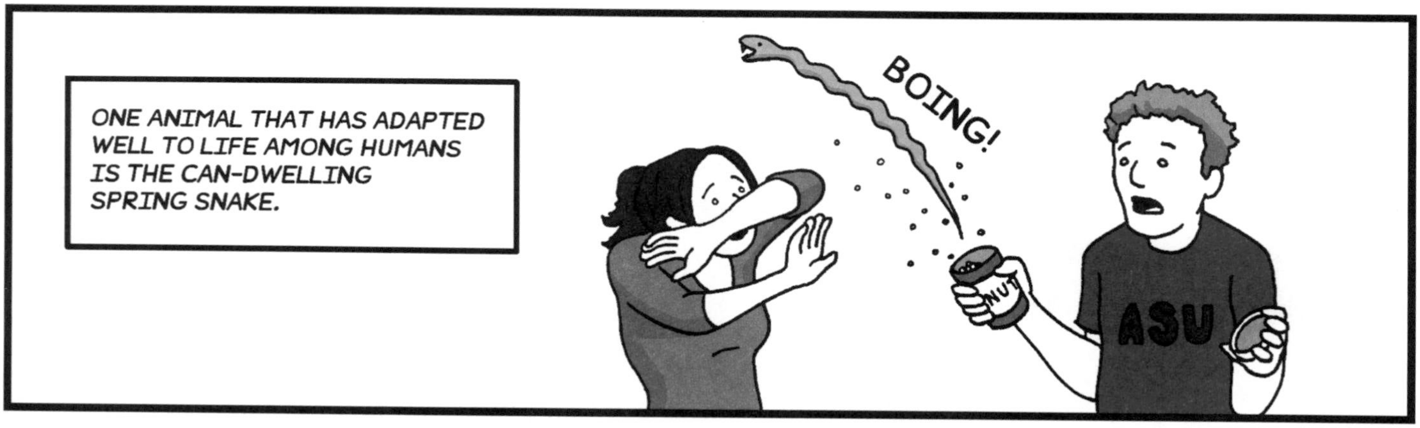
ONE ANIMAL THAT HAS ADAPTED WELL TO LIFE AMONG HUMANS IS THE CAN-DWELLING SPRING SNAKE.
BOING!
NUT
ASU

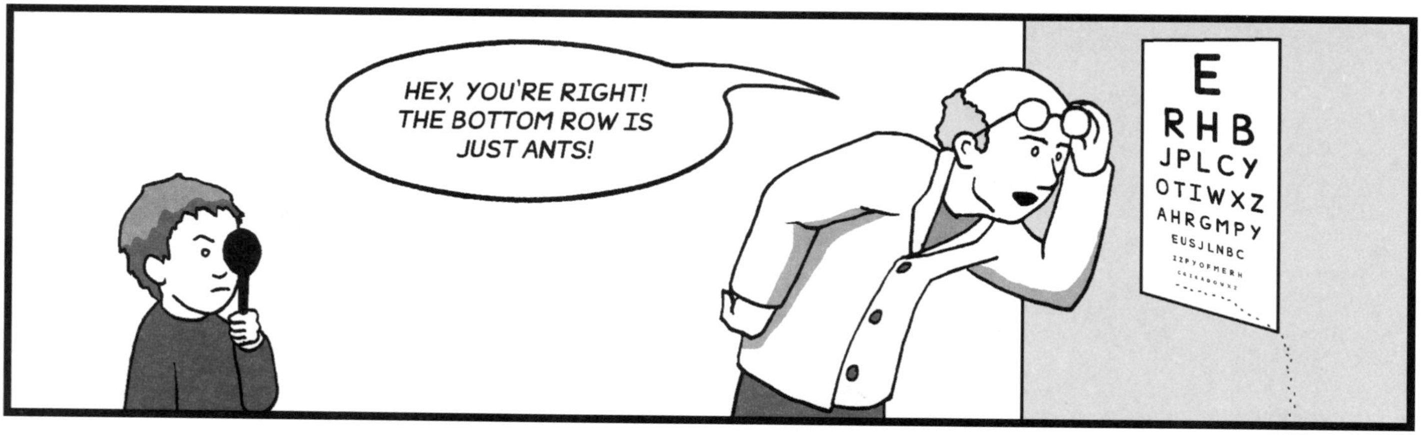
HEY, YOU'RE RIGHT! THE BOTTOM ROW IS JUST ANTS!
E
RHB
JPLCY
OTIWXZ
AHRGMPY
EUSJLNBC

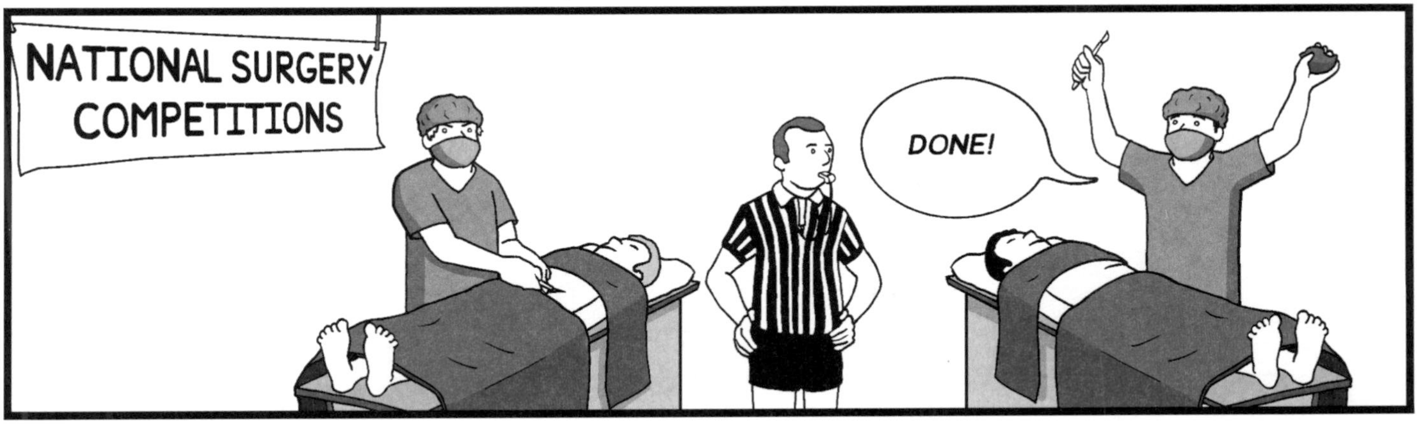
NATIONAL SURGERY COMPETITIONS
DONE!

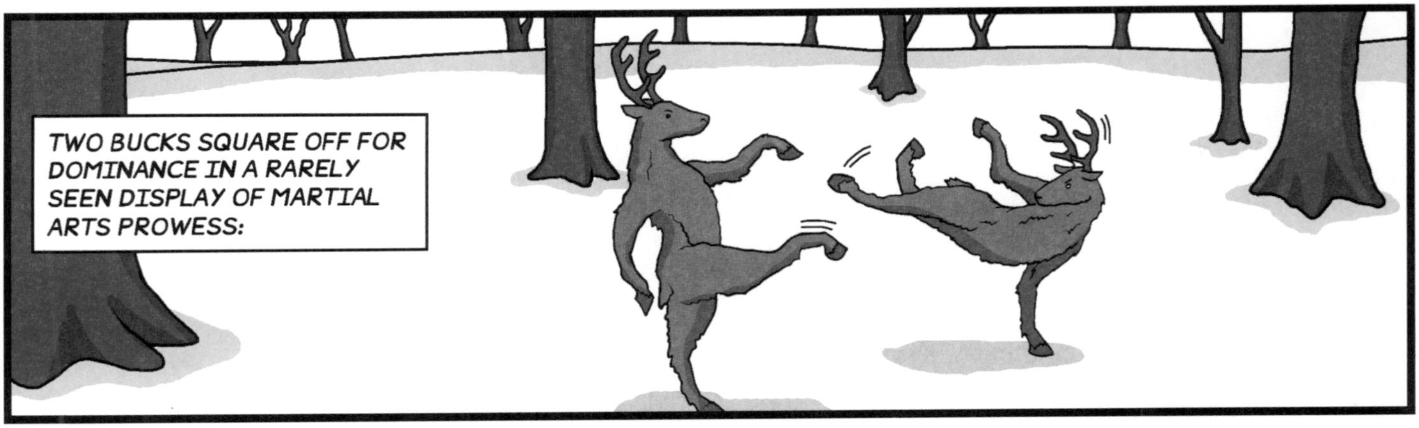
TWO BUCKS SQUARE OFF FOR DOMINANCE IN A RARELY SEEN DISPLAY OF MARTIAL ARTS PROWESS:

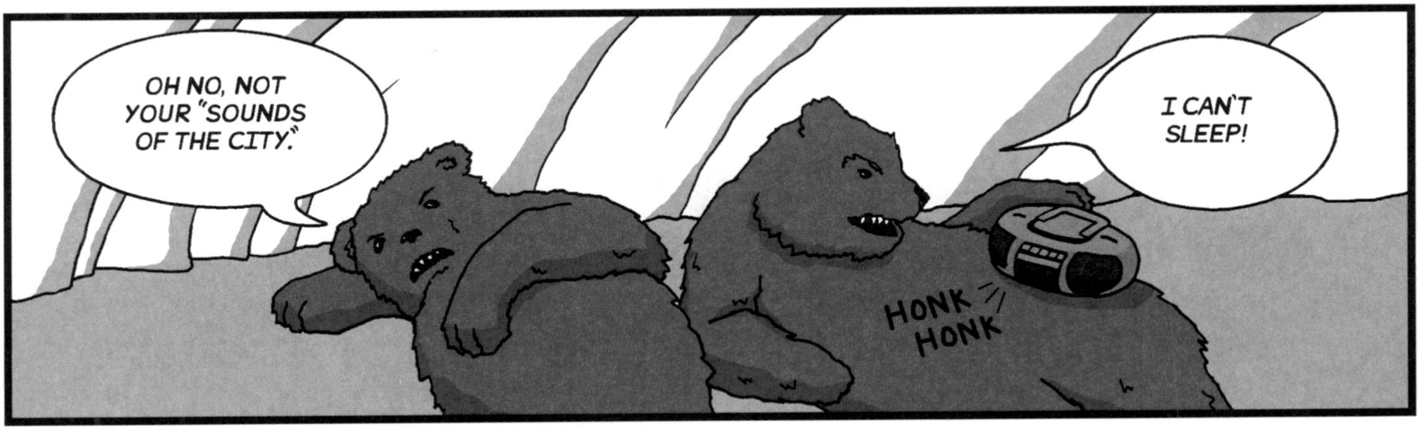
OH NO, NOT YOUR "SOUNDS OF THE CITY."
I CAN'T SLEEP!
HONK HONK

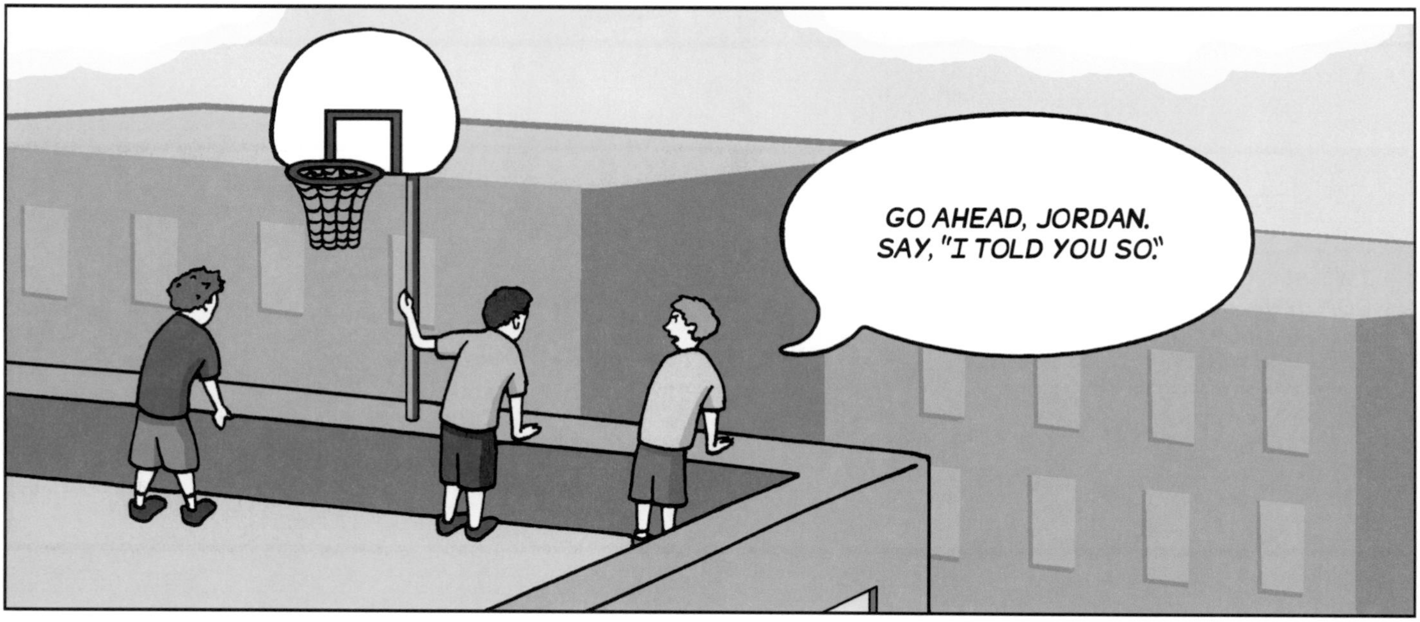
GO AHEAD, JORDAN.
SAY, "I TOLD YOU SO."

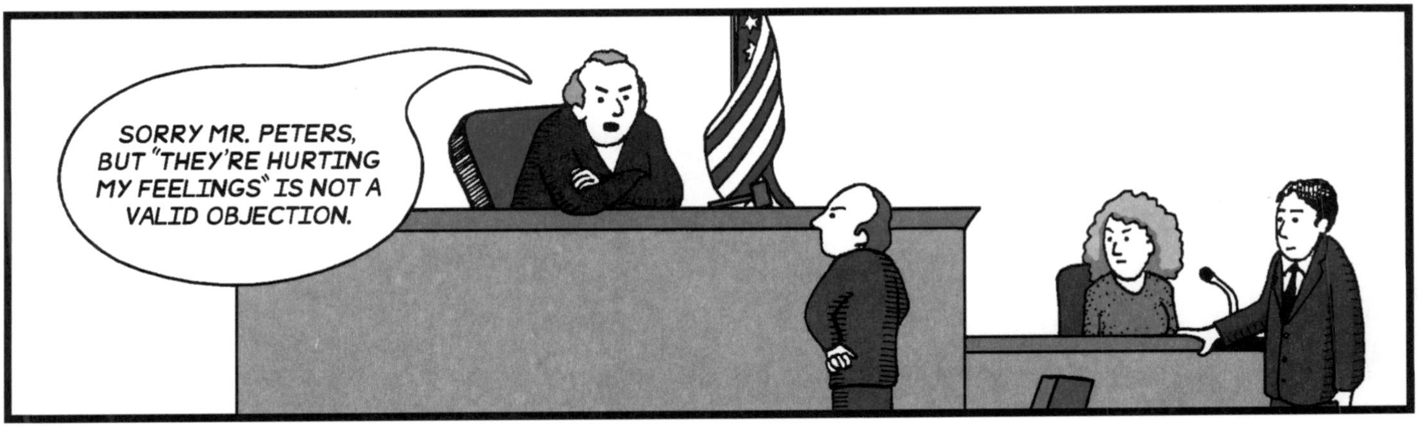
SORRY MR. PETERS, BUT "THEY'RE HURTING MY FEELINGS" IS NOT A VALID OBJECTION.

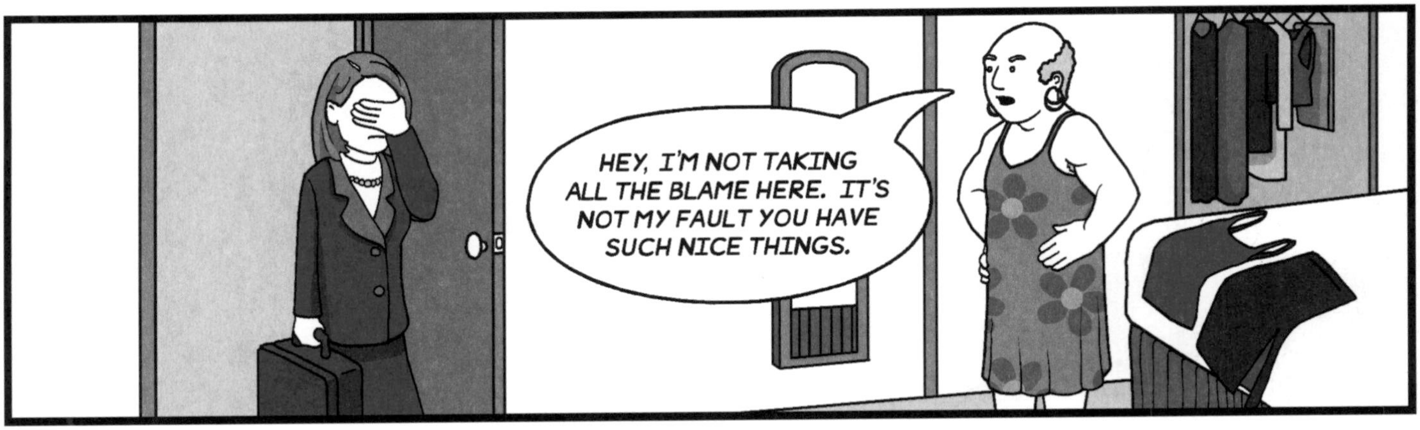
HEY, I'M NOT TAKING ALL THE BLAME HERE. IT'S NOT MY FAULT YOU HAVE SUCH NICE THINGS.

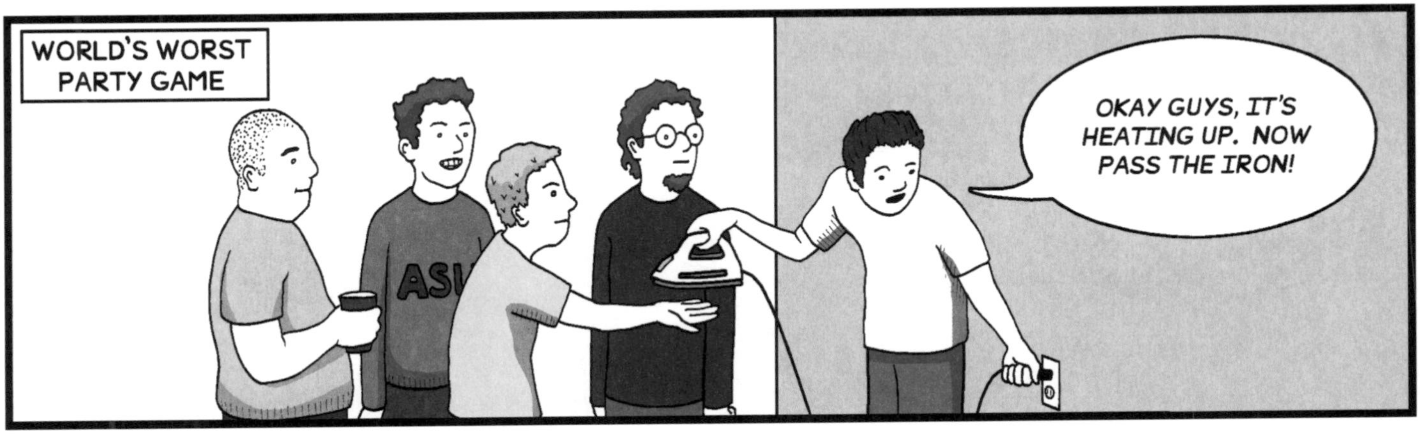
WORLD'S WORST PARTY GAME
OKAY GUYS, IT'S HEATING UP. NOW PASS THE IRON!
ASU

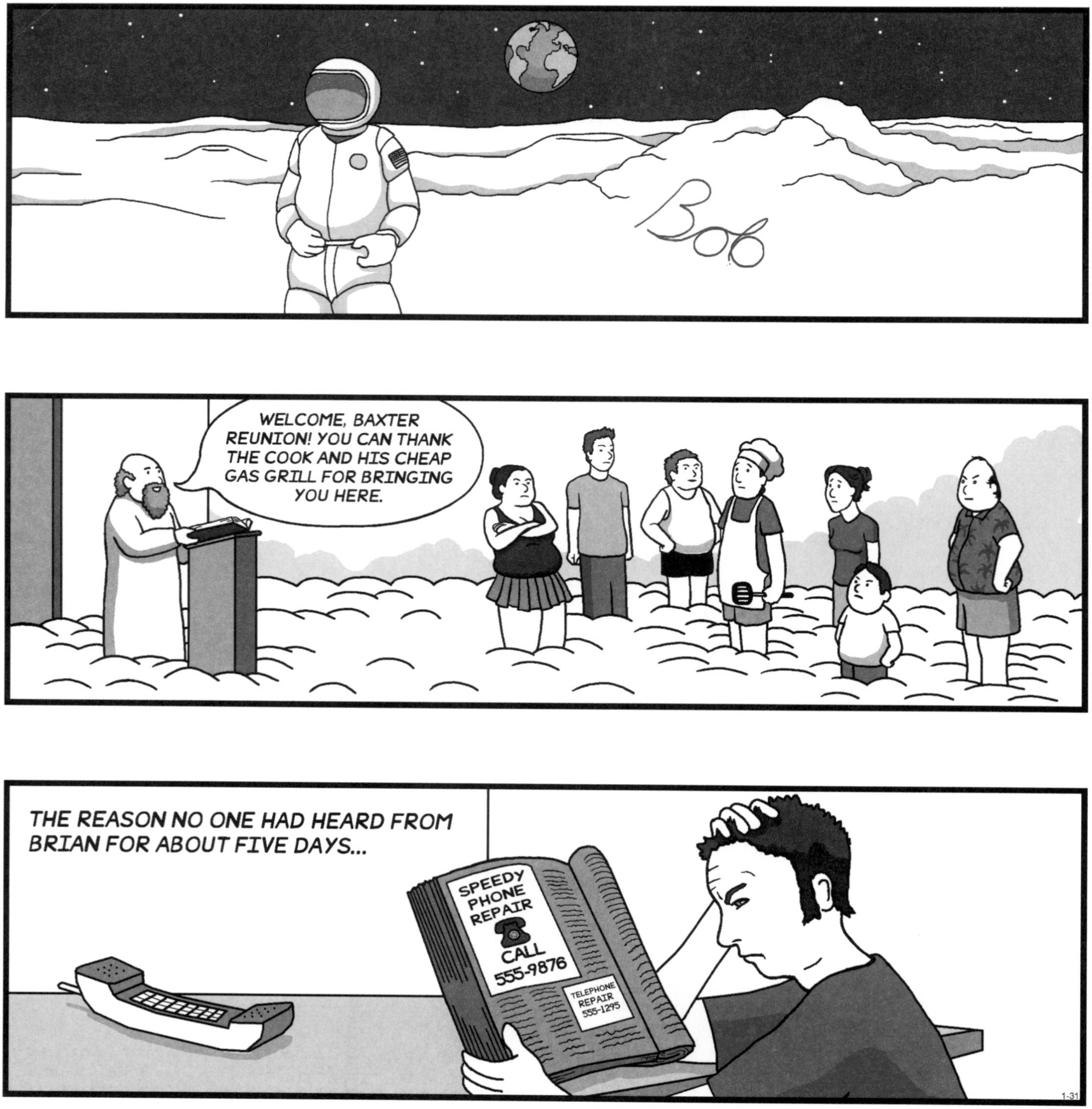
Bob
WELCOME, BAXTER REUNION! YOU CAN THANK THE COOK AND HIS CHEAP GAS GRILL FOR BRINGING YOU HERE.
THE REASON NO ONE HAD HEARD FROM BRIAN FOR ABOUT FIVE DAYS...
SPEEDY PHONE REPAIR
CALL 555-9876
TELEPHONE REPAIR 555-1295
1-31

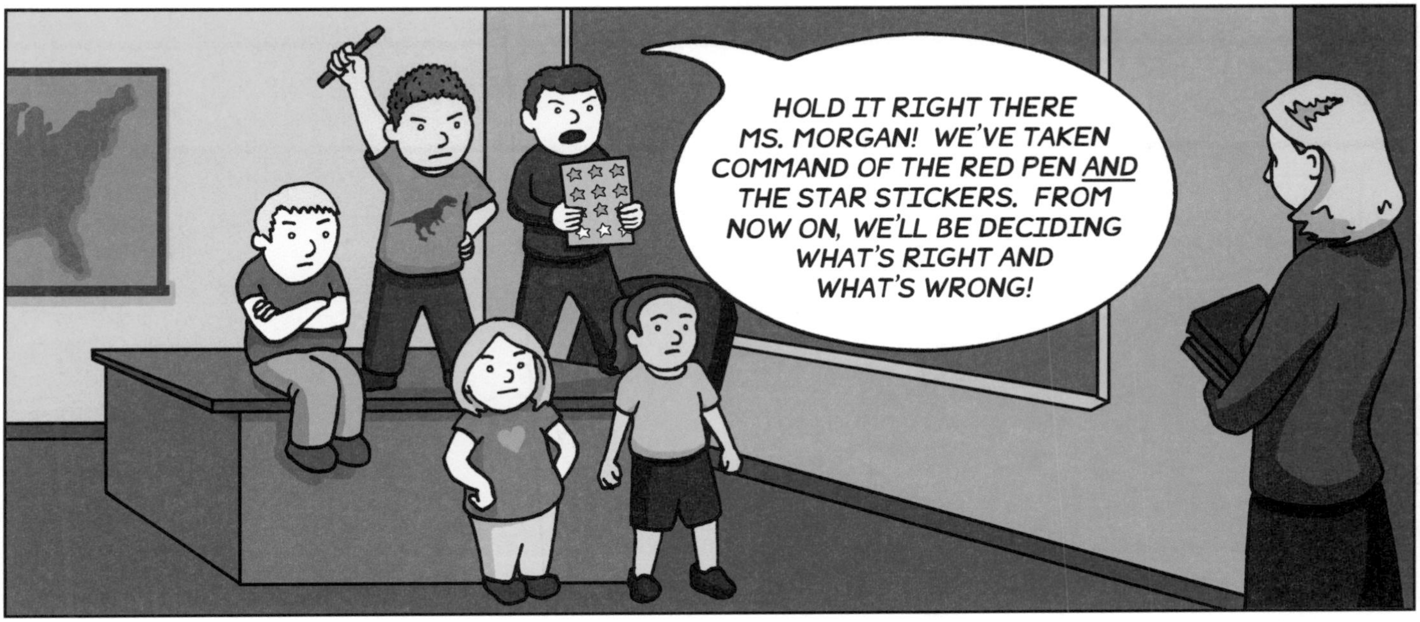
HOLD IT RIGHT THERE MS. MORGAN! WE'VE TAKEN COMMAND OF THE RED PEN AND THE STAR STICKERS. FROM NOW ON, WE'LL BE DECIDING WHAT'S RIGHT AND WHAT'S WRONG!

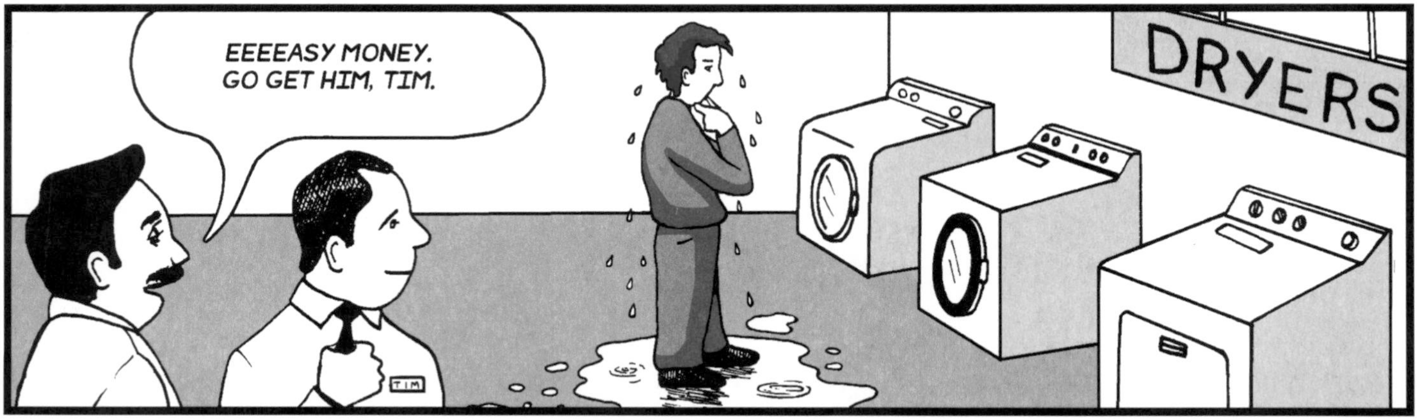
EEEEASY MONEY.
GO GET HIM, TIM.
DRYERS
TIM

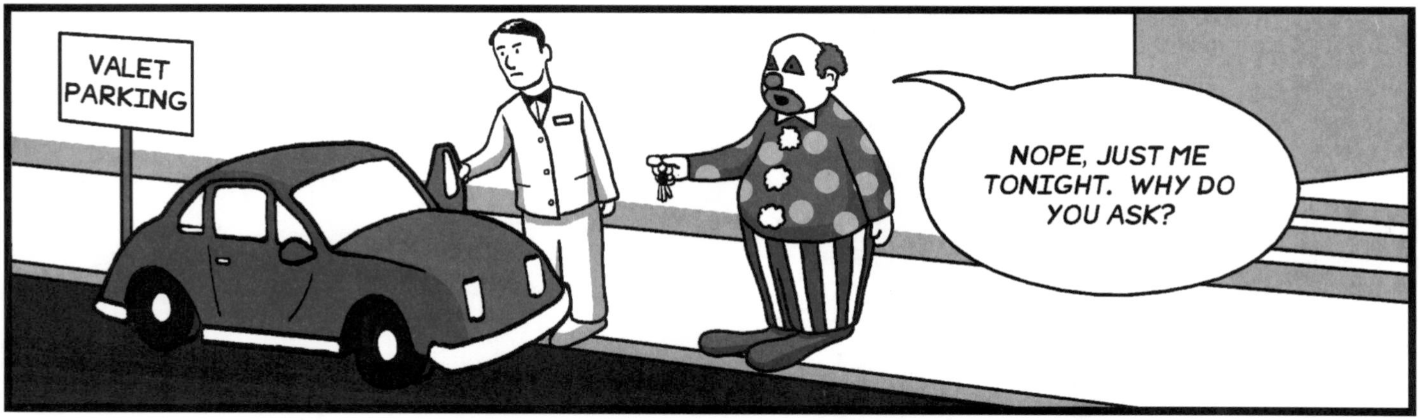
VALET
PARKING
NOPE, JUST ME TONIGHT. WHY DO YOU ASK?

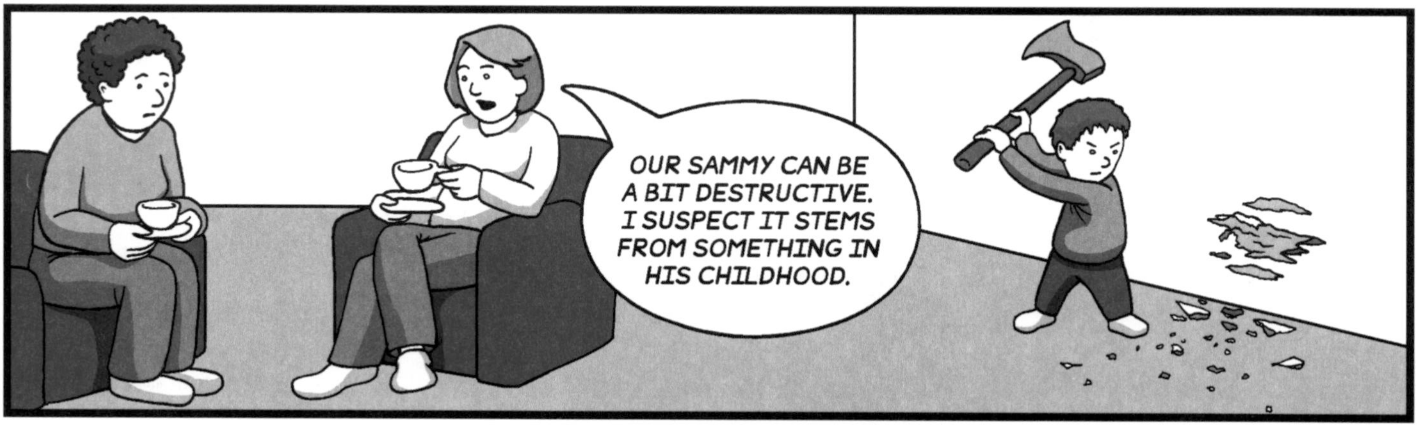
OUR SAMMY CAN BE A BIT DESTRUCTIVE. I SUSPECT IT STEMS FROM SOMETHING IN HIS CHILDHOOD.

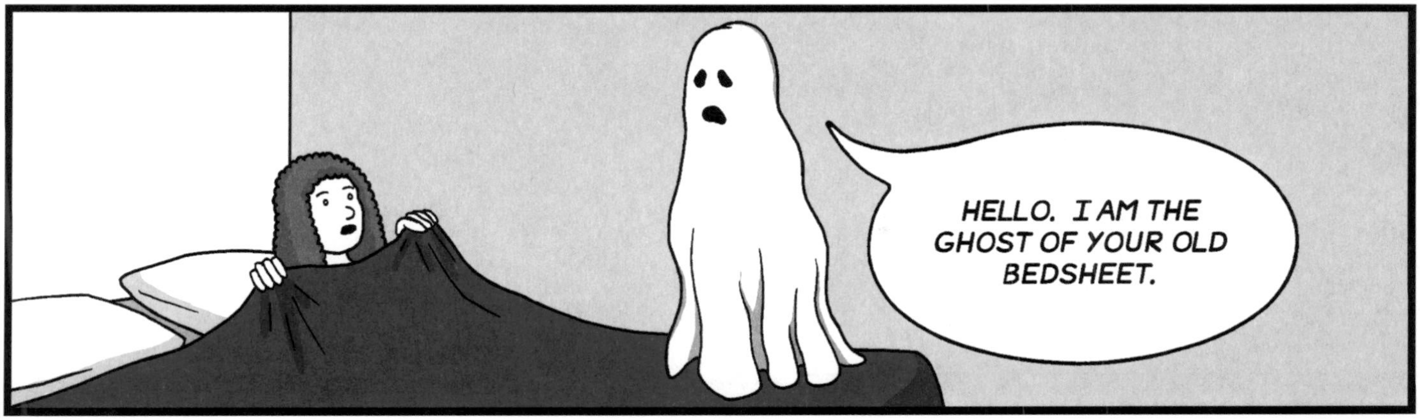
HELLO. I AM THE GHOST OF YOUR OLD BEDSHEET.

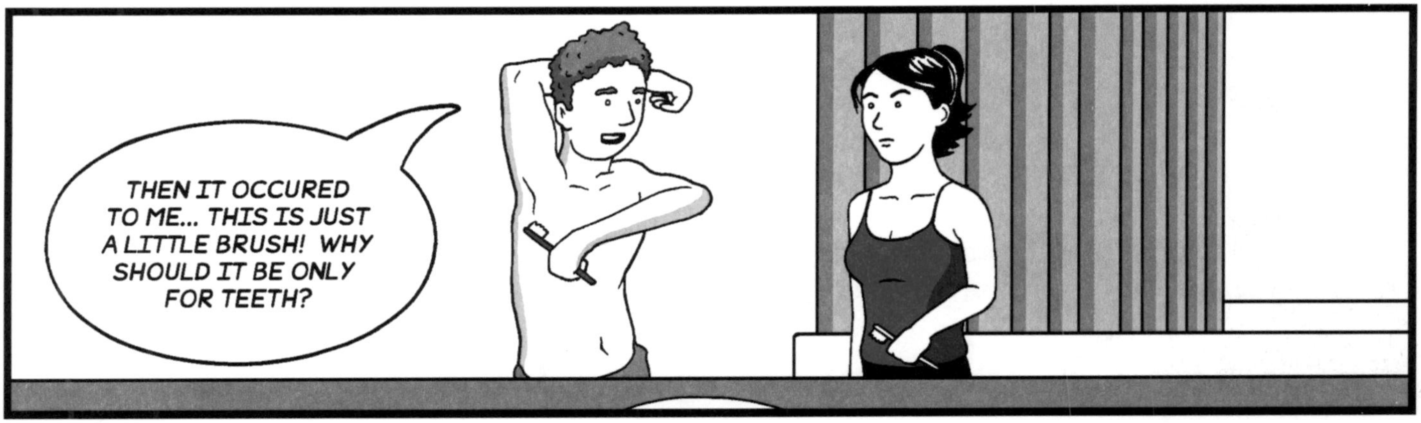
THEN IT OCCURED TO ME... THIS IS JUST A LITTLE BRUSH! WHY SHOULD IT BE ONLY FOR TEETH?

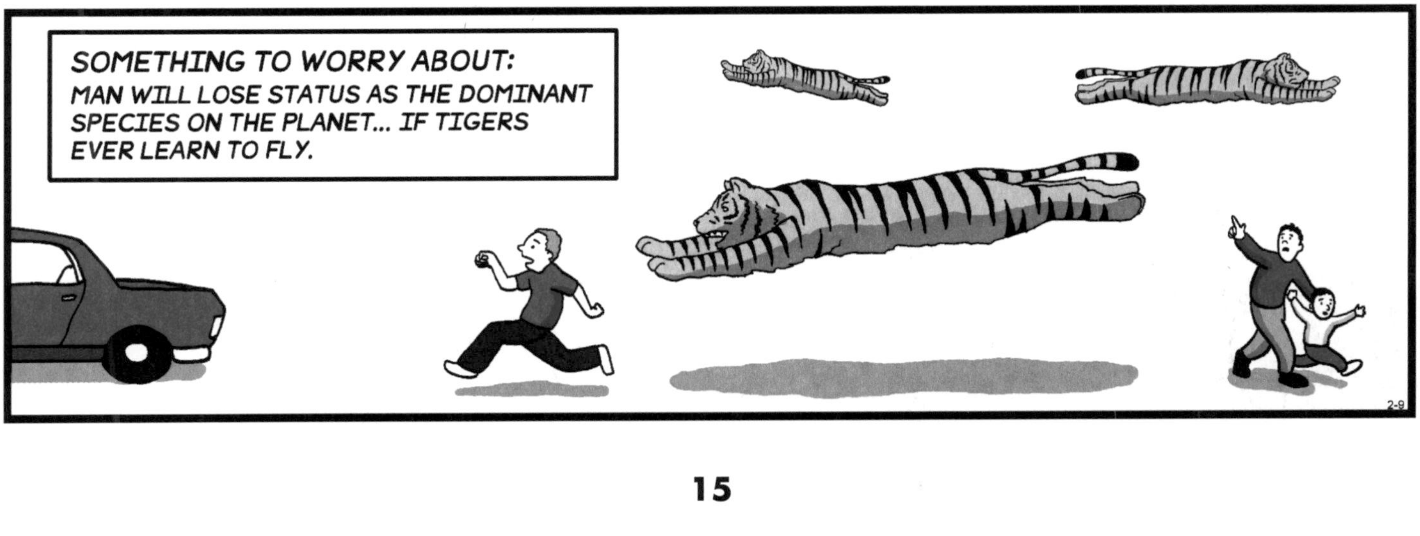
SOMETHING TO WORRY ABOUT:
MAN WILL LOSE STATUS AS THE DOMINANT SPECIES ON THE PLANET... IF TIGERS EVER LEARN TO FLY.

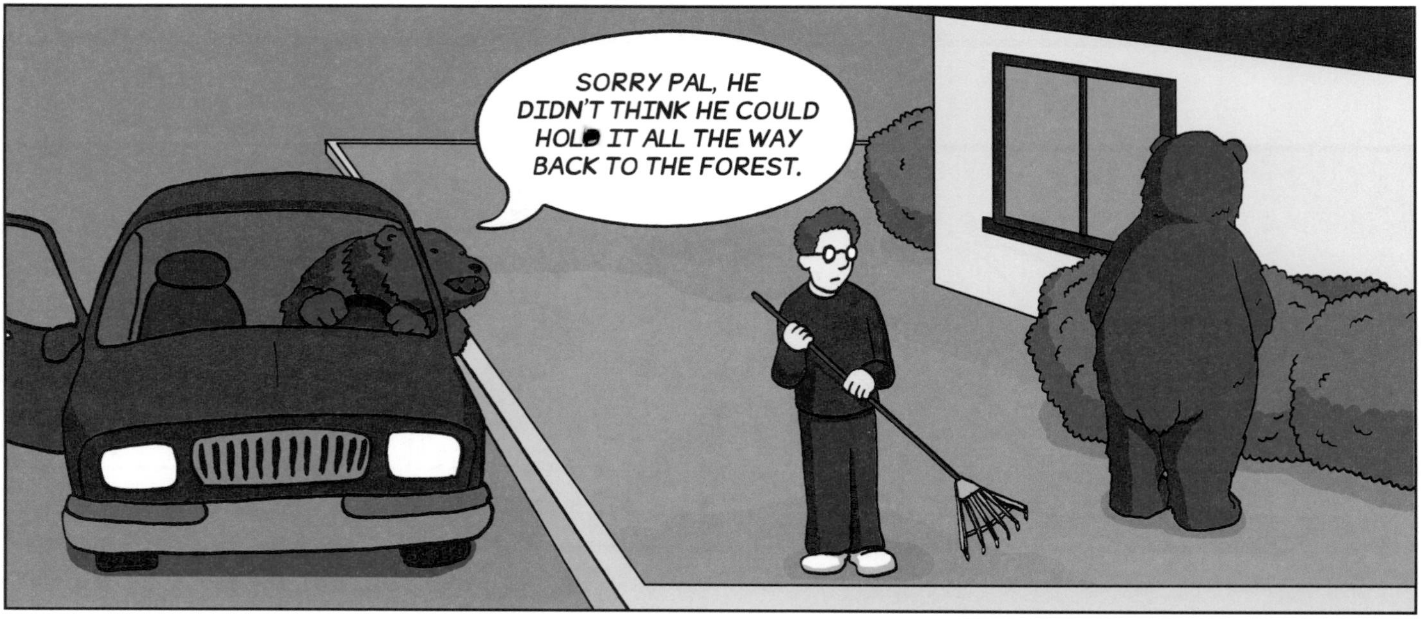
SORRY PAL, HE DIDN'T THINK HE COULD HOLD IT ALL THE WAY BACK TO THE FOREST.

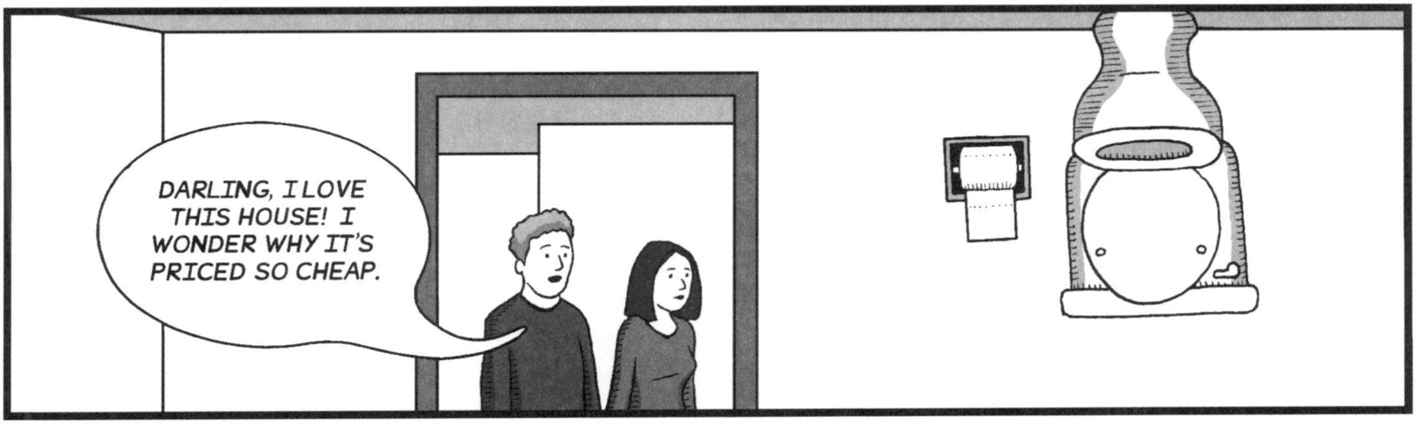
DARLING, I LOVE THIS HOUSE! I WONDER WHY IT'S PRICED SO CHEAP.

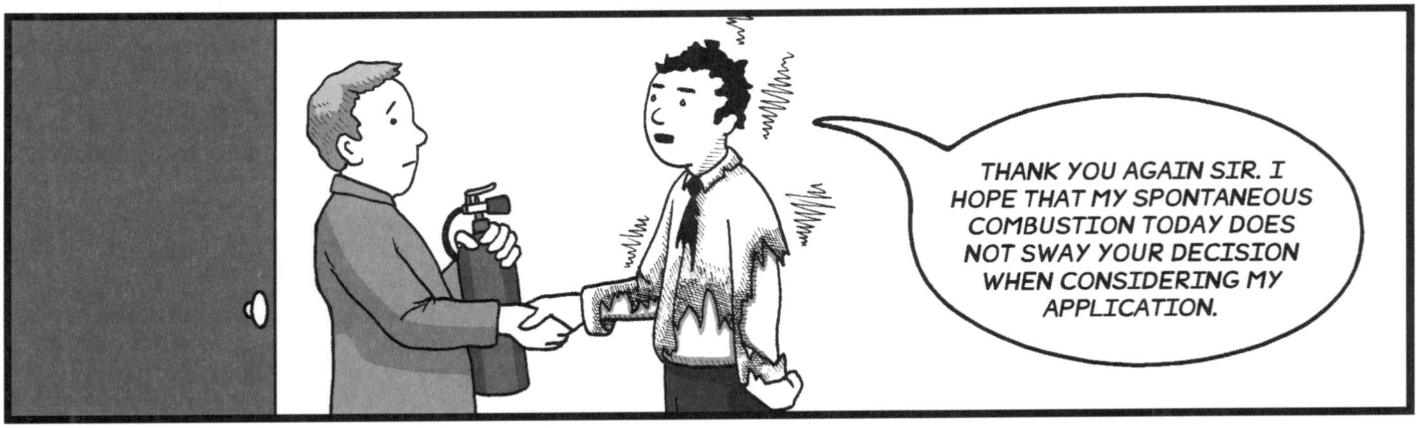
THANK YOU AGAIN SIR. I HOPE THAT MY SPONTANEOUS COMBUSTION TODAY DOES NOT SWAY YOUR DECISION WHEN CONSIDERING MY APPLICATION.

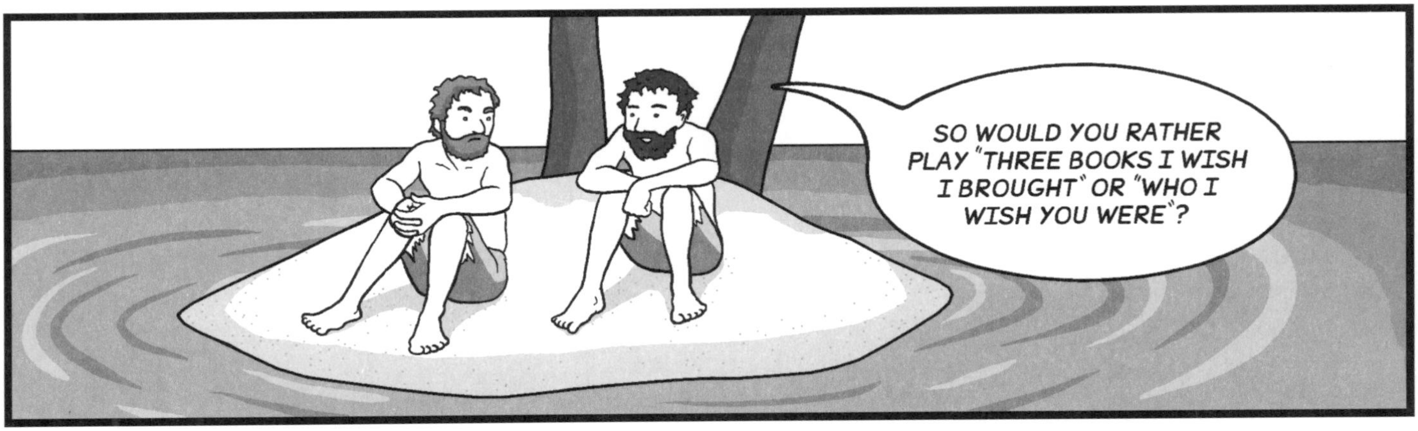
SO WOULD YOU RATHER PLAY "THREE BOOKS I WISH I BROUGHT" OR "WHO I WISH YOU WERE"?

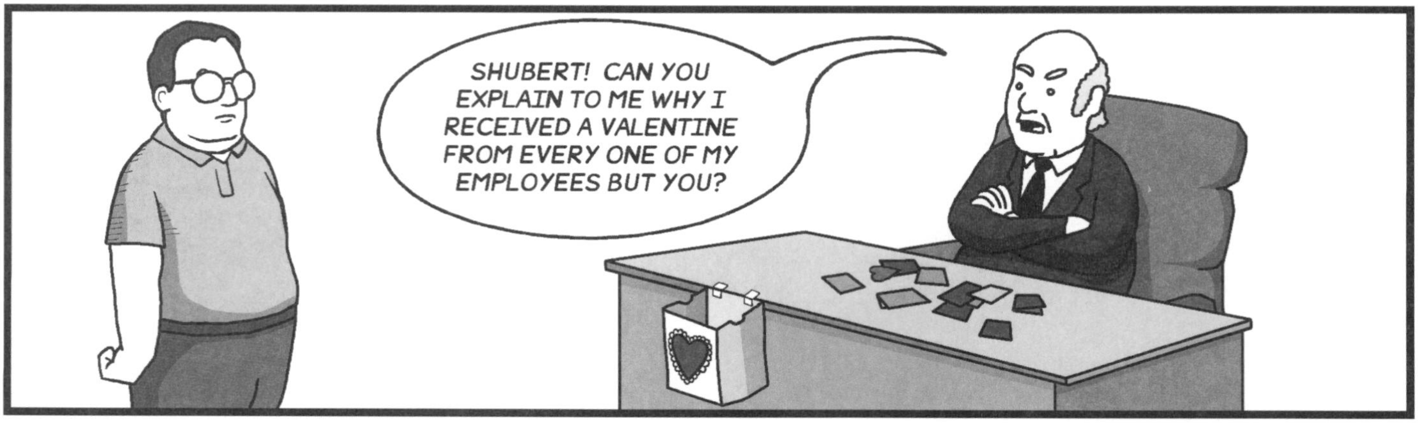
SHUBERT! CAN YOU EXPLAIN TO ME WHY I RECEIVED A VALENTINE FROM EVERY ONE OF MY EMPLOYEES BUT YOU?

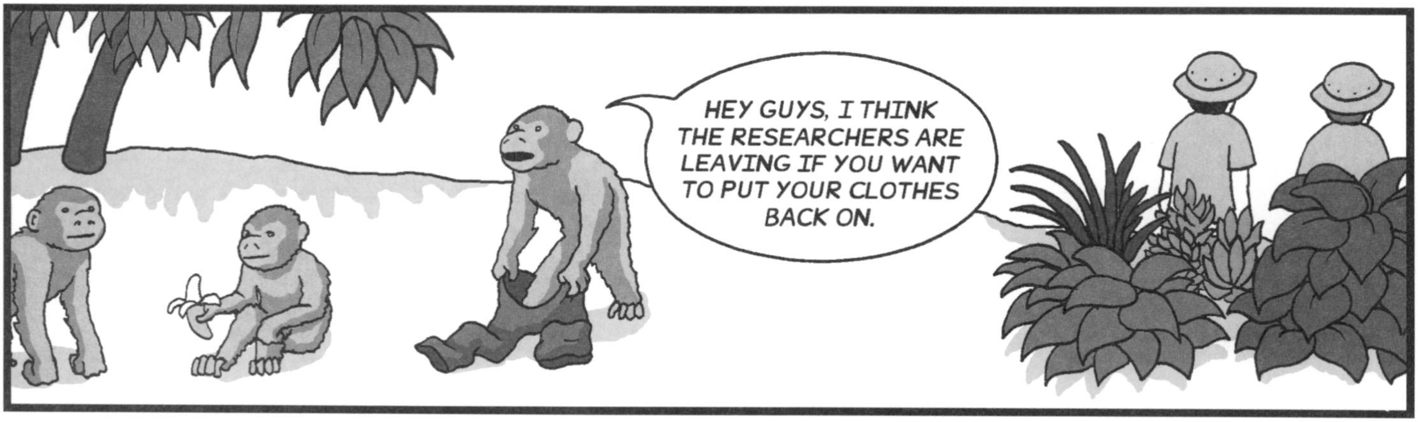
HEY GUYS, I THINK THE RESEARCHERS ARE LEAVING IF YOU WANT TO PUT YOUR CLOTHES BACK ON.

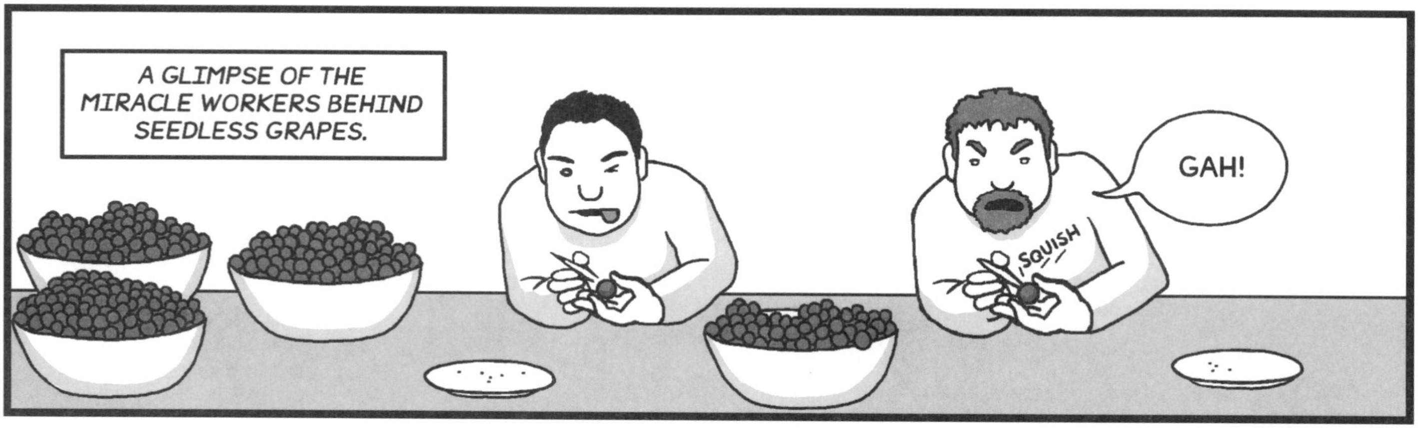
A GLIMPSE OF THE MIRACLE WORKERS BEHIND SEEDLESS GRAPES.
SQUISH
GAH!

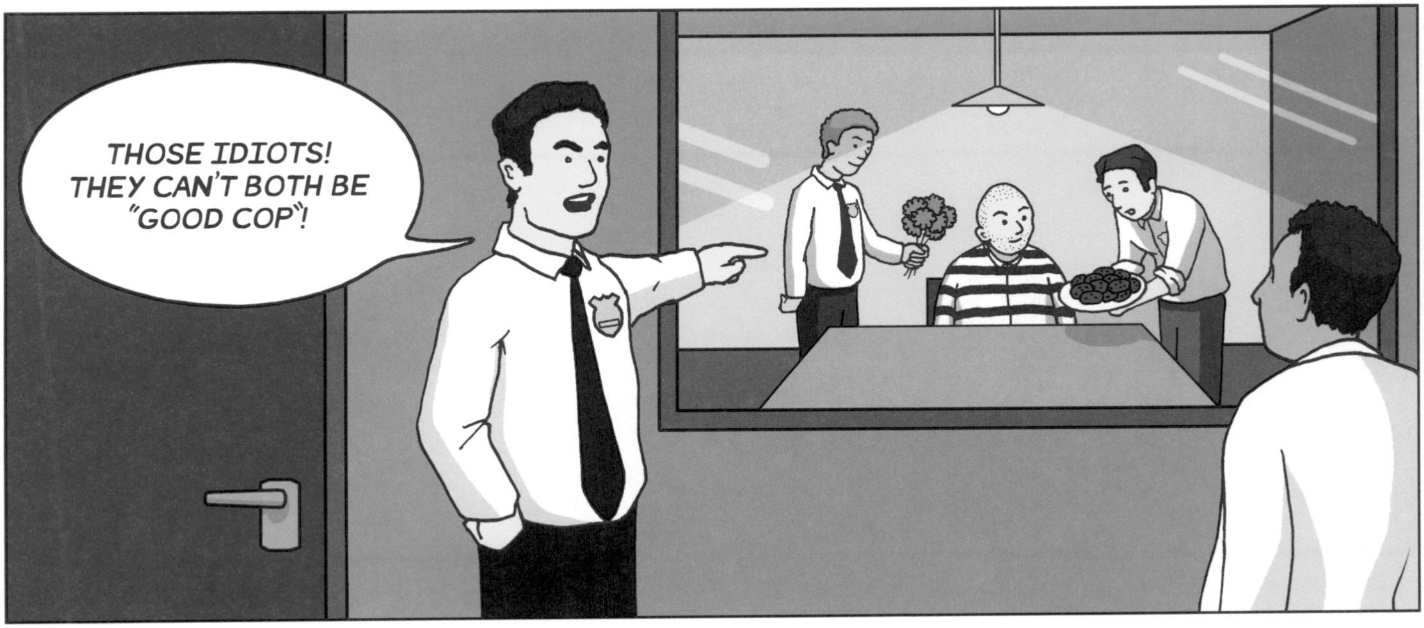
THOSE IDIOTS! THEY CAN'T BOTH BE "GOOD COP"!

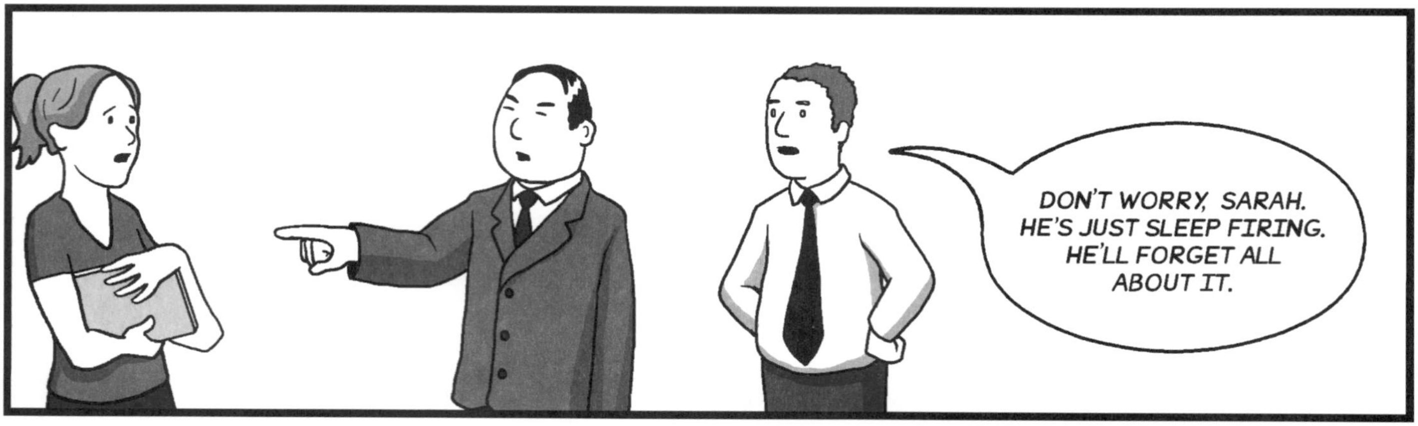
DON'T WORRY, SARAH. HE'S JUST SLEEP FIRING. HE'LL FORGET ALL ABOUT IT.

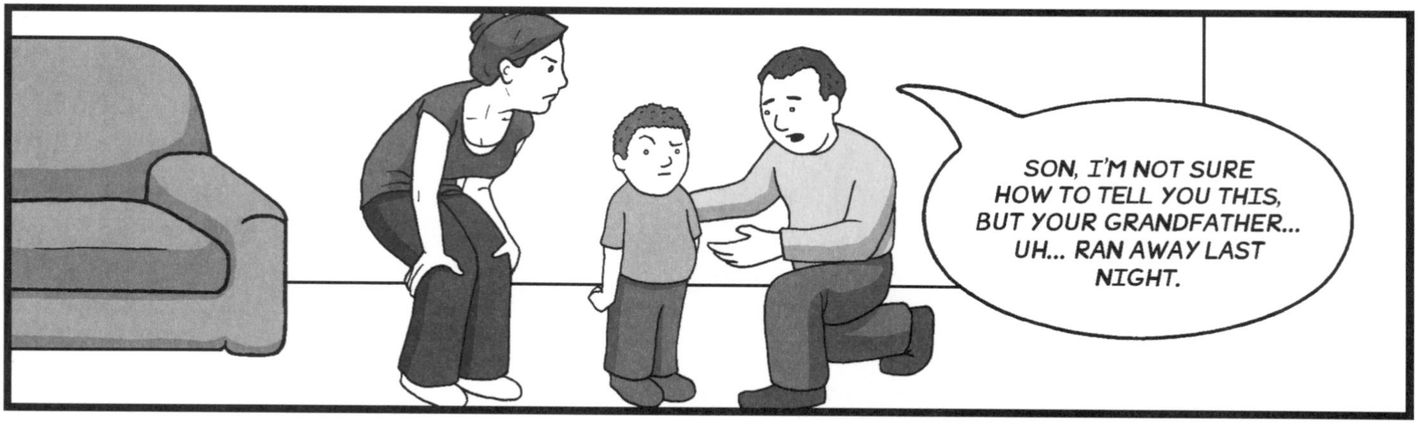
SON, I'M NOT SURE HOW TO TELL YOU THIS, BUT YOUR GRANDFATHER... UH... RAN AWAY LAST NIGHT.

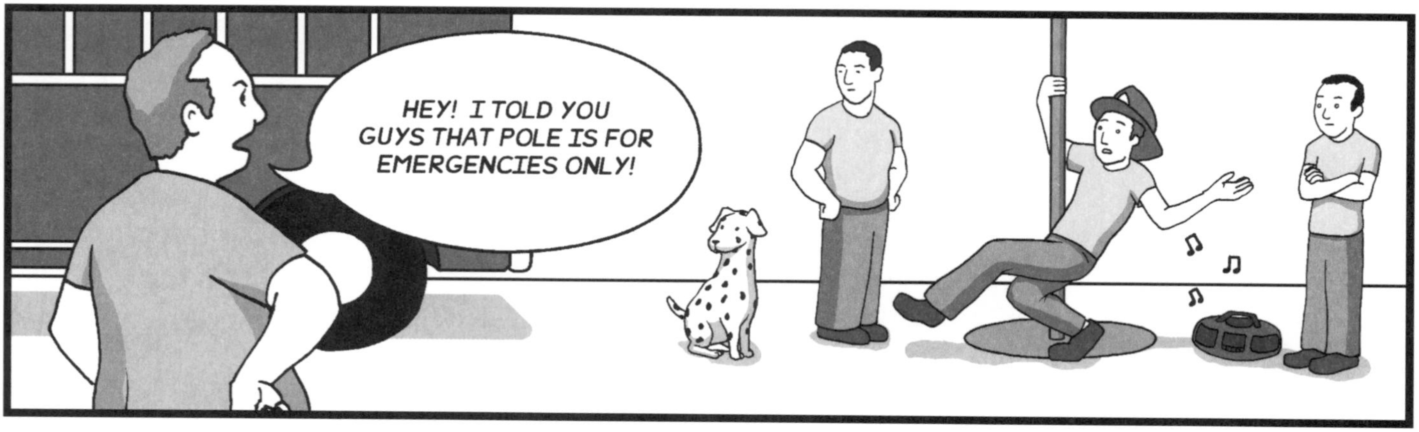
HEY! I TOLD YOU GUYS THAT POLE IS FOR EMERGENCIES ONLY!

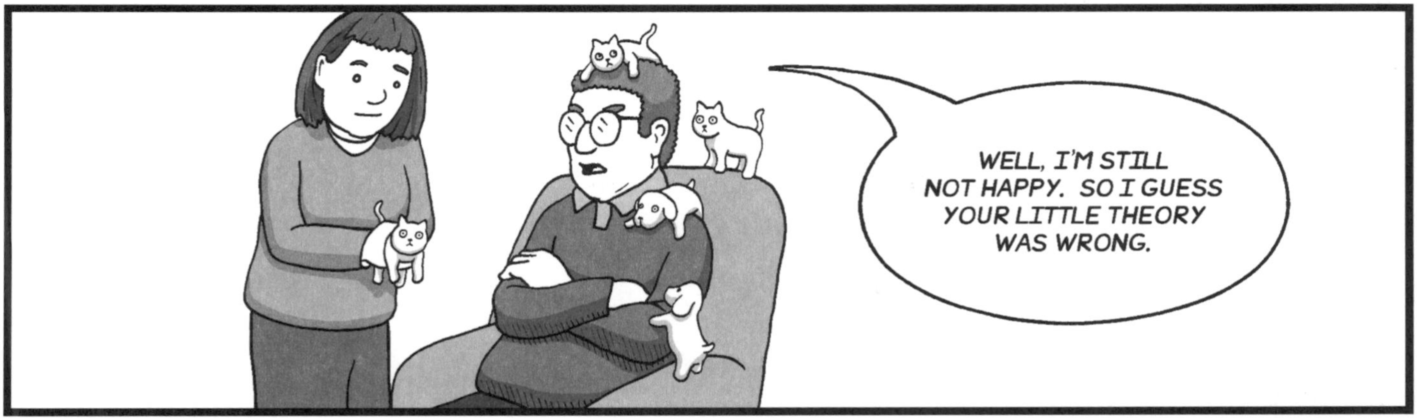
WELL, I'M STILL NOT HAPPY. SO I GUESS YOUR LITTLE THEORY WAS WRONG.

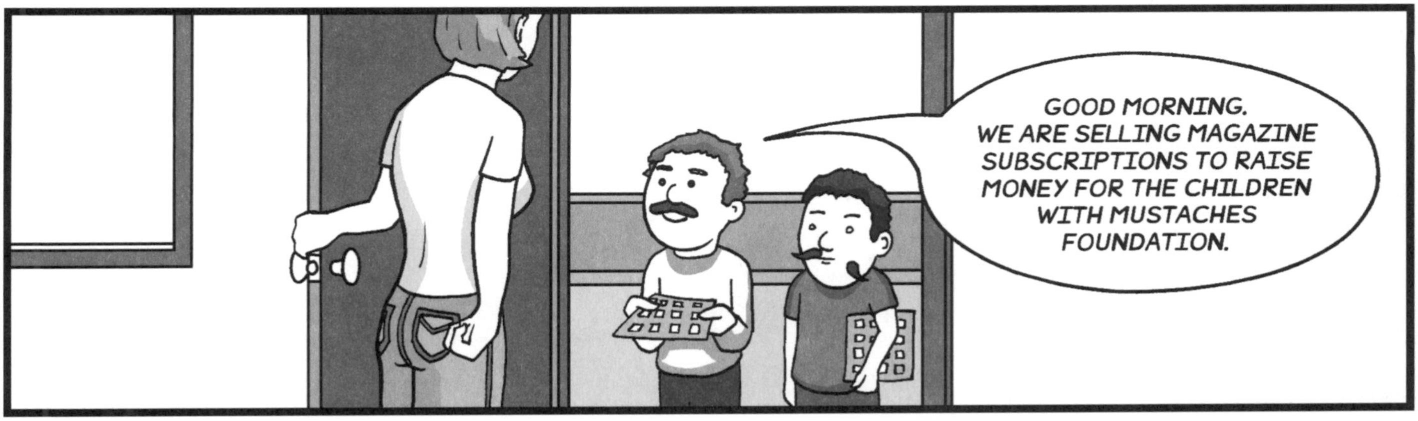
GOOD MORNING. WE ARE SELLING MAGAZINE SUBSCRIPTIONS TO RAISE MONEY FOR THE CHILDREN WITH MUSTACHES FOUNDATION.

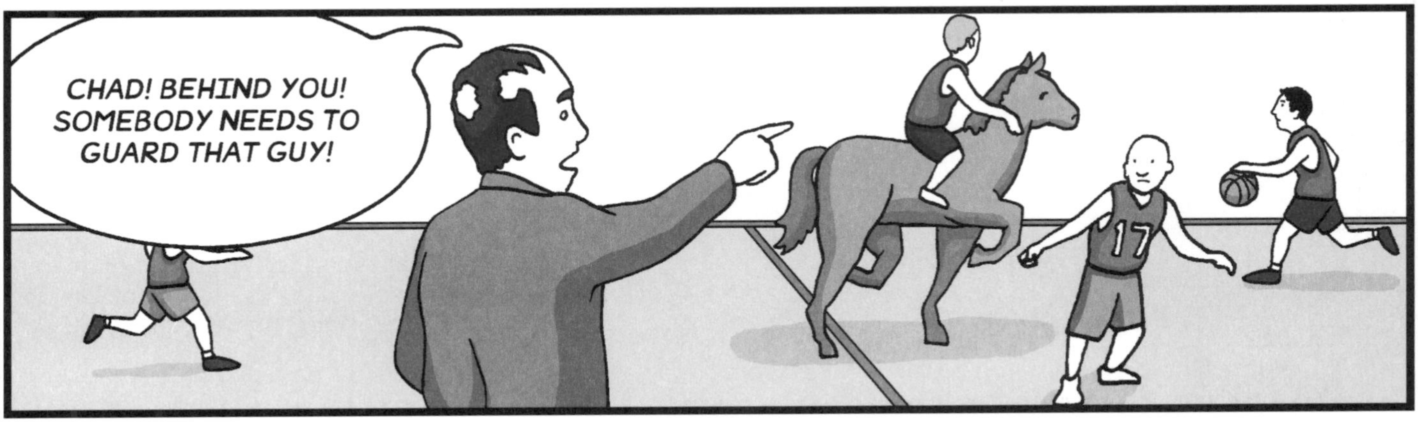
CHAD! BEHIND YOU! SOMEBODY NEEDS TO GUARD THAT GUY!
17

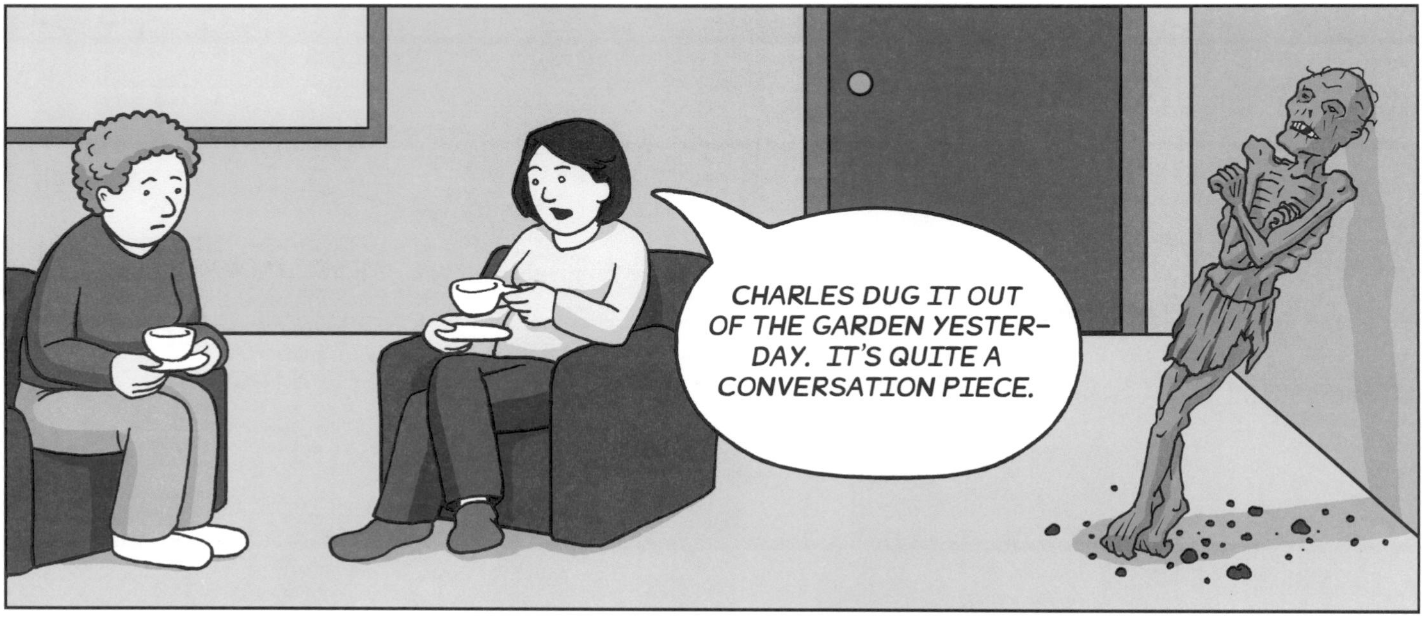
CHARLES DUG IT OUT OF THE GARDEN YESTER-DAY. IT'S QUITE A CONVERSATION PIECE.

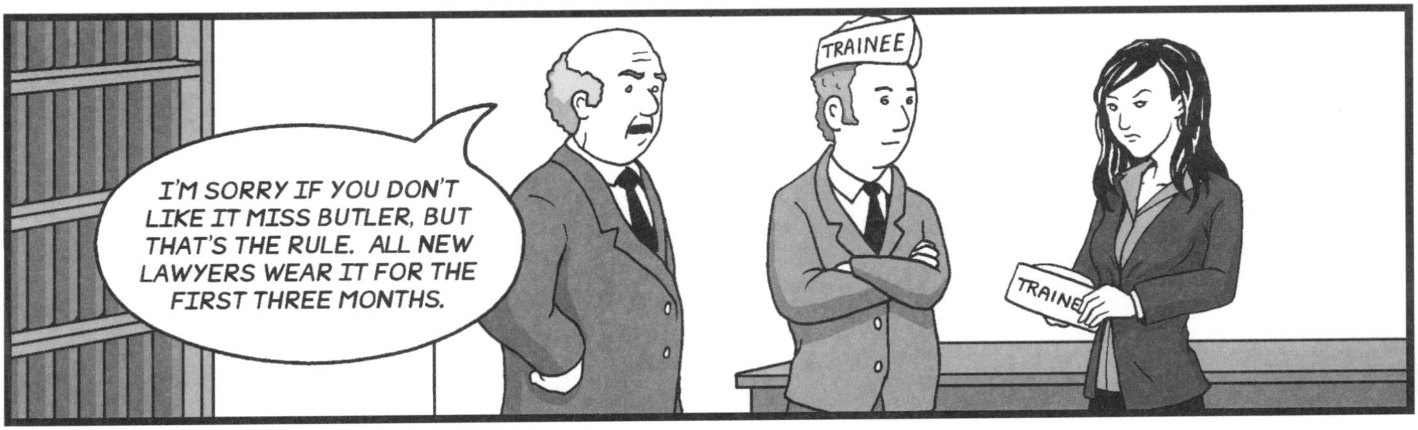
TRAINEE
I'M SORRY IF YOU DON'T LIKE IT MISS BUTLER, BUT THAT'S THE RULE. ALL NEW LAWYERS WEAR IT FOR THE FIRST THREE MONTHS.

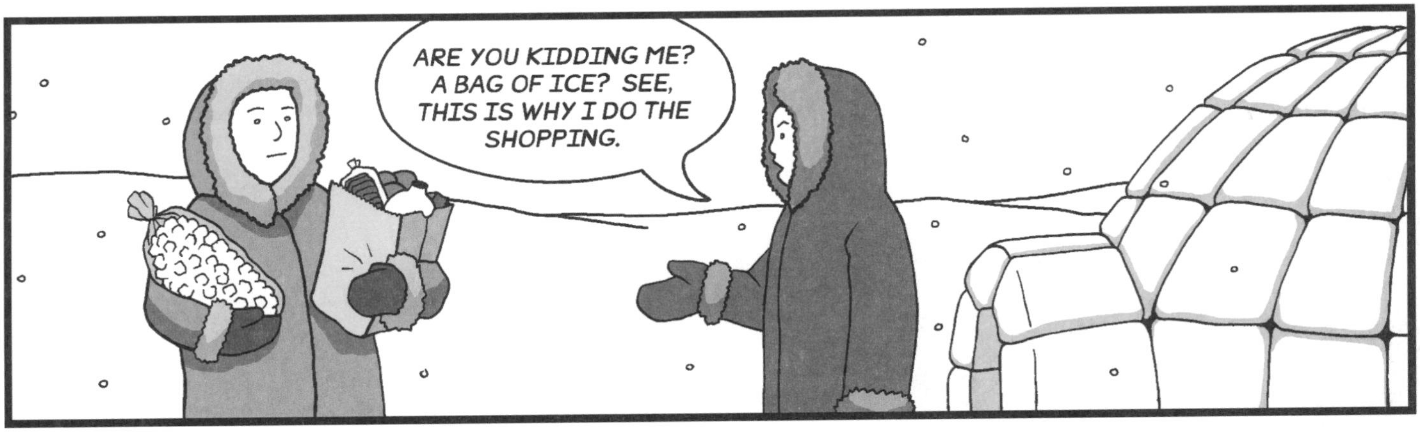
ARE YOU KIDDING ME? A BAG OF ICE? SEE, THIS IS WHY I DO THE SHOPPING.

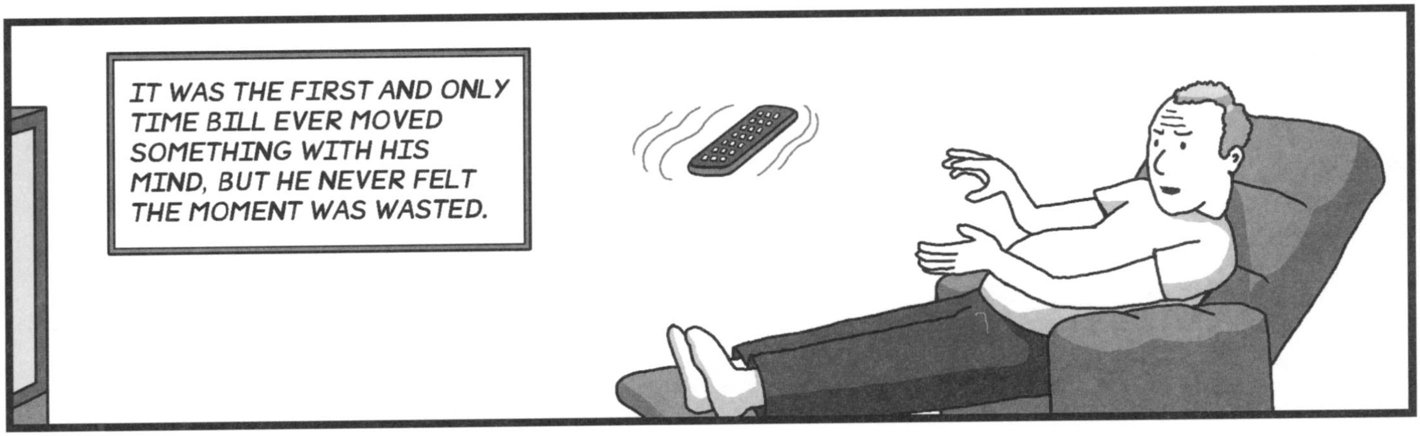
IT WAS THE FIRST AND ONLY TIME BILL EVER MOVED SOMETHING WITH HIS MIND, BUT HE NEVER FELT THE MOMENT WAS WASTED.

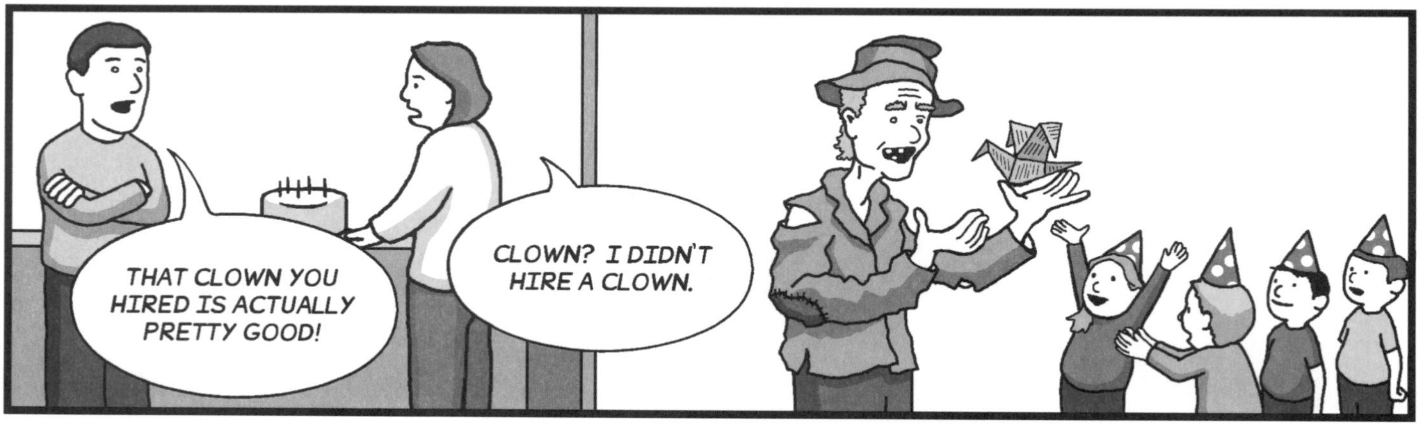
THAT CLOWN YOU HIRED IS ACTUALLY PRETTY GOOD!
CLOWN? I DIDN'T HIRE A CLOWN.

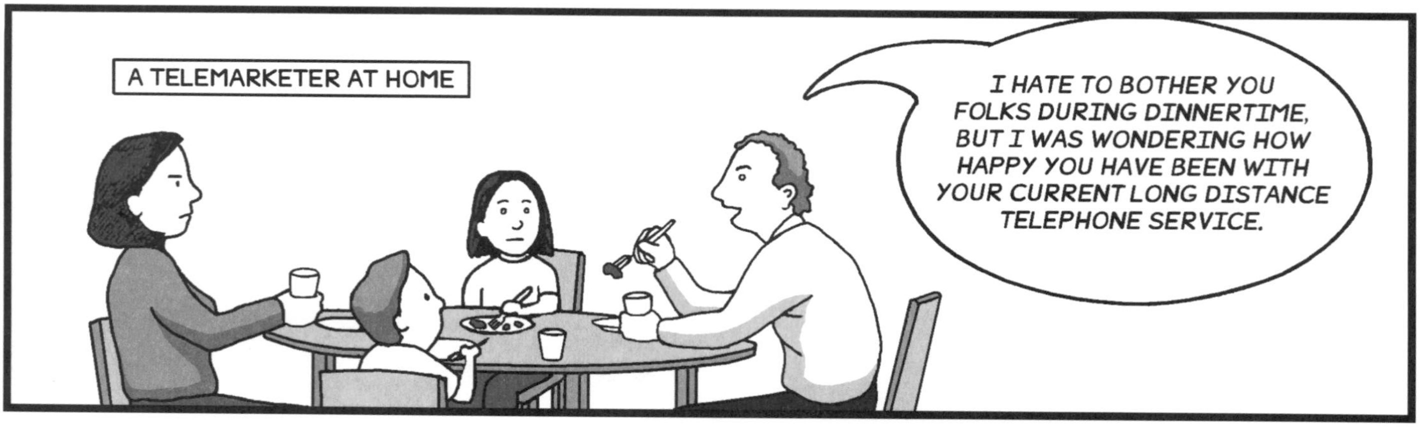
A TELEMARKETER AT HOME
I HATE TO BOTHER YOU FOLKS DURING DINNERTIME, BUT I WAS WONDERING HOW HAPPY YOU HAVE BEEN WITH YOUR CURRENT LONG DISTANCE TELEPHONE SERVICE.

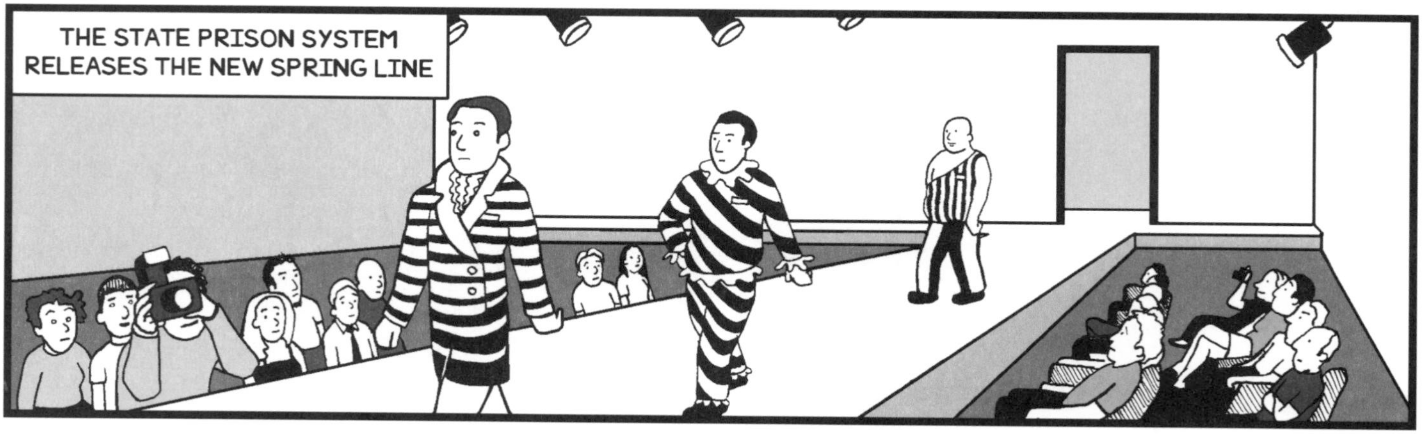
THE STATE PRISON SYSTEM RELEASES THE NEW SPRING LINE

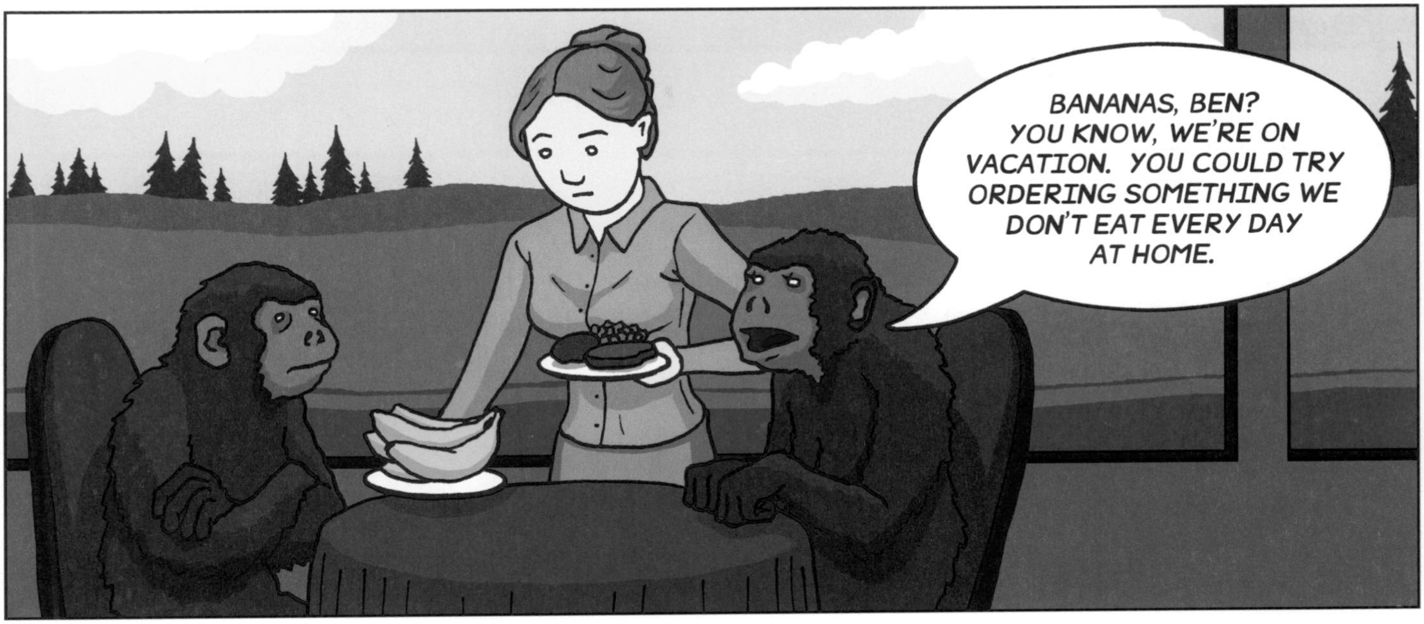
BANANAS, BEN? YOU KNOW, WE'RE ON VACATION. YOU COULD TRY ORDERING SOMETHING WE DON'T EAT EVERY DAY AT HOME.

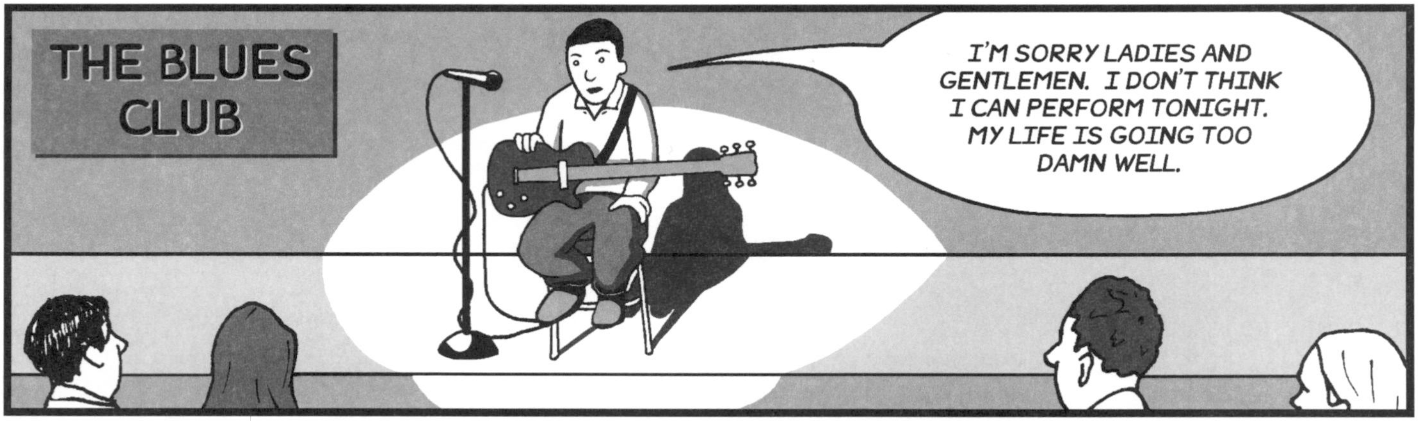
THE BLUES CLUB
I'M SORRY LADIES AND GENTLEMEN. I DON'T THINK I CAN PERFORM TONIGHT. MY LIFE IS GOING TOO DAMN WELL.

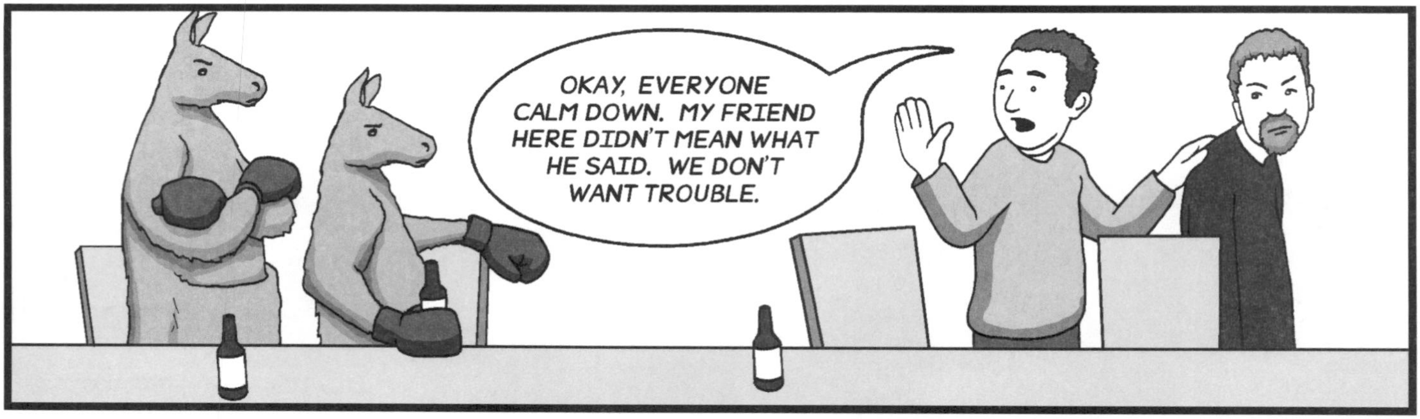
OKAY, EVERYONE CALM DOWN. MY FRIEND HERE DIDN'T MEAN WHAT HE SAID. WE DON'T WANT TROUBLE.

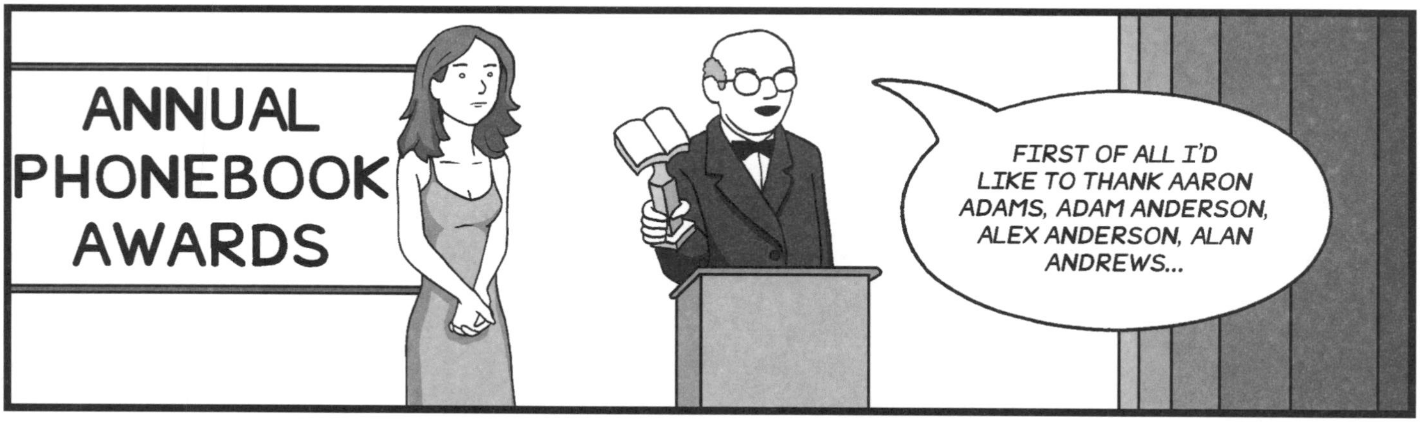
ANNUAL PHONEBOOK AWARDS
FIRST OF ALL I'D LIKE TO THANK AARON ADAMS, ADAM ANDERSON, ALEX ANDERSON, ALAN ANDREWS...

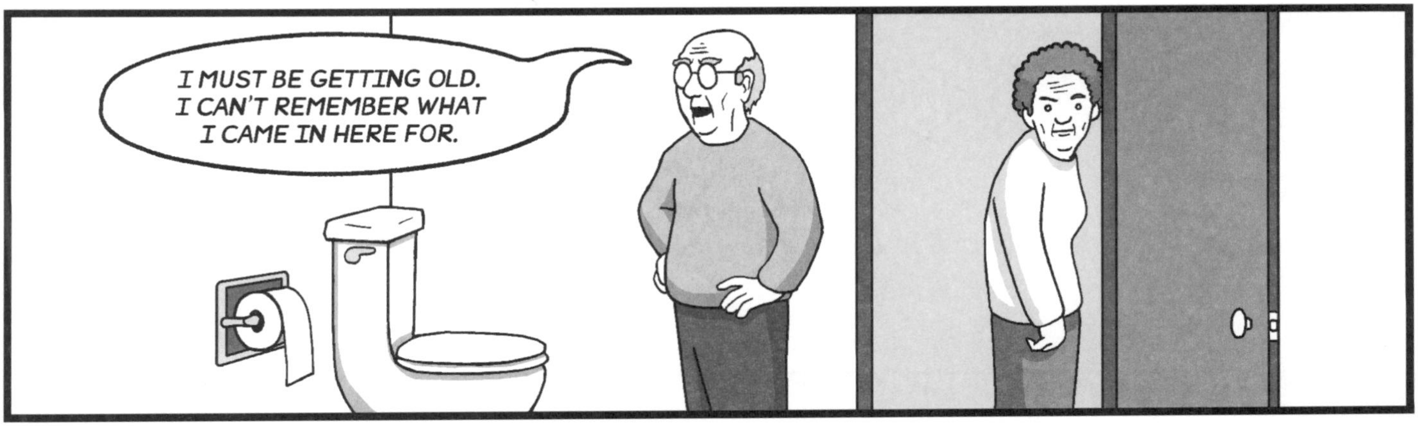
I MUST BE GETTING OLD. I CAN'T REMEMBER WHAT I CAME IN HERE FOR.

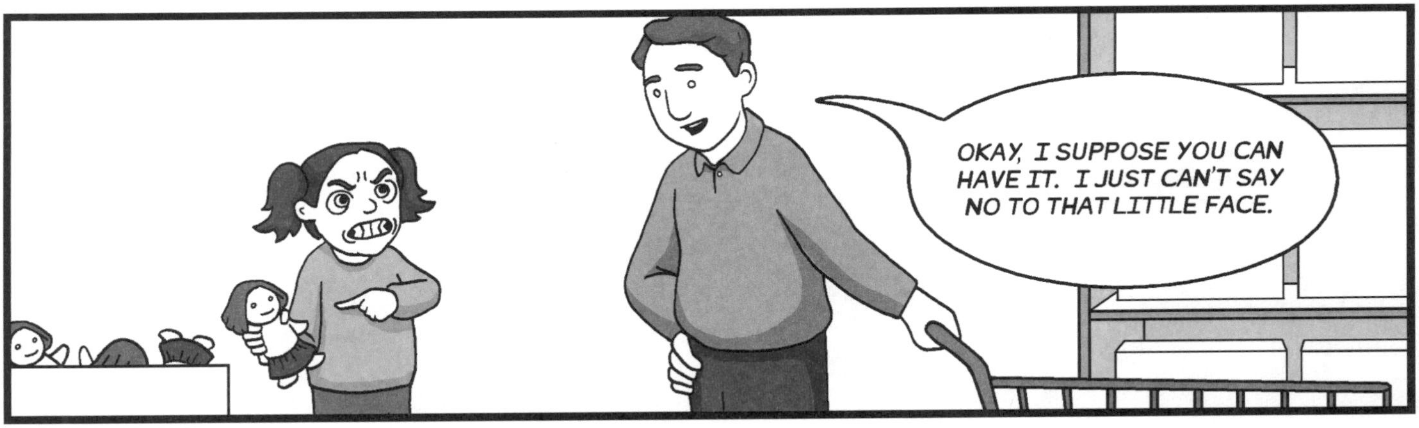
OKAY, I SUPPOSE YOU CAN HAVE IT. I JUST CAN'T SAY NO TO THAT LITTLE FACE.

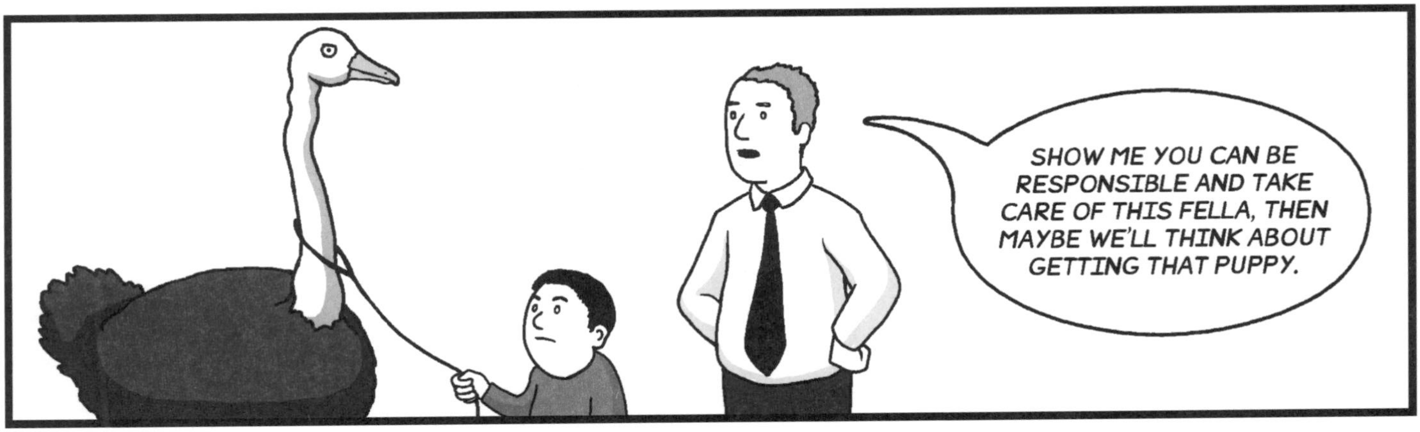
SHOW ME YOU CAN BE RESPONSIBLE AND TAKE CARE OF THIS FELLA, THEN MAYBE WE'LL THINK ABOUT GETTING THAT PUPPY.

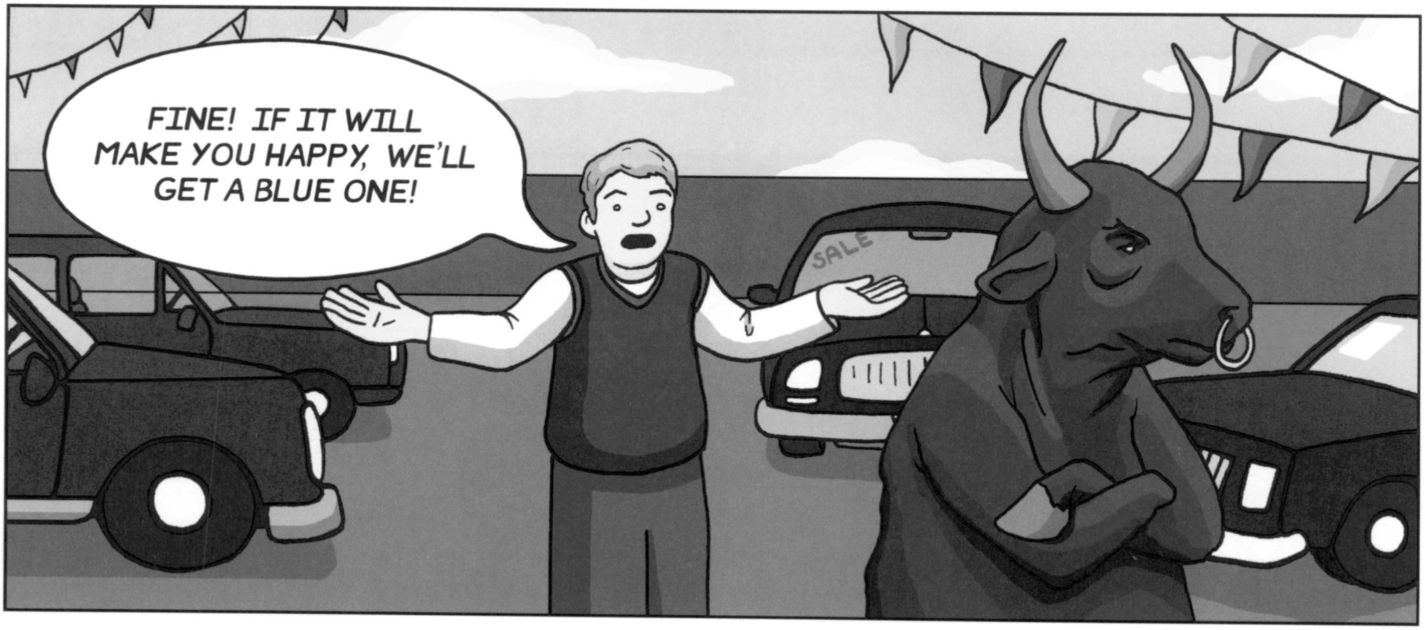
FINE! IF IT WILL MAKE YOU HAPPY, WE'LL GET A BLUE ONE!
SALE

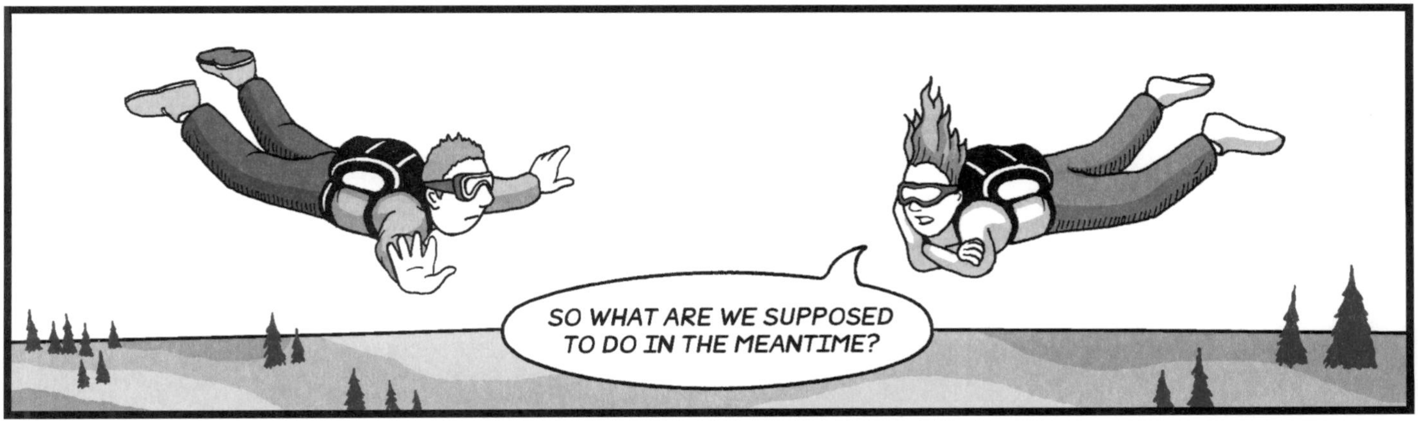
SO WHAT ARE WE SUPPOSED TO DO IN THE MEANTIME?

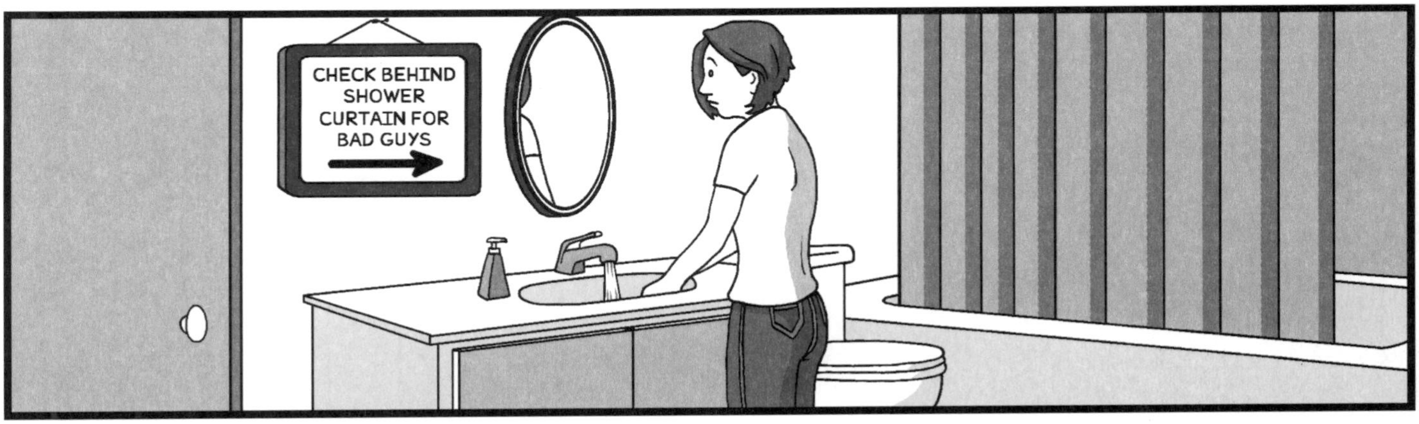
CHECK BEHIND SHOWER CURTAIN FOR BAD GUYS

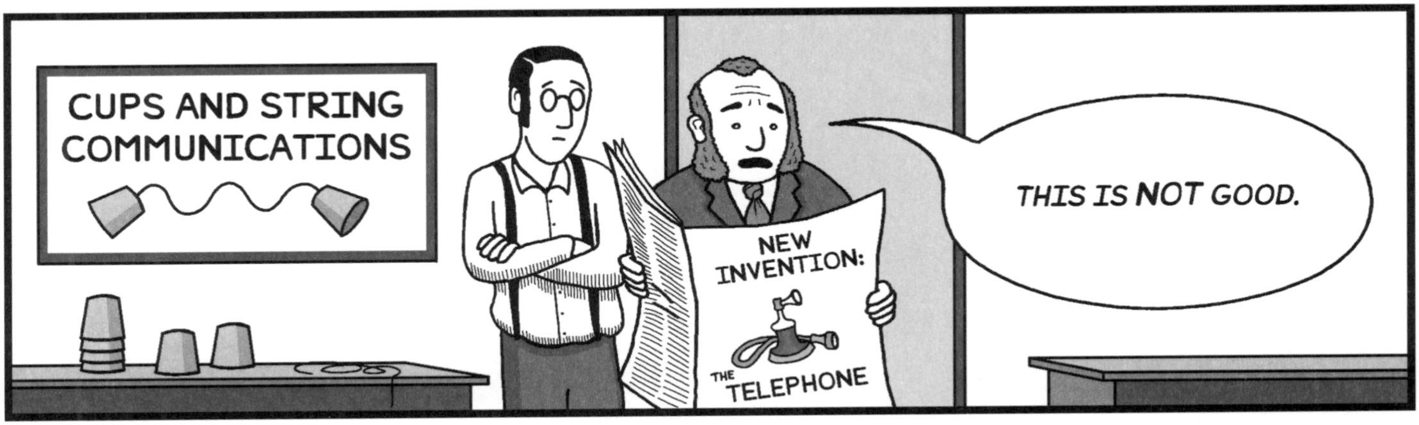
CUPS AND STRING COMMUNICATIONS
NEW INVENTION:
THE TELEPHONE
THIS IS **NOT** GOOD.

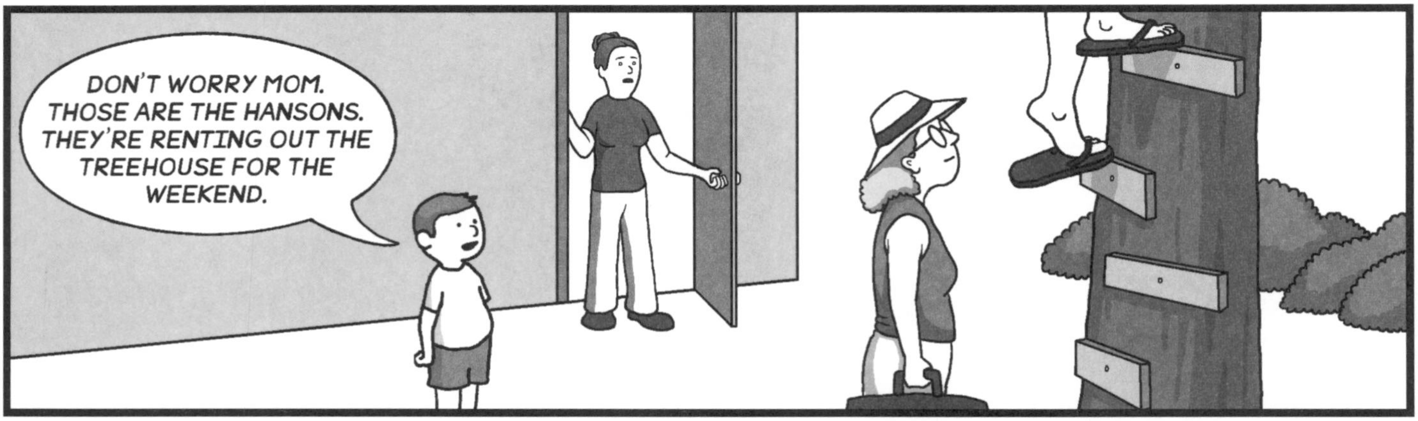
DON'T WORRY MOM. THOSE ARE THE HANSONS. THEY'RE RENTING OUT THE TREEHOUSE FOR THE WEEKEND.

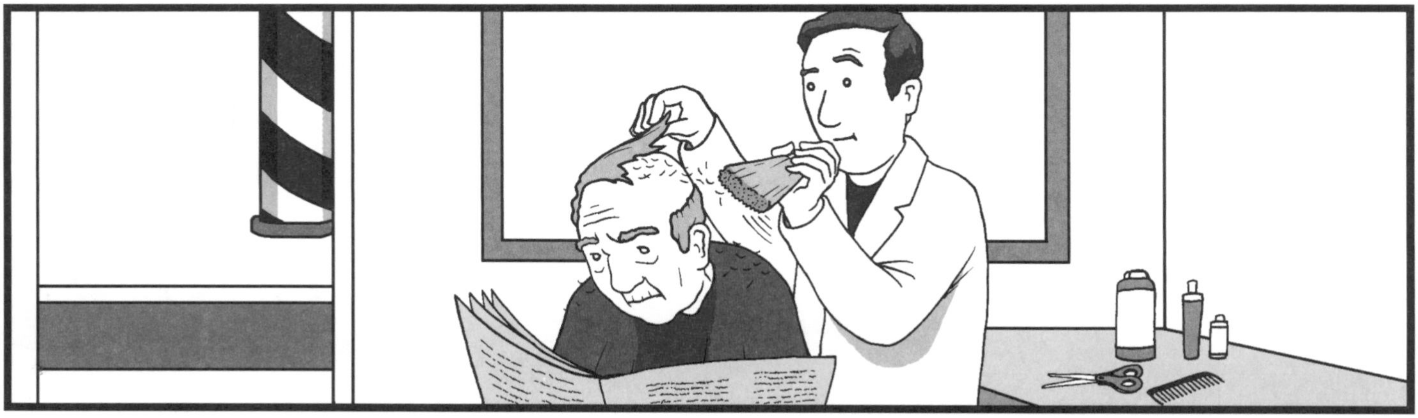

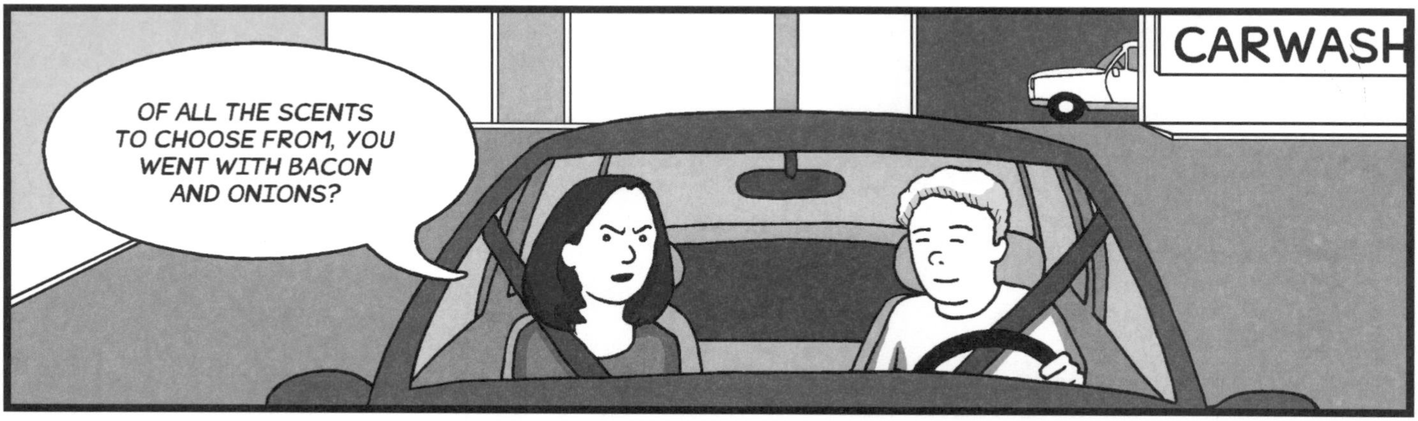
CARWASH
OF ALL THE SCENTS TO CHOOSE FROM, YOU WENT WITH BACON AND ONIONS?

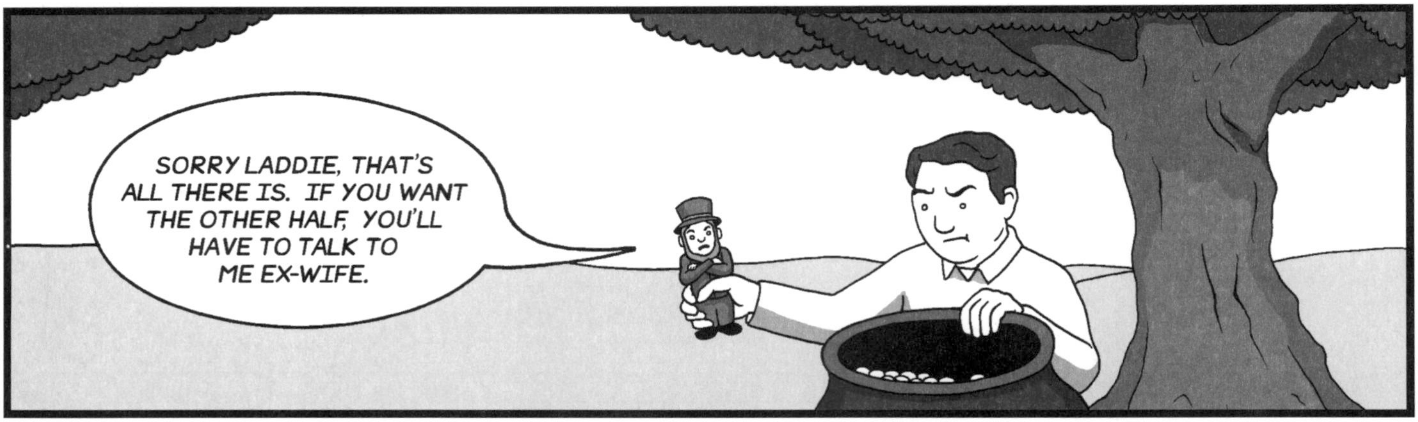
SORRY LADDIE, THAT'S ALL THERE IS. IF YOU WANT THE OTHER HALF, YOU'LL HAVE TO TALK TO ME EX-WIFE.

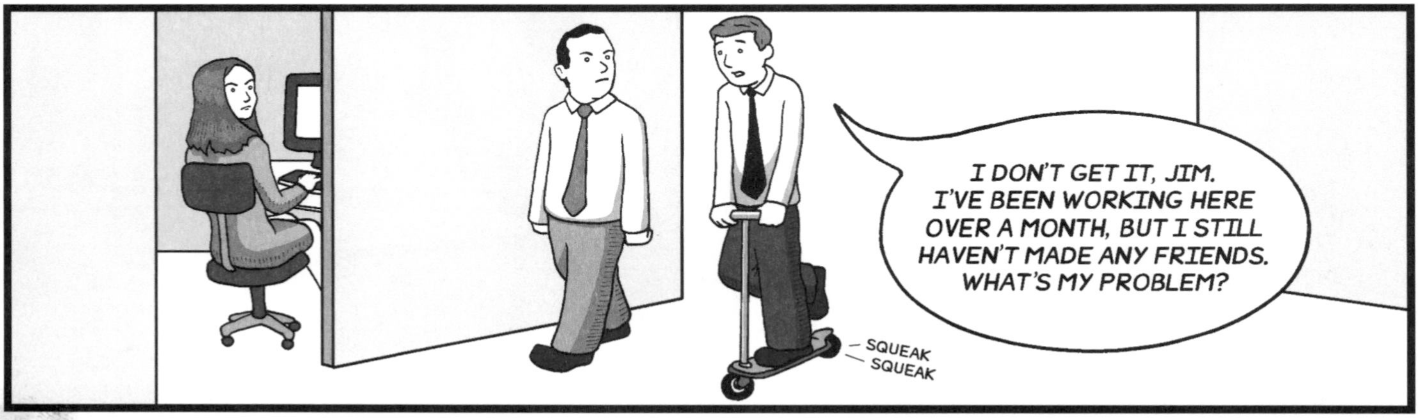
I DON'T GET IT, JIM. I'VE BEEN WORKING HERE OVER A MONTH, BUT I STILL HAVEN'T MADE ANY FRIENDS. WHAT'S MY PROBLEM?
SQUEAK
SQUEAK

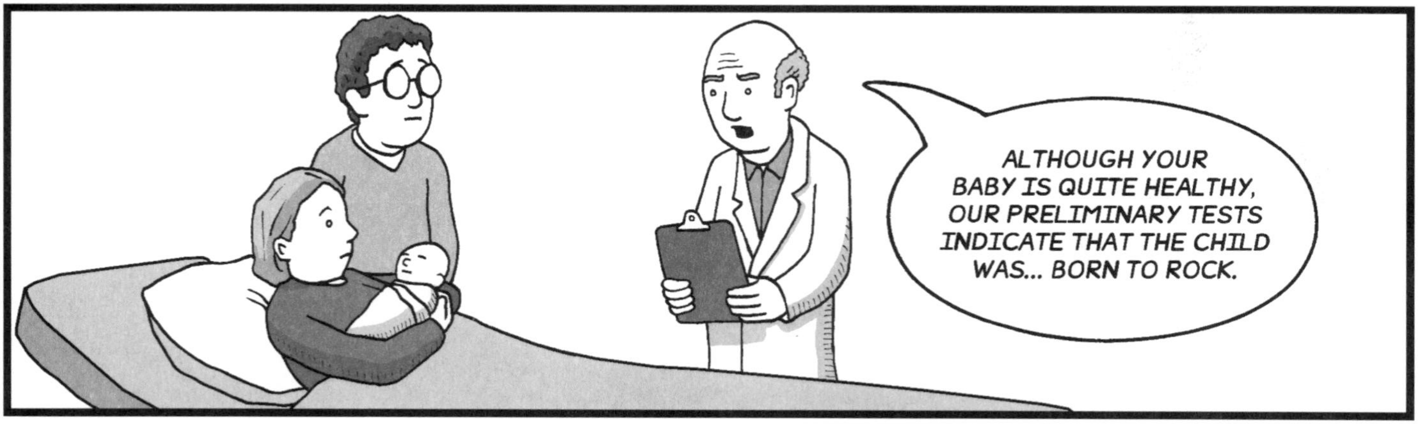
ALTHOUGH YOUR BABY IS QUITE HEALTHY, OUR PRELIMINARY TESTS INDICATE THAT THE CHILD WAS... BORN TO ROCK.

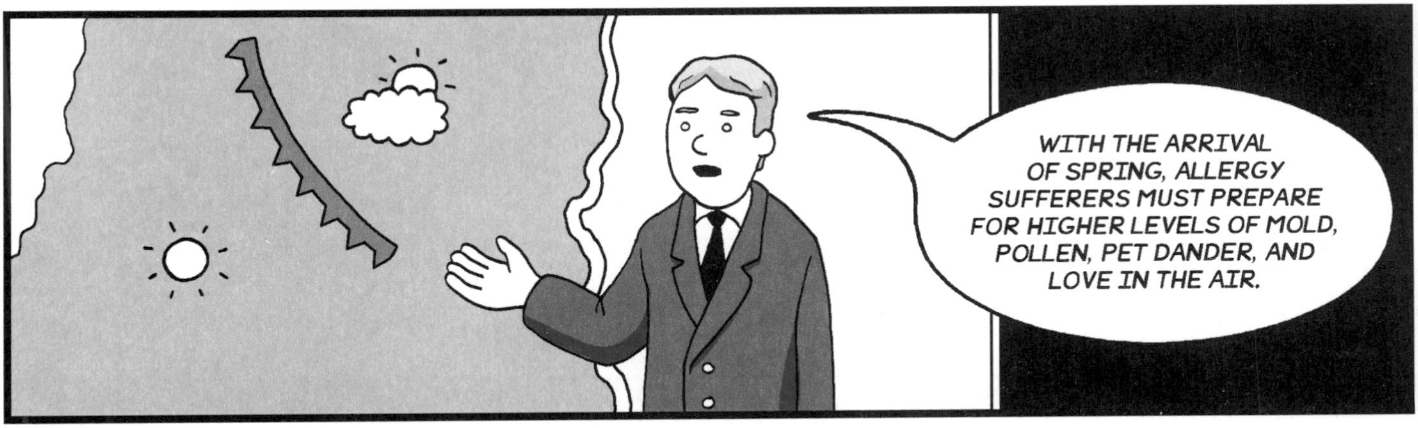
WITH THE ARRIVAL OF SPRING, ALLERGY SUFFERERS MUST PREPARE FOR HIGHER LEVELS OF MOLD, POLLEN, PET DANDER, AND LOVE IN THE AIR.

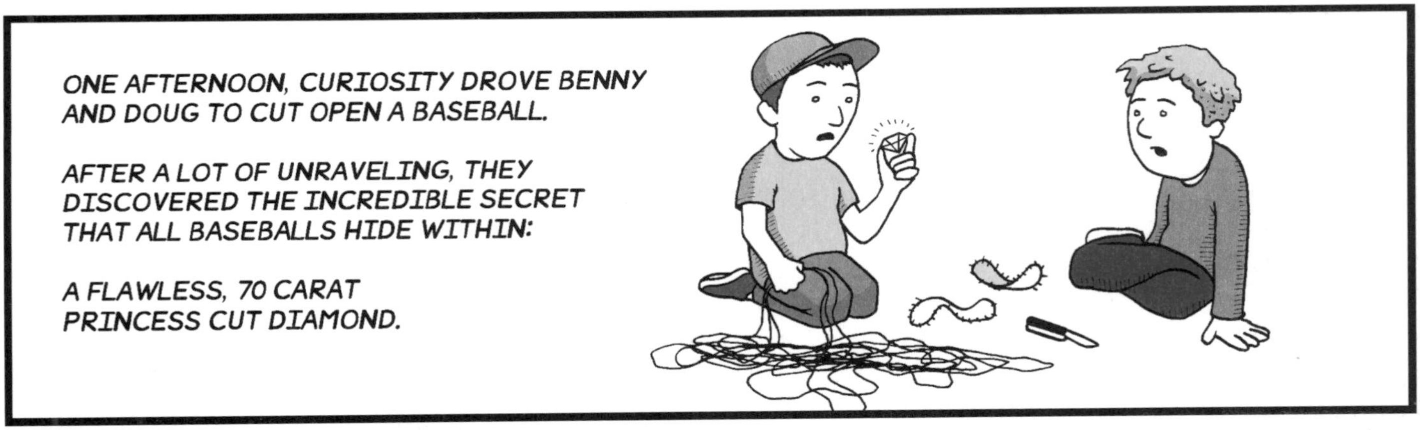
ONE AFTERNOON, CURIOSITY DROVE BENNY AND DOUG TO CUT OPEN A BASEBALL.
AFTER A LOT OF UNRAVELING, THEY DISCOVERED THE INCREDIBLE SECRET THAT ALL BASEBALLS HIDE WITHIN:
A FLAWLESS, 70 CARAT PRINCESS CUT DIAMOND.

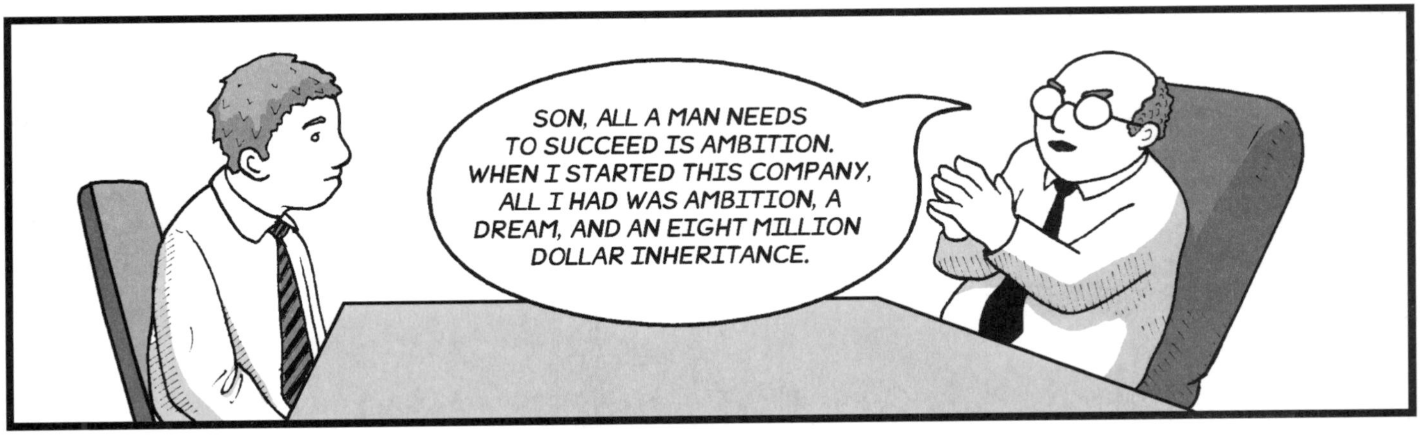
SON, ALL A MAN NEEDS TO SUCCEED IS AMBITION. WHEN I STARTED THIS COMPANY, ALL I HAD WAS AMBITION, A DREAM, AND AN EIGHT MILLION DOLLAR INHERITANCE.

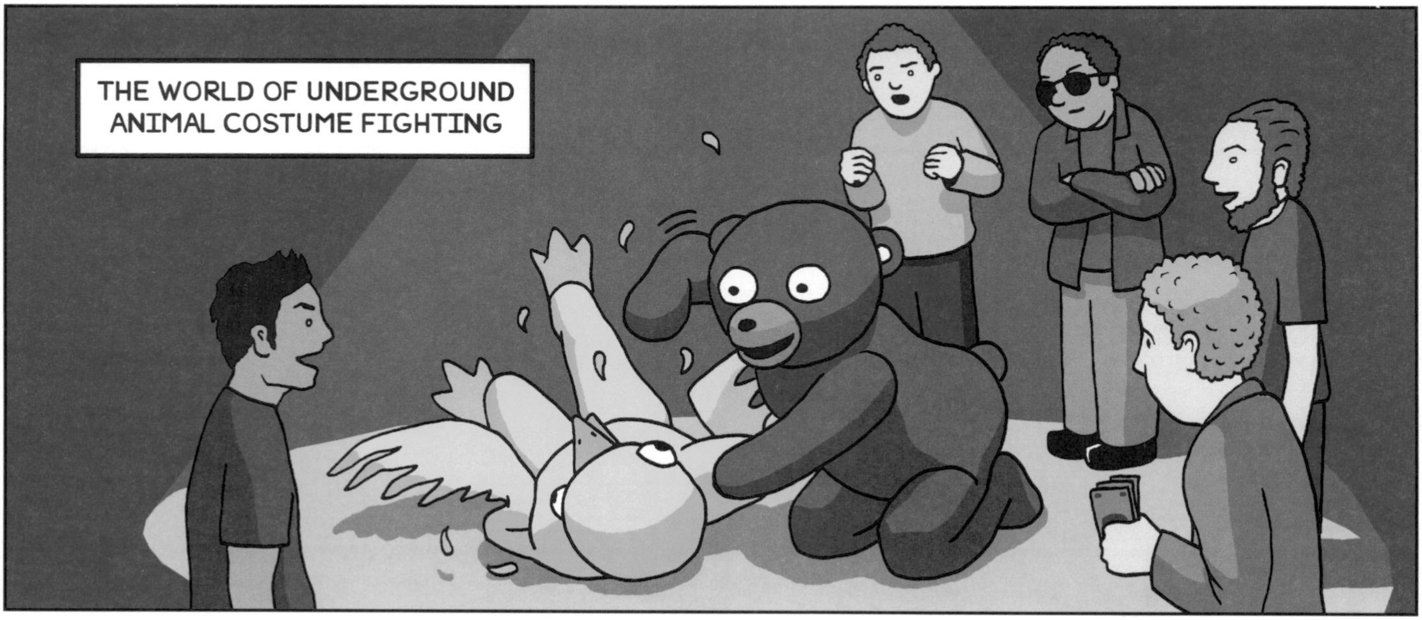
THE WORLD OF UNDERGROUND
ANIMAL COSTUME FIGHTING

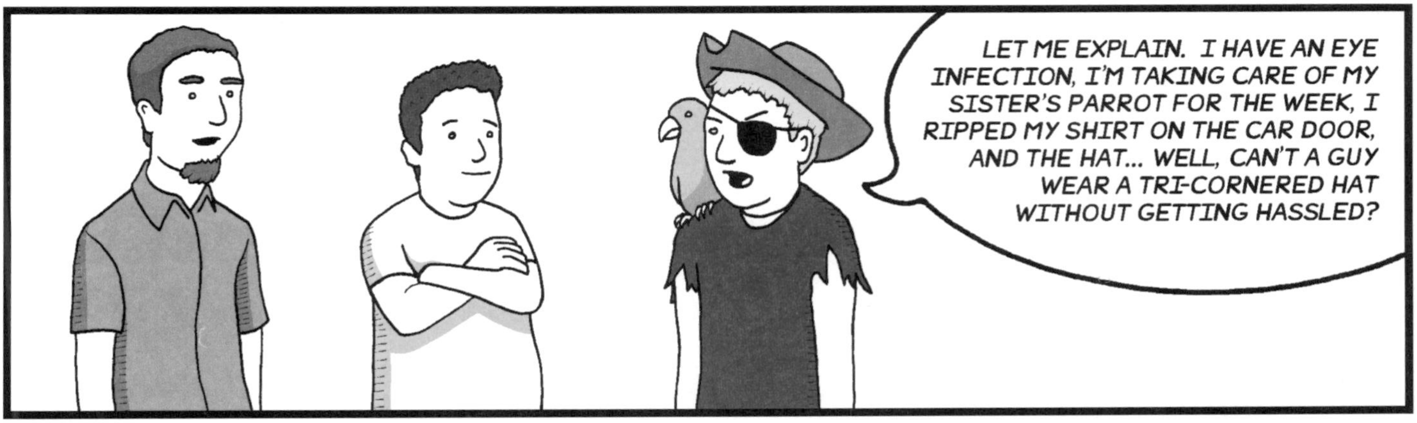
LET ME EXPLAIN. I HAVE AN EYE INFECTION, I'M TAKING CARE OF MY SISTER'S PARROT FOR THE WEEK, I RIPPED MY SHIRT ON THE CAR DOOR, AND THE HAT... WELL, CAN'T A GUY WEAR A TRI-CORNERED HAT WITHOUT GETTING HASSLED?

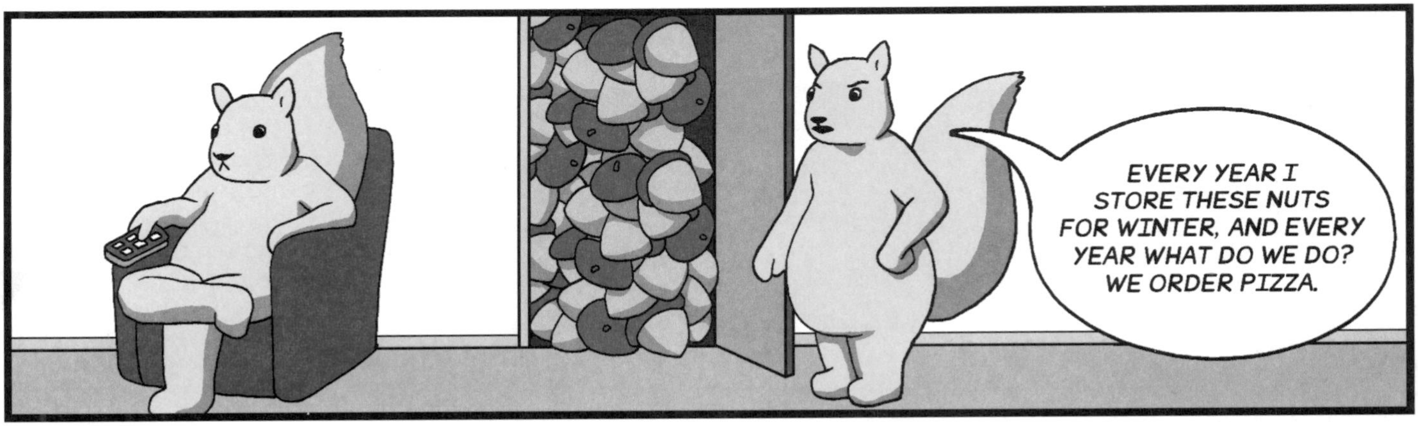
EVERY YEAR I STORE THESE NUTS FOR WINTER, AND EVERY YEAR WHAT DO WE DO? WE ORDER PIZZA.

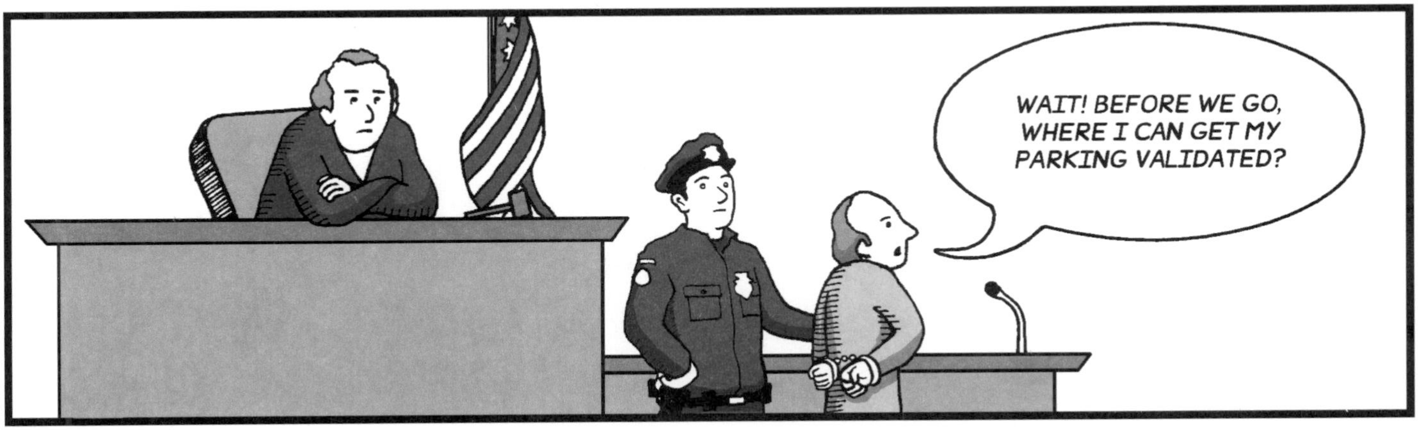
WAIT! BEFORE WE GO, WHERE I CAN GET MY PARKING VALIDATED?

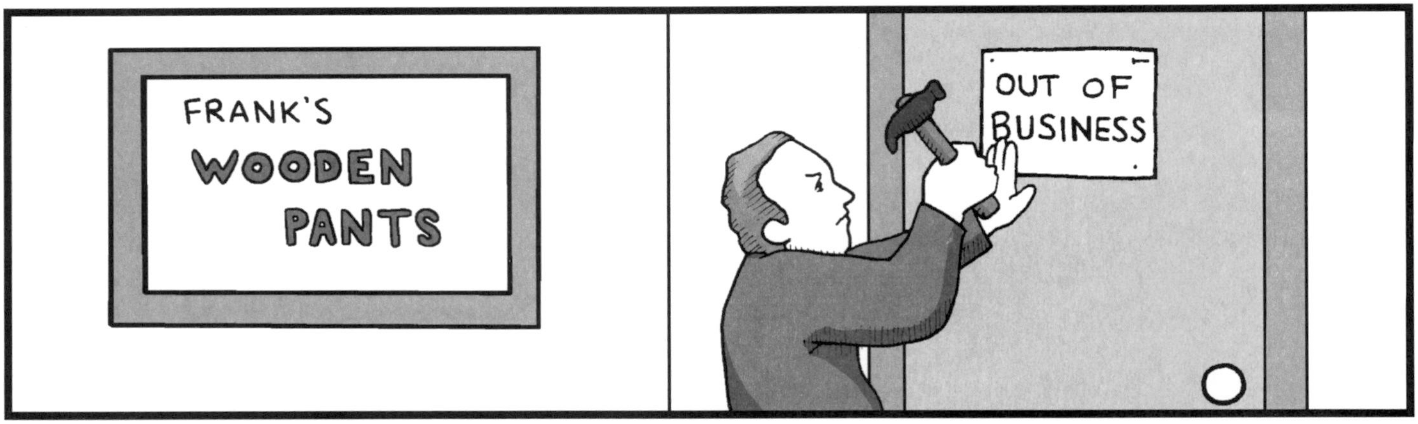
FRANK'S
WOODEN
PANTS
OUT OF BUSINESS

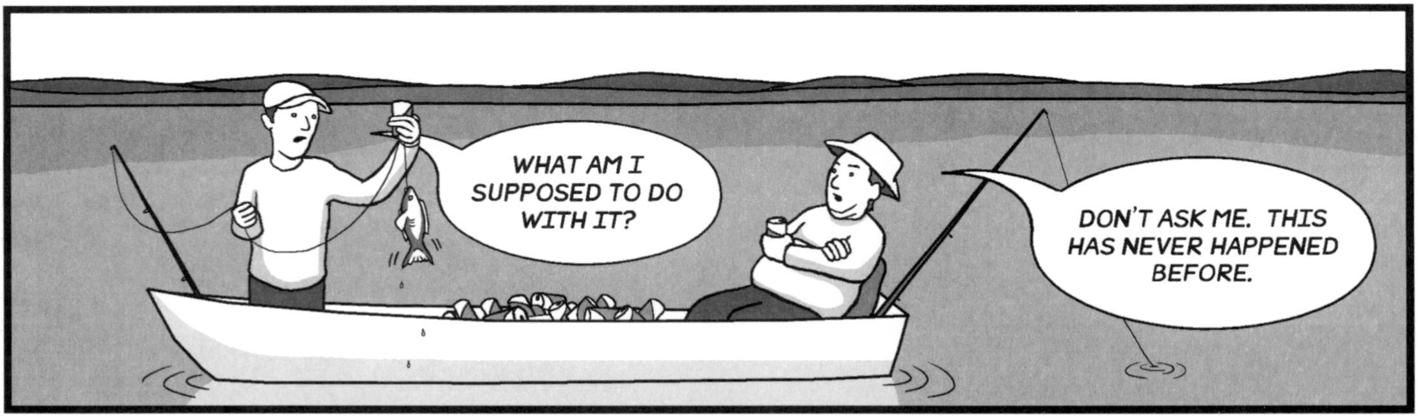
WHAT AM I SUPPOSED TO DO WITH IT?
DON'T ASK ME. THIS HAS NEVER HAPPENED BEFORE.

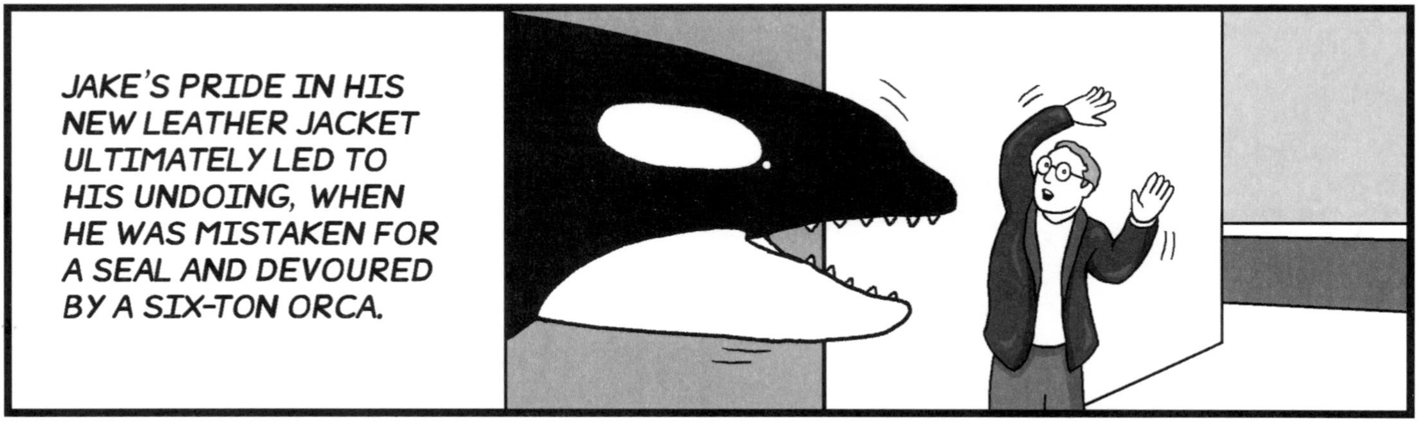
JAKE'S PRIDE IN HIS NEW LEATHER JACKET ULTIMATELY LED TO HIS UNDOING, WHEN HE WAS MISTAKEN FOR A SEAL AND DEVOURED BY A SIX-TON ORCA.

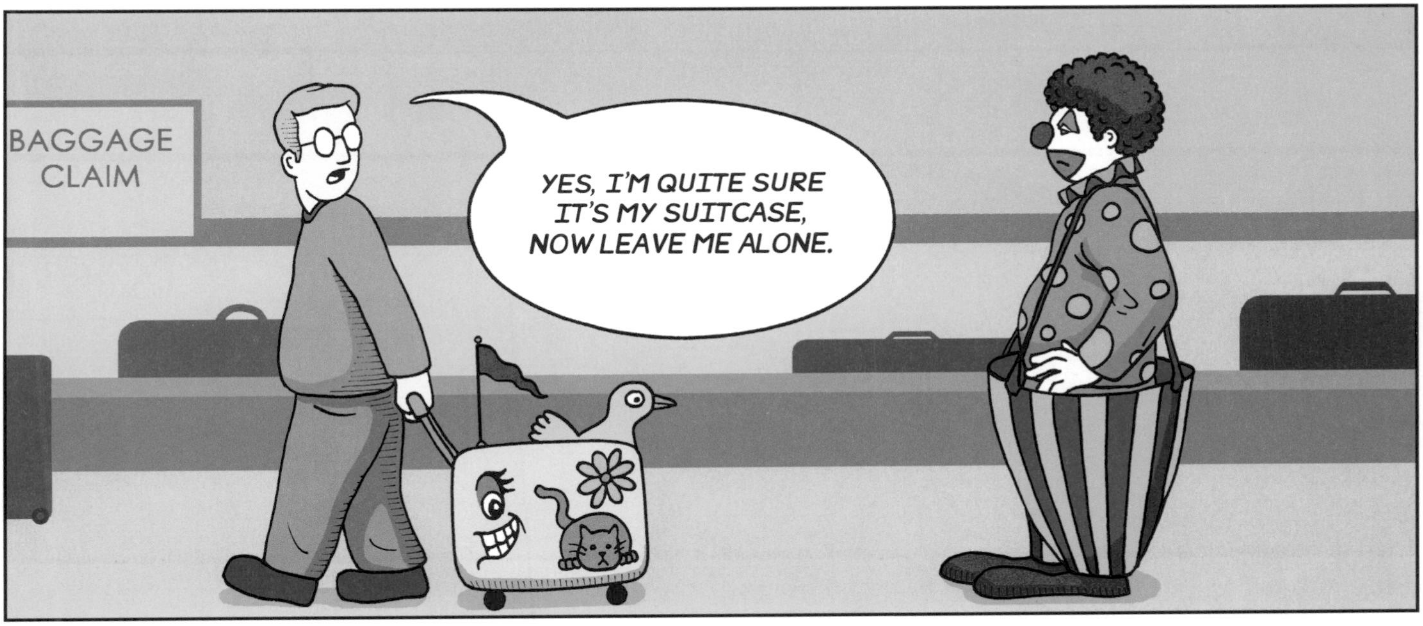
BAGGAGE CLAIM
YES, I'M QUITE SURE IT'S MY SUITCASE, NOW LEAVE ME ALONE.

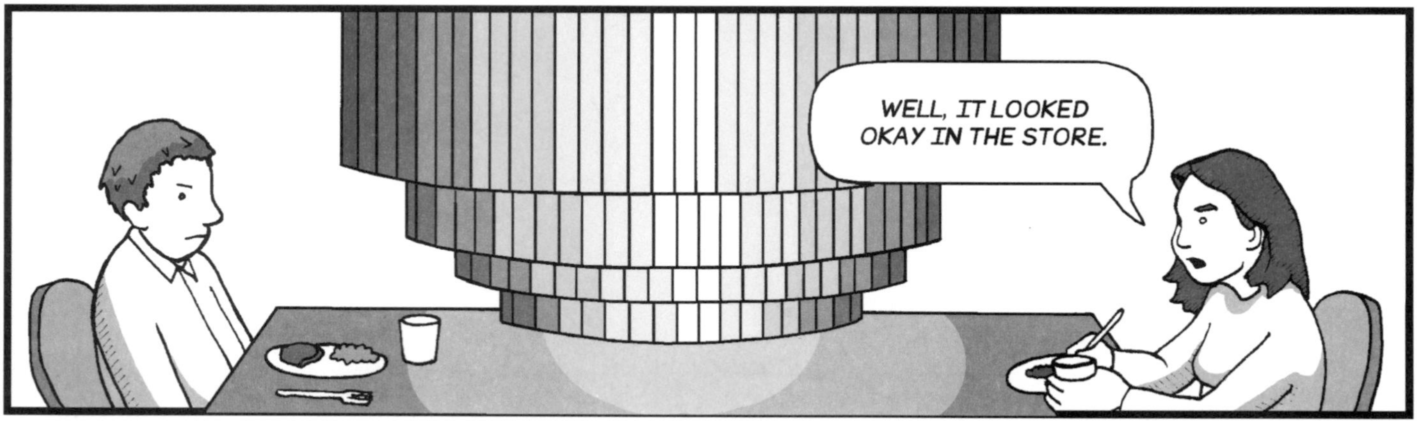
WELL, IT LOOKED OKAY IN THE STORE.

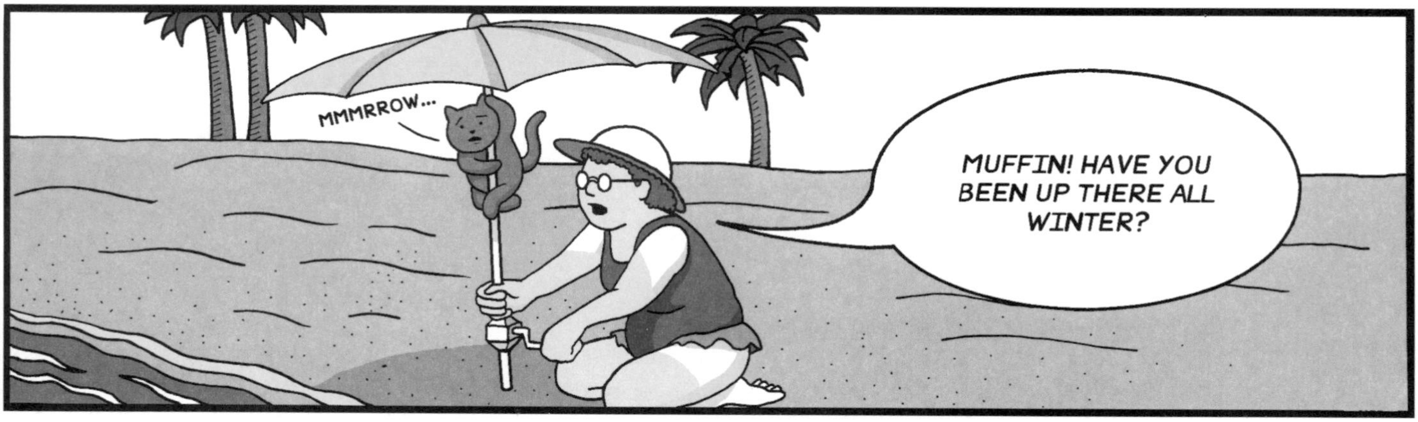
MMMRROW...
MUFFIN! HAVE YOU BEEN UP THERE ALL WINTER?

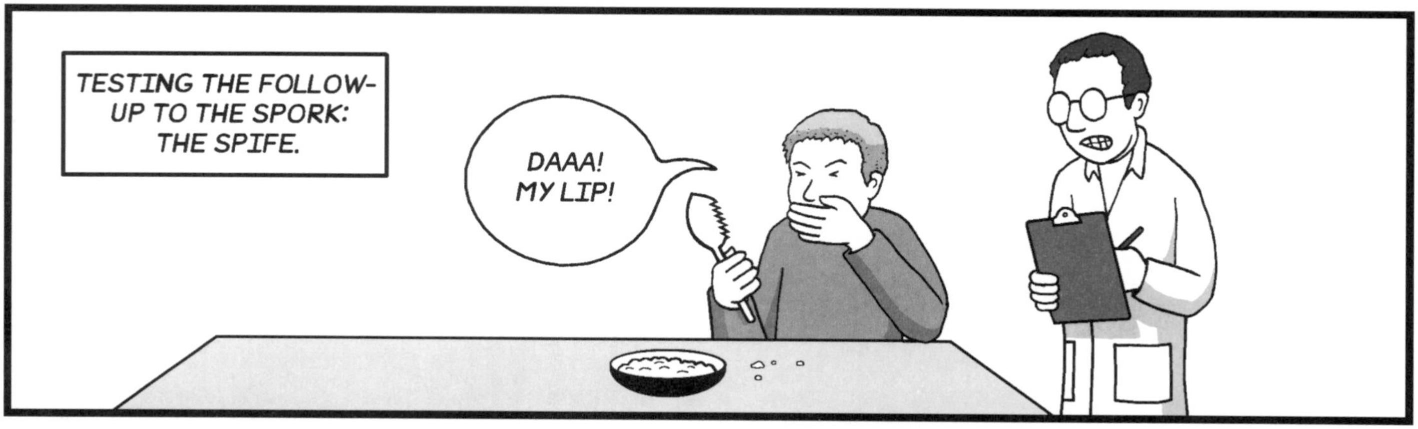
TESTING THE FOLLOW-UP TO THE SPORK: THE SPIFE.
DAAA! MY LIP!

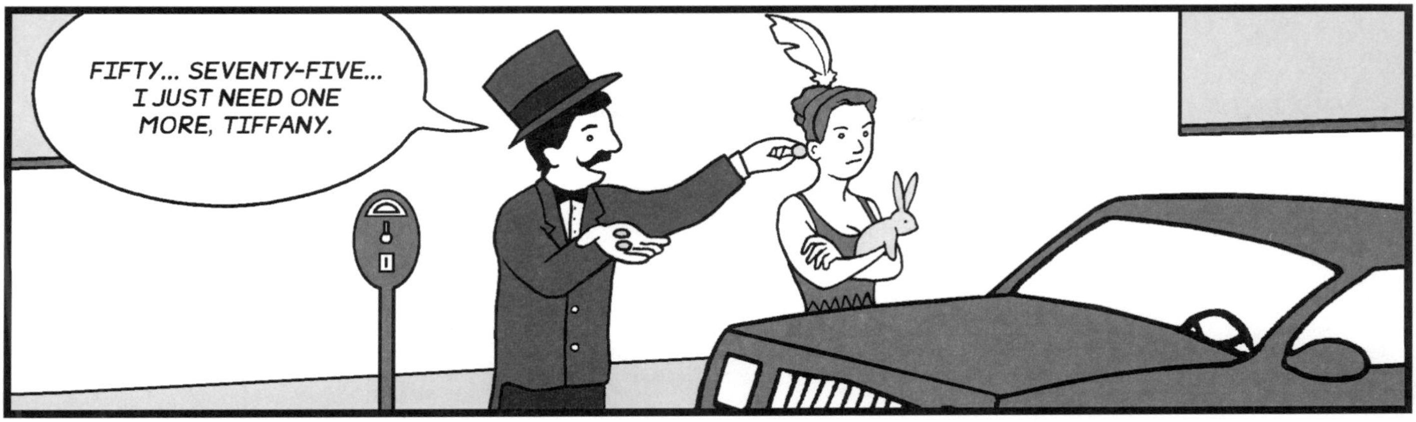
FIFTY... SEVENTY-FIVE... I JUST NEED ONE MORE, TIFFANY.

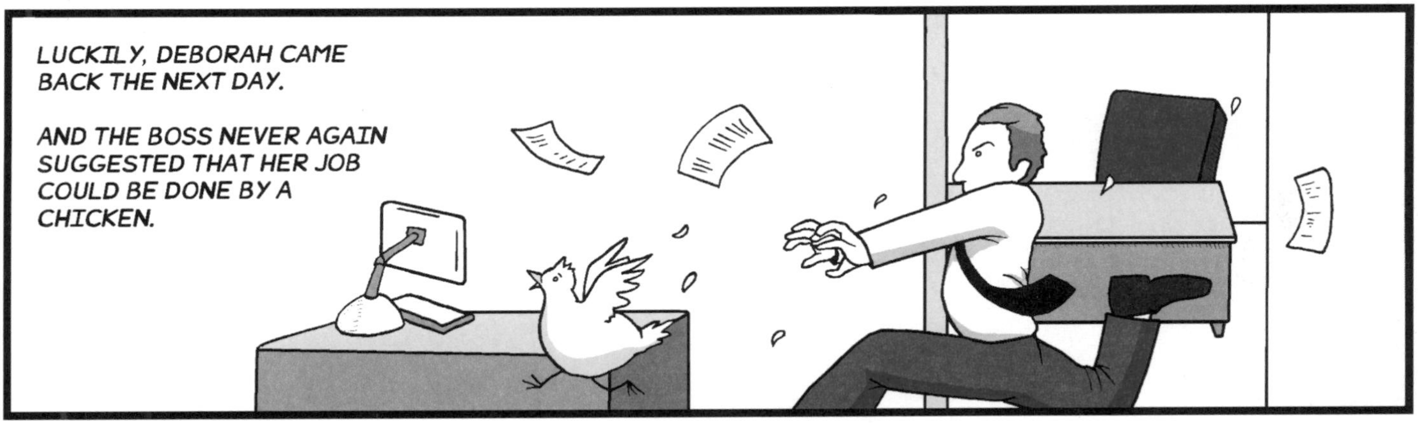
LUCKILY, DEBORAH CAME BACK THE NEXT DAY.
AND THE BOSS NEVER AGAIN SUGGESTED THAT HER JOB COULD BE DONE BY A CHICKEN.

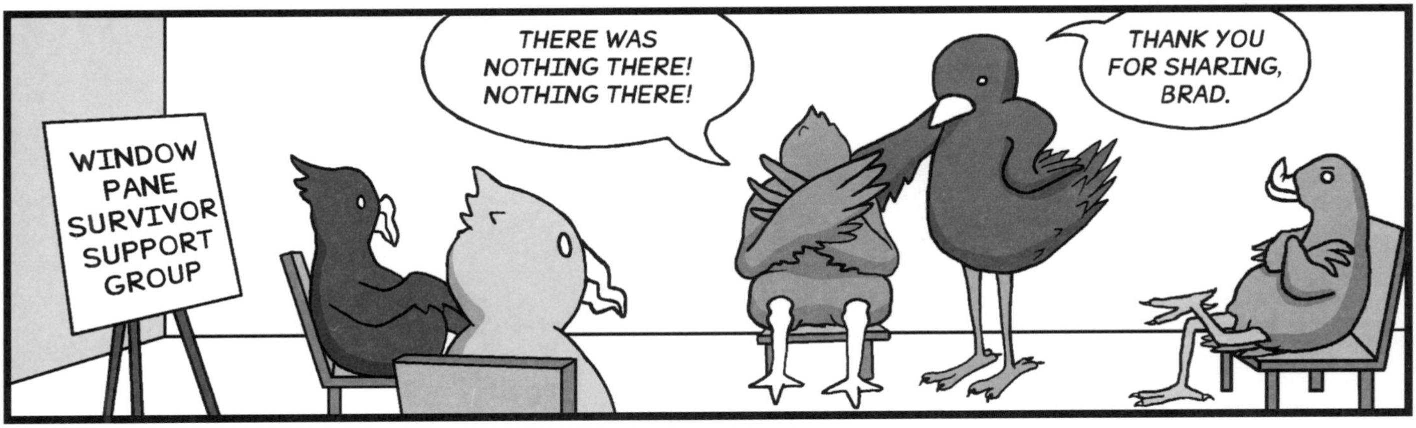
WINDOW PANE SURVIVOR SUPPORT GROUP
THERE WAS NOTHING THERE! NOTHING THERE!
THANK YOU FOR SHARING, BRAD.

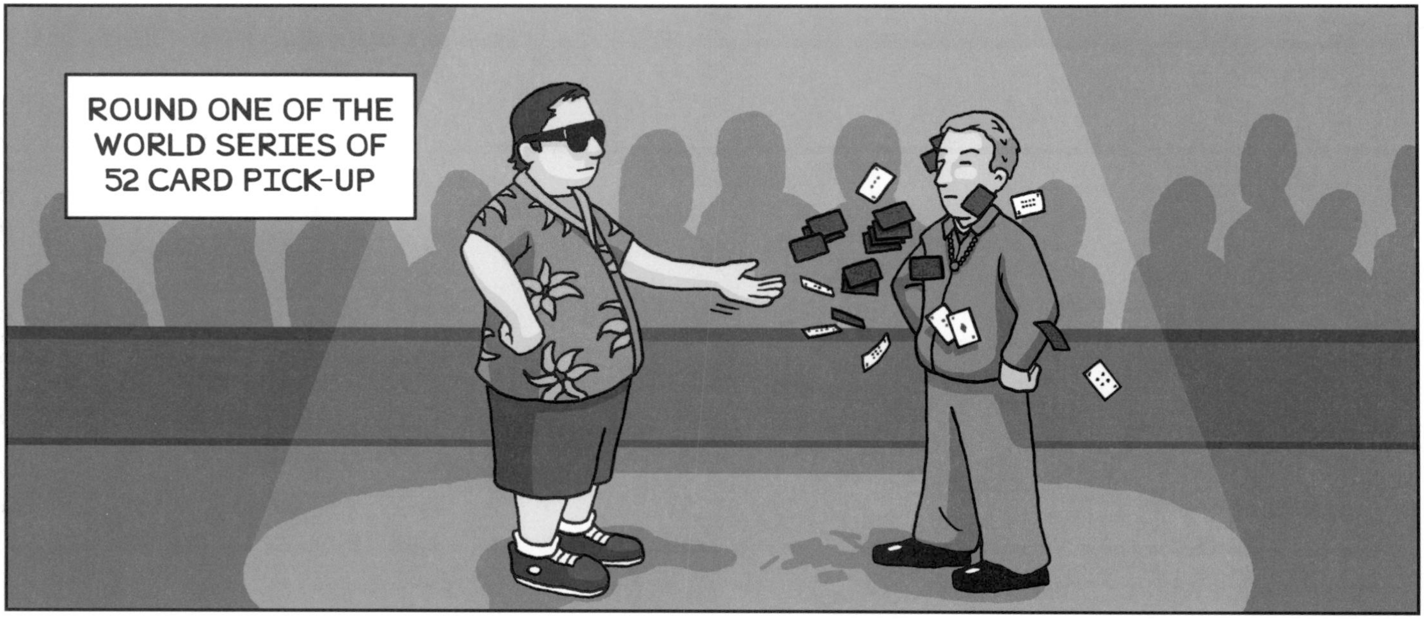
ROUND ONE OF THE WORLD SERIES OF 52 CARD PICK-UP

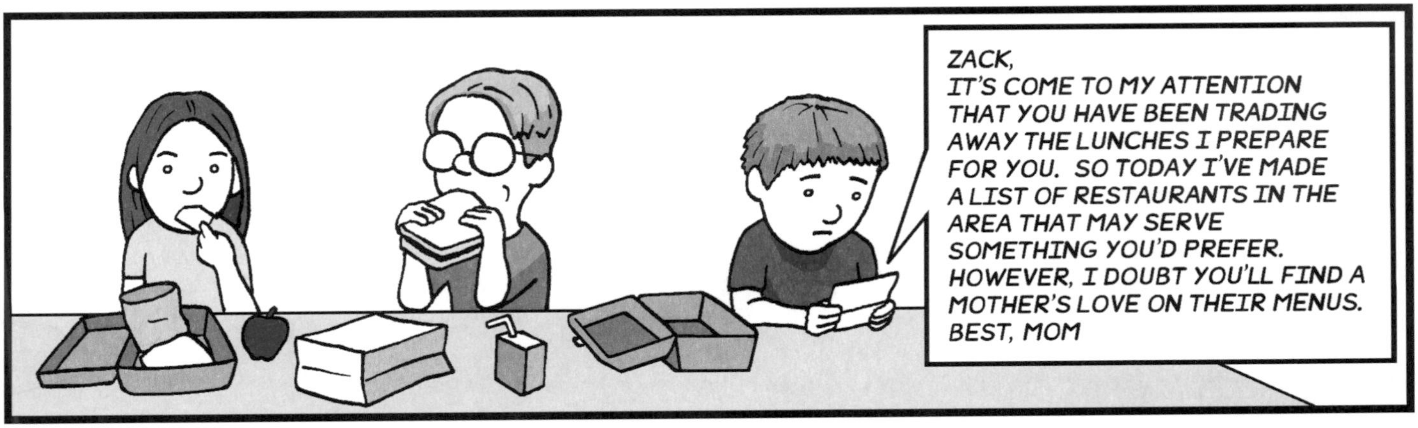
ZACK,
IT'S COME TO MY ATTENTION THAT YOU HAVE BEEN TRADING AWAY THE LUNCHES I PREPARE FOR YOU. SO TODAY I'VE MADE A LIST OF RESTAURANTS IN THE AREA THAT MAY SERVE SOMETHING YOU'D PREFER. HOWEVER, I DOUBT YOU'LL FIND A MOTHER'S LOVE ON THEIR MENUS.
BEST, MOM

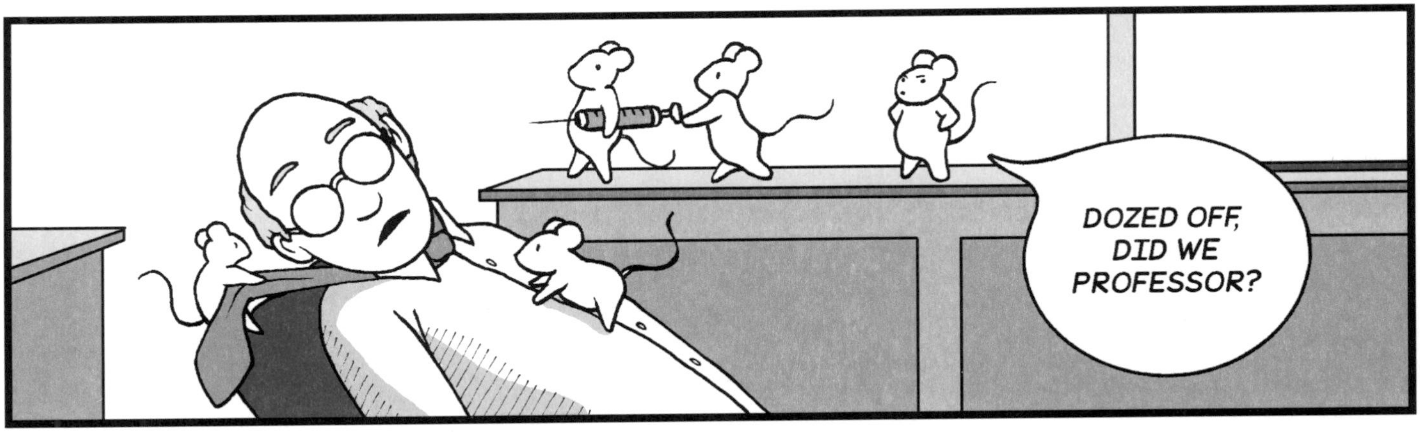
DOZED OFF, DID WE PROFESSOR?

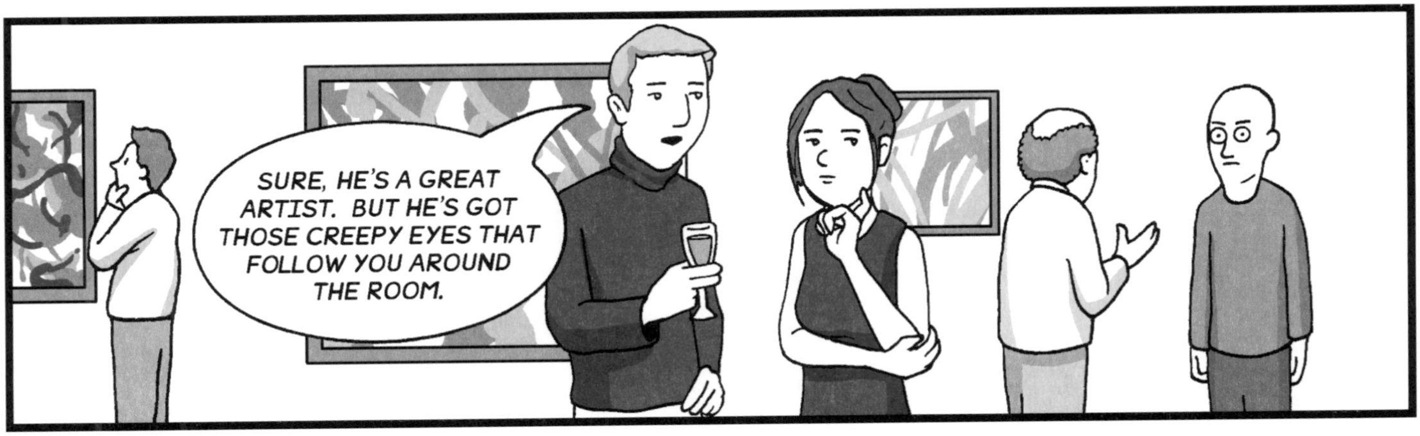
SURE, HE'S A GREAT ARTIST. BUT HE'S GOT THOSE CREEPY EYES THAT FOLLOW YOU AROUND THE ROOM.

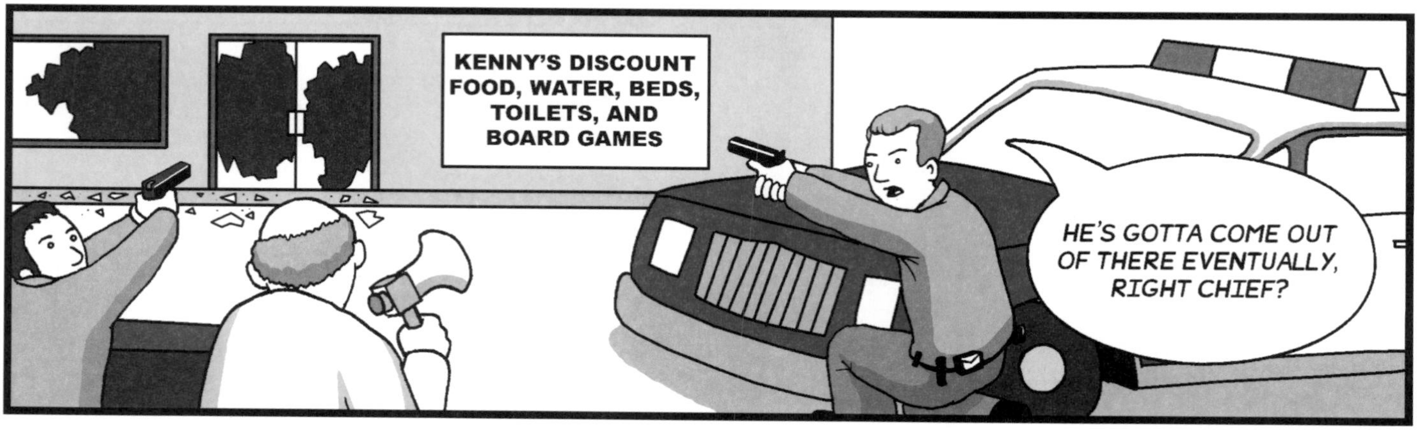
KENNY'S DISCOUNT FOOD, WATER, BEDS, TOILETS, AND BOARD GAMES
HE'S GOTTA COME OUT OF THERE EVENTUALLY, RIGHT CHIEF?

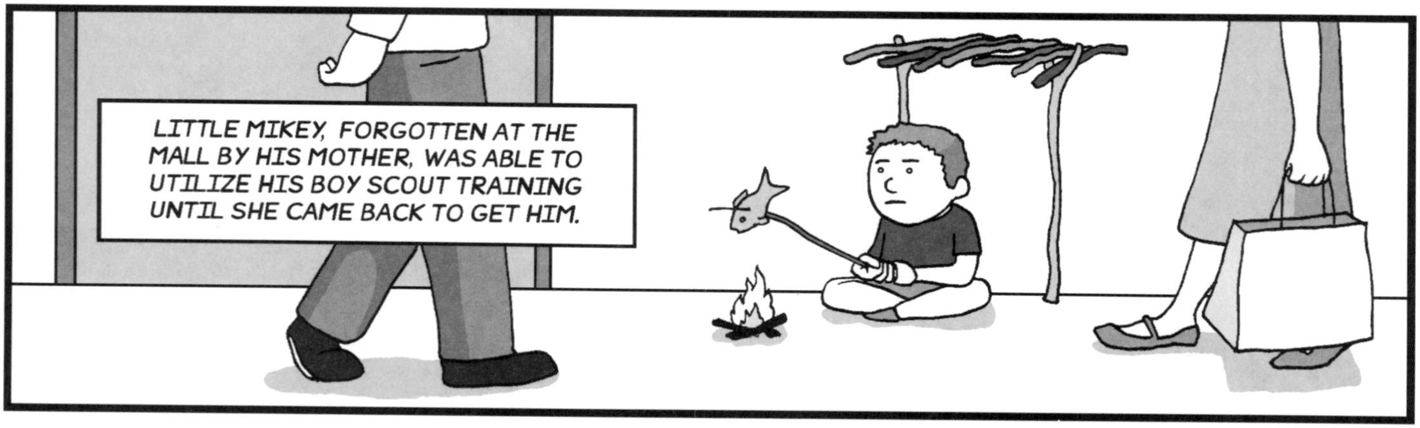
LITTLE MIKEY, FORGOTTEN AT THE MALL BY HIS MOTHER, WAS ABLE TO UTILIZE HIS BOY SCOUT TRAINING UNTIL SHE CAME BACK TO GET HIM.

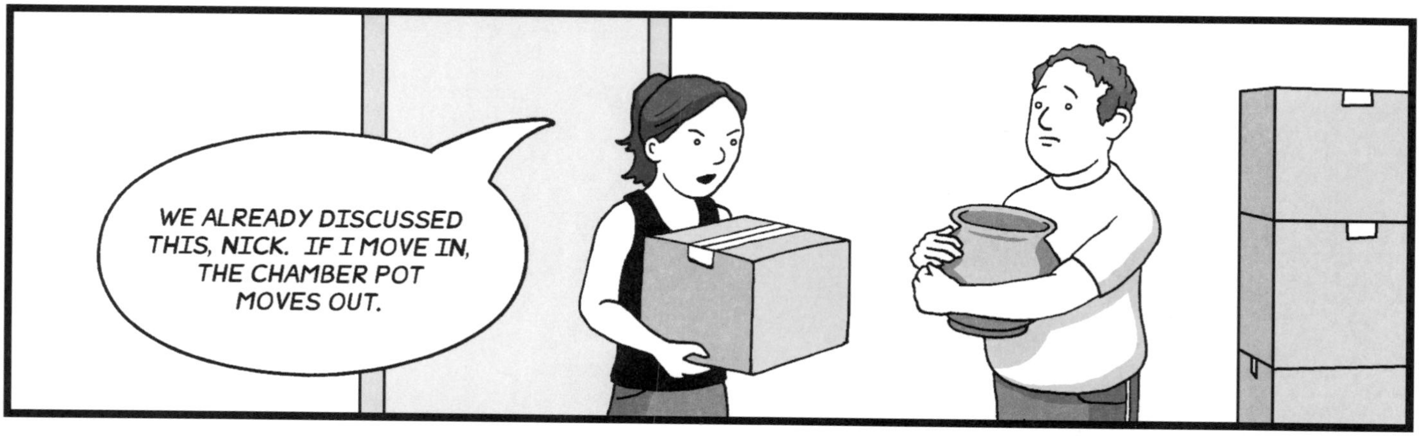
WE ALREADY DISCUSSED THIS, NICK. IF I MOVE IN, THE CHAMBER POT MOVES OUT.

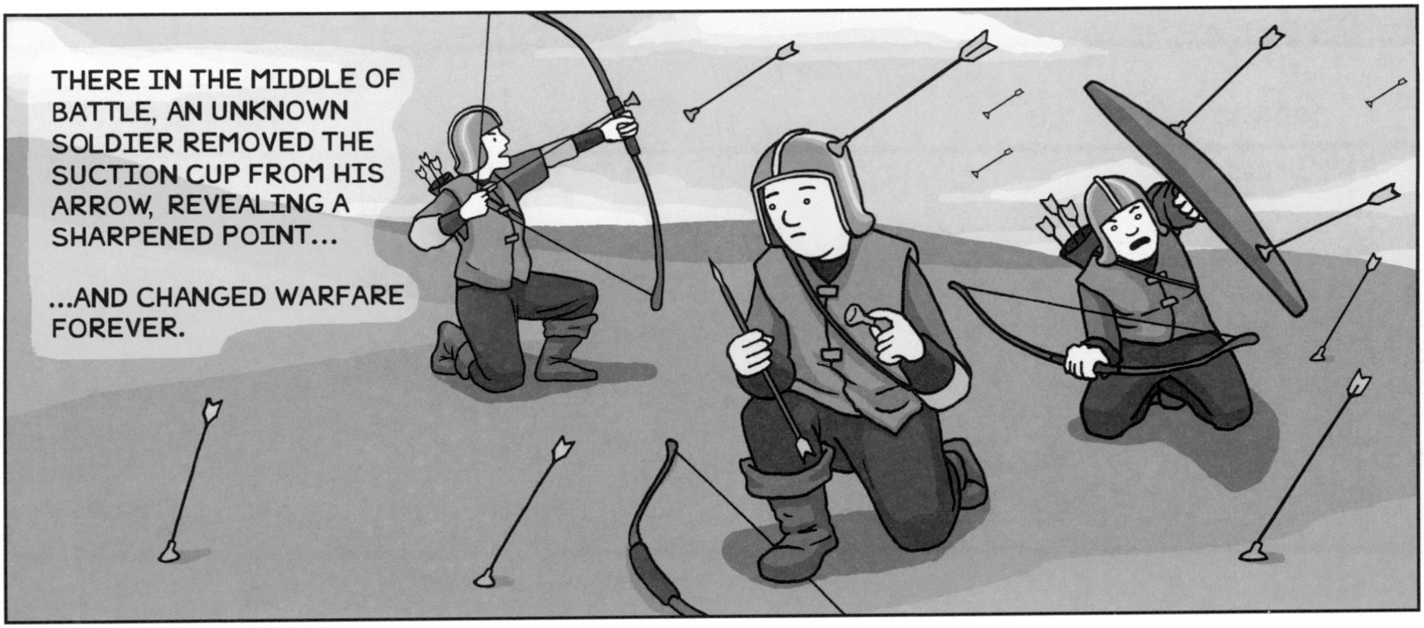
THERE IN THE MIDDLE OF BATTLE, AN UNKNOWN SOLDIER REMOVED THE SUCTION CUP FROM HIS ARROW, REVEALING A SHARPENED POINT...
...AND CHANGED WARFARE FOREVER.

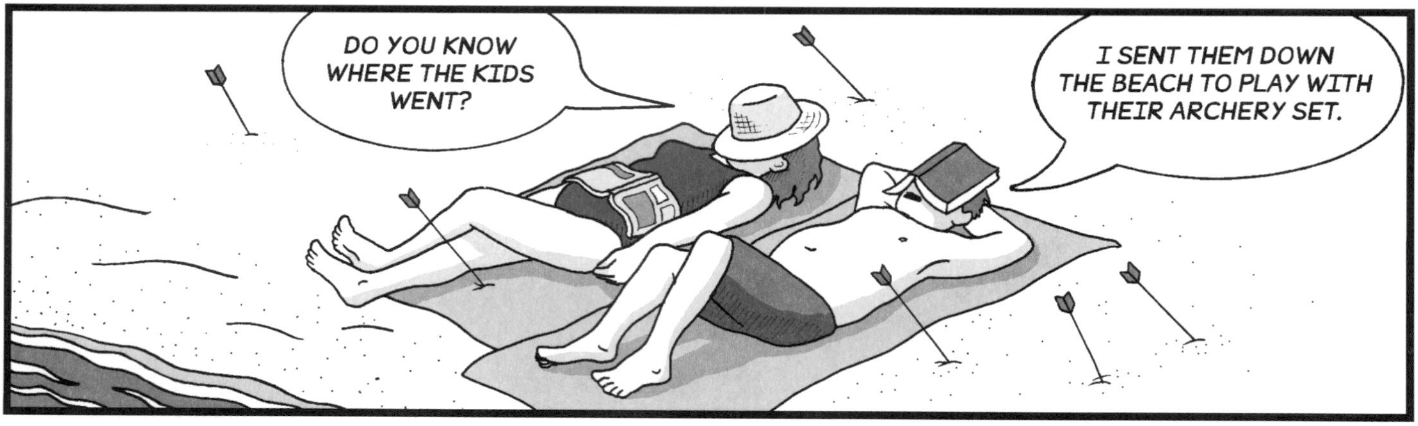
DO YOU KNOW WHERE THE KIDS WENT?
I SENT THEM DOWN THE BEACH TO PLAY WITH THEIR ARCHERY SET.

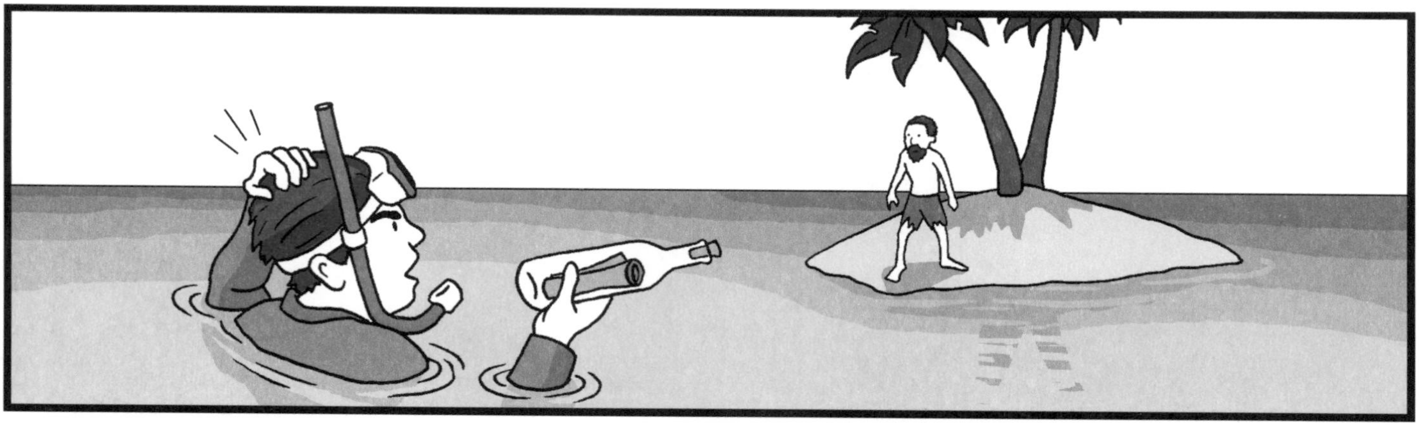

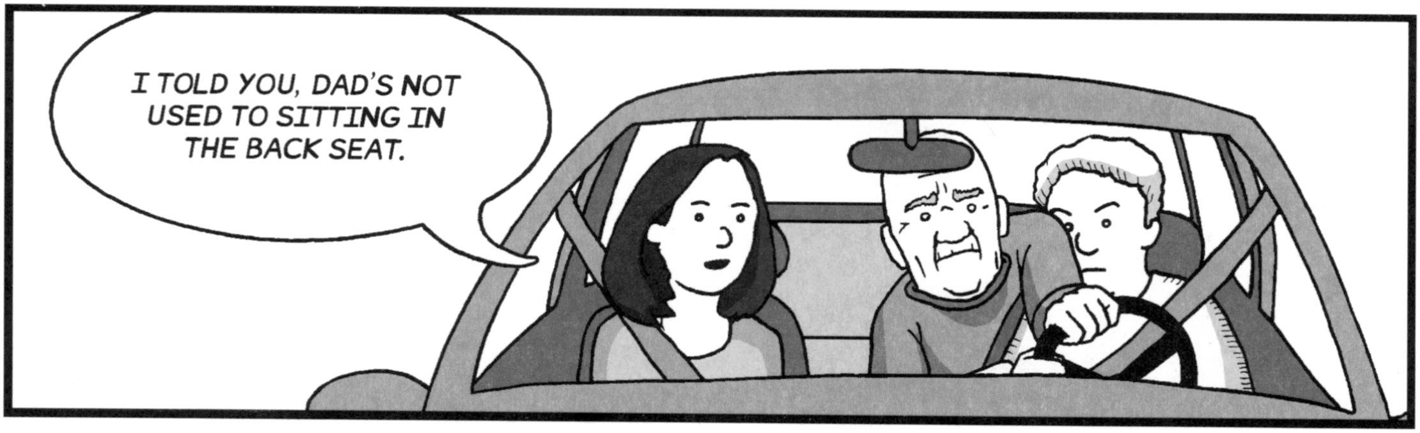
I TOLD YOU, DAD'S NOT USED TO SITTING IN THE BACK SEAT.

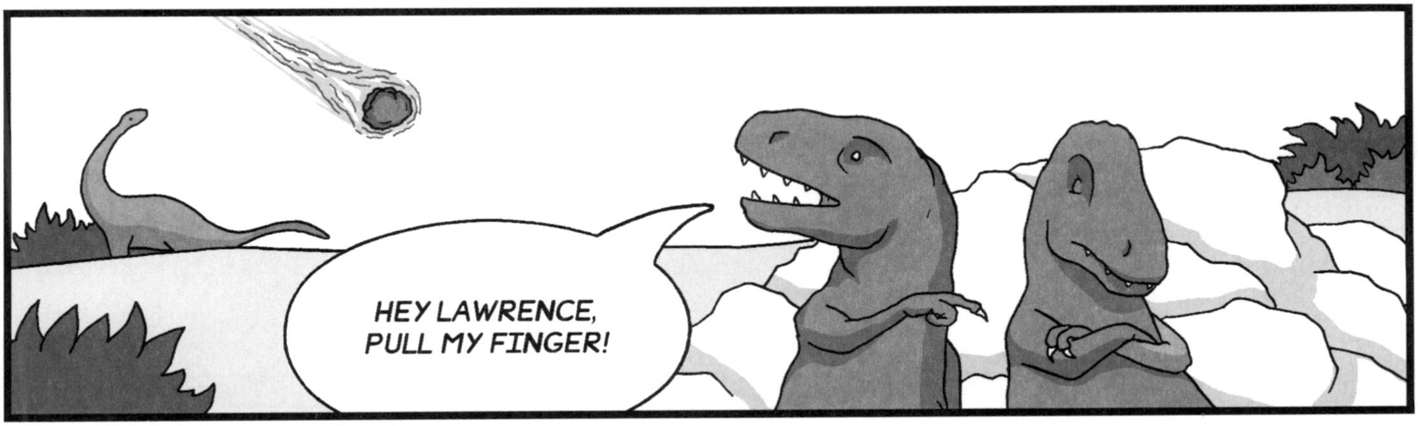
HEY LAWRENCE, PULL MY FINGER!

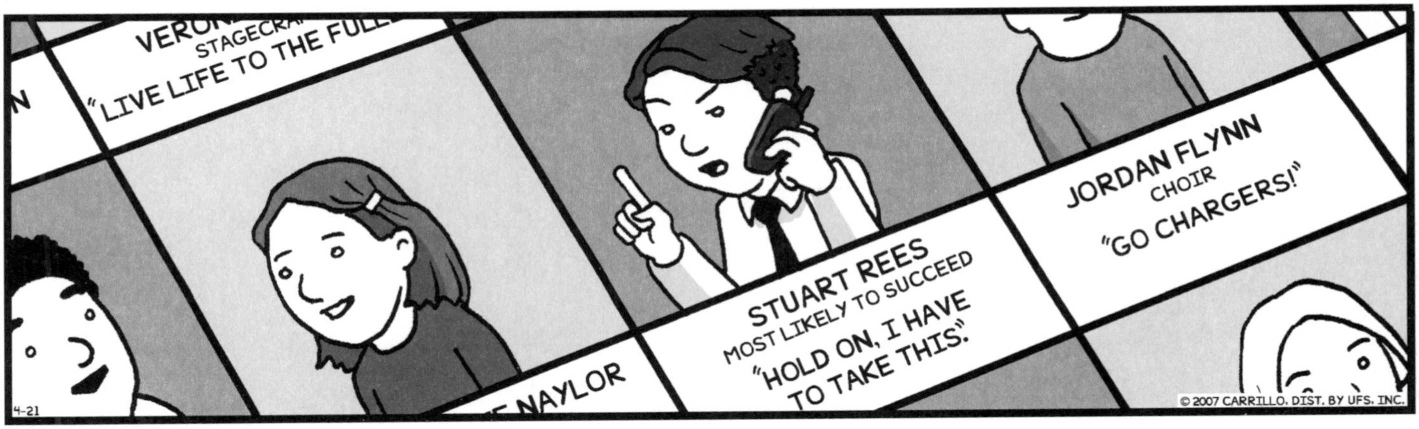
“LIVE LIFE TO THE
STUART REES
MOST LIKELY TO SUCCEED
“HOLD ON, I HAVE TO TAKE THIS.”
JORDAN FLYNN
CHOIR
“GO CHARGERS!”
NAYLOR
4-21
© 2007 CARRILLO. DIST. BY UFS, INC.

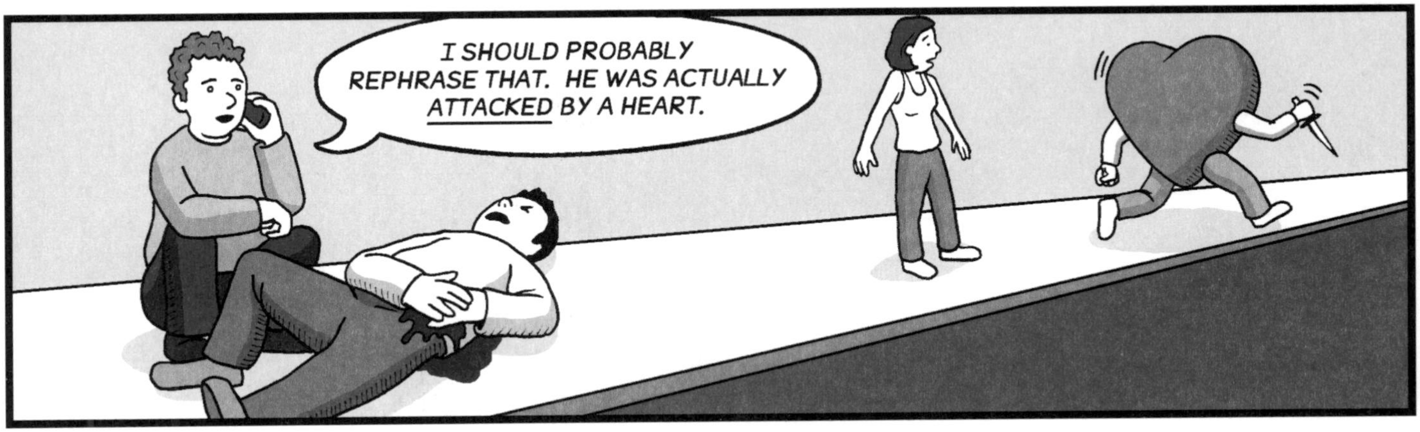
I SHOULD PROBABLY REPHRASE THAT. HE WAS ACTUALLY ATTACKED BY A HEART.

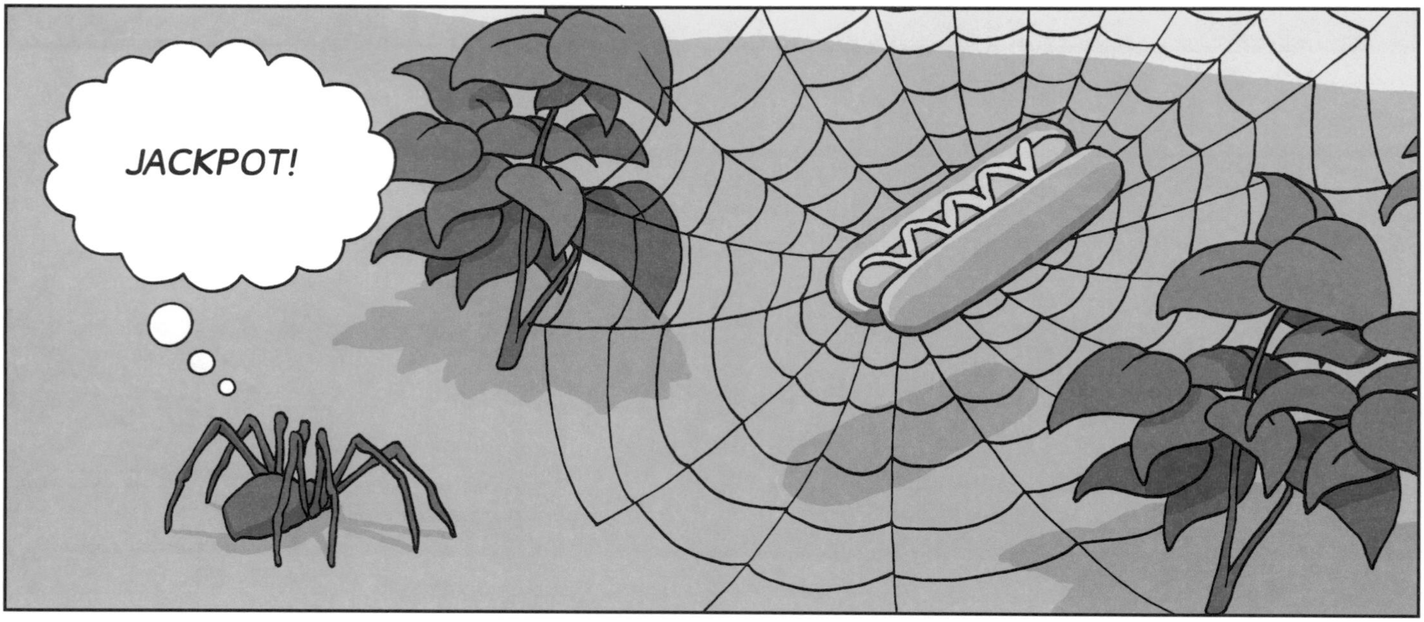
JACKPOT!

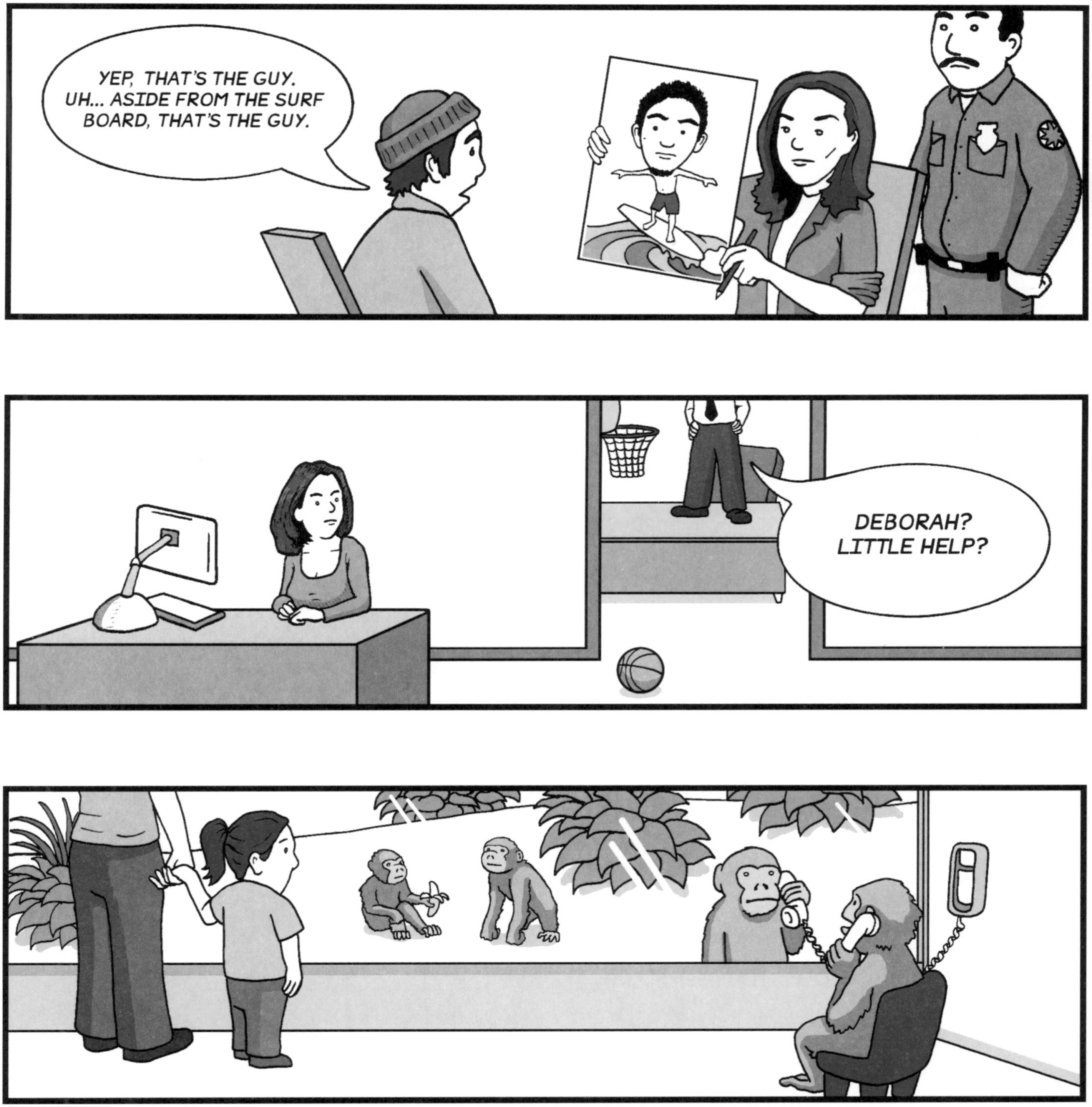
YEP, THAT'S THE GUY. UH... ASIDE FROM THE SURF BOARD, THAT'S THE GUY.
DEBORAH? LITTLE HELP?

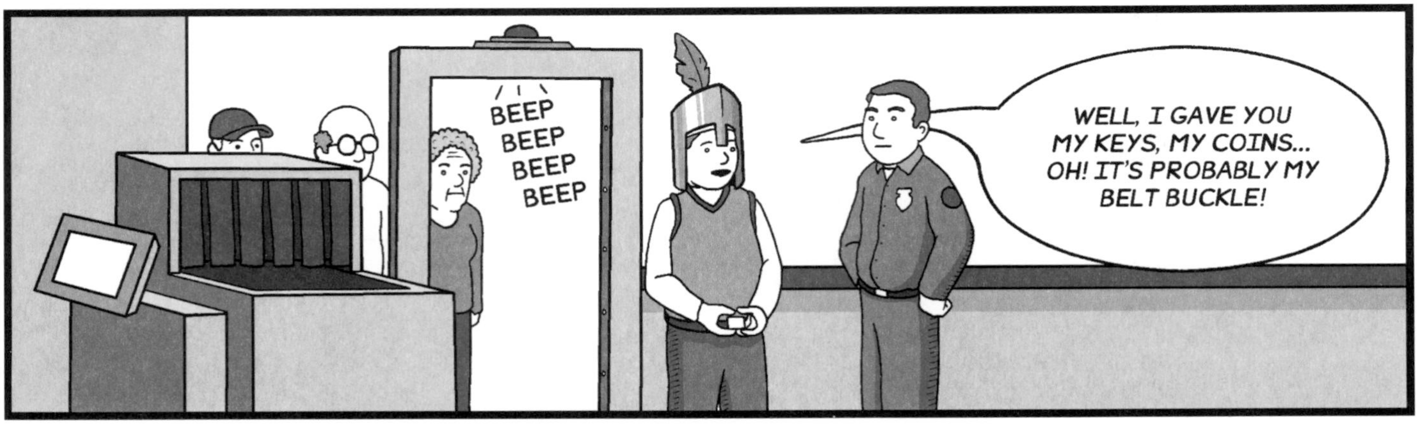
BEEP
BEEP
BEEP
BEEP
WELL, I GAVE YOU MY KEYS, MY COINS... OH! IT'S PROBABLY MY BELT BUCKLE!

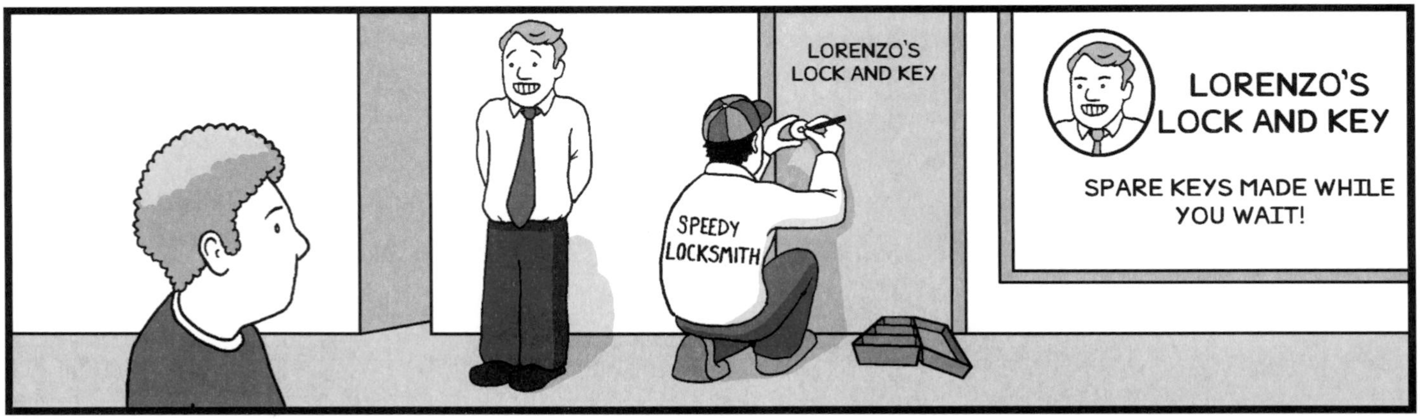
LORENZO'S LOCK AND KEY
SPEEDY LOCKSMITH
LORENZO'S LOCK AND KEY
SPARE KEYS MADE WHILE YOU WAIT!

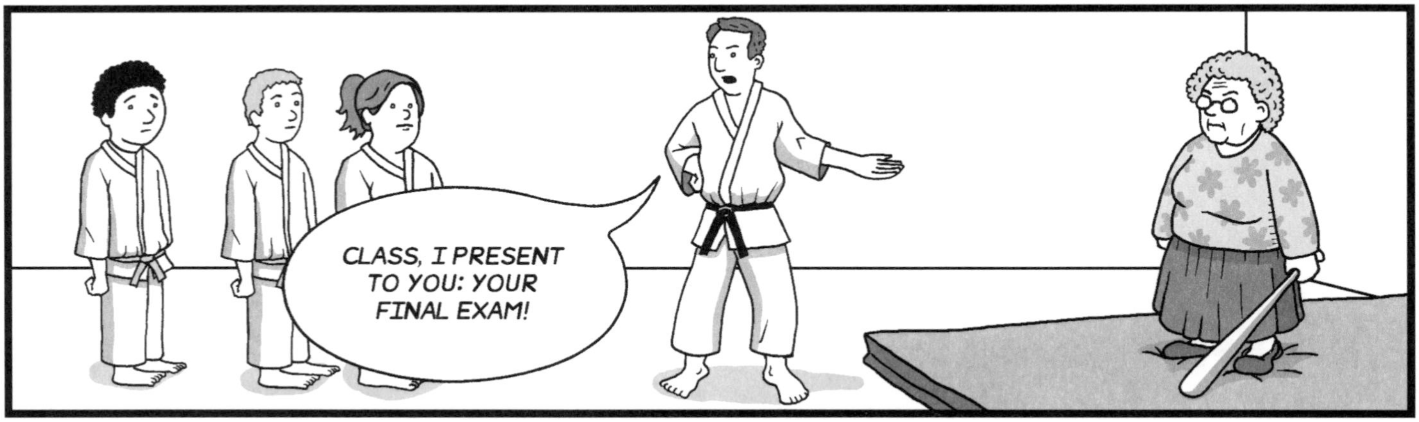
CLASS, I PRESENT TO YOU: YOUR FINAL EXAM!

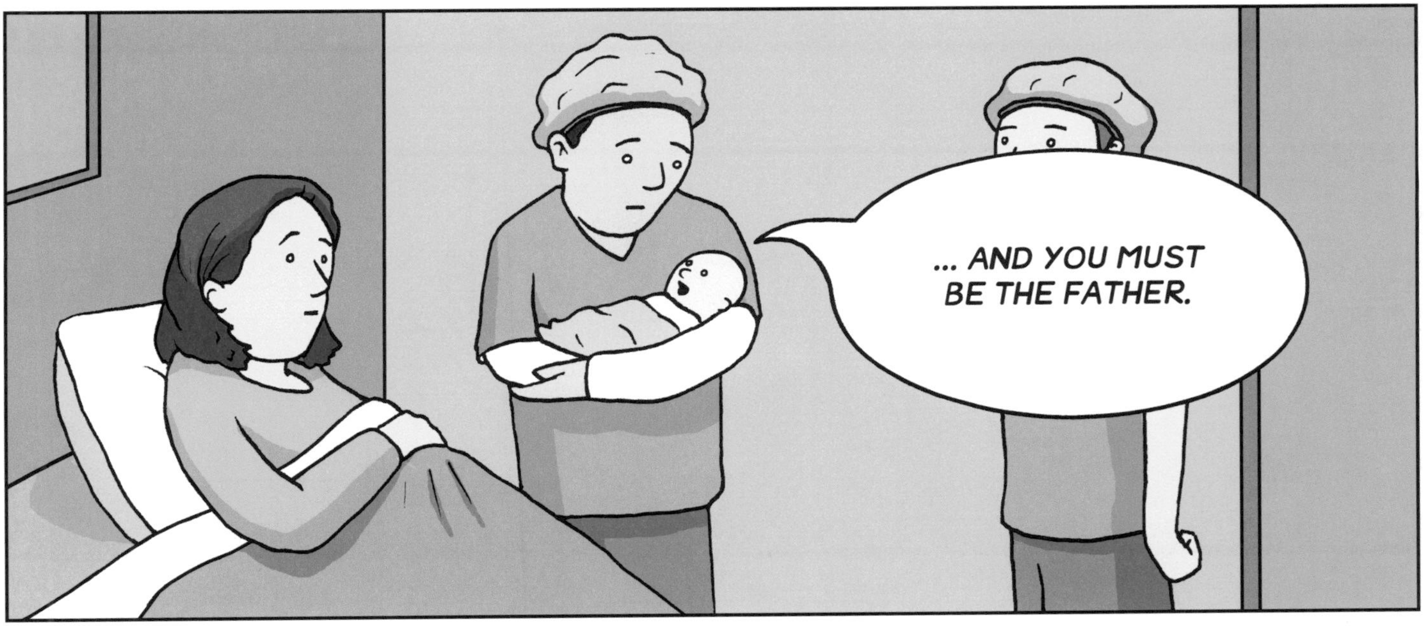
... AND YOU MUST BE THE FATHER.

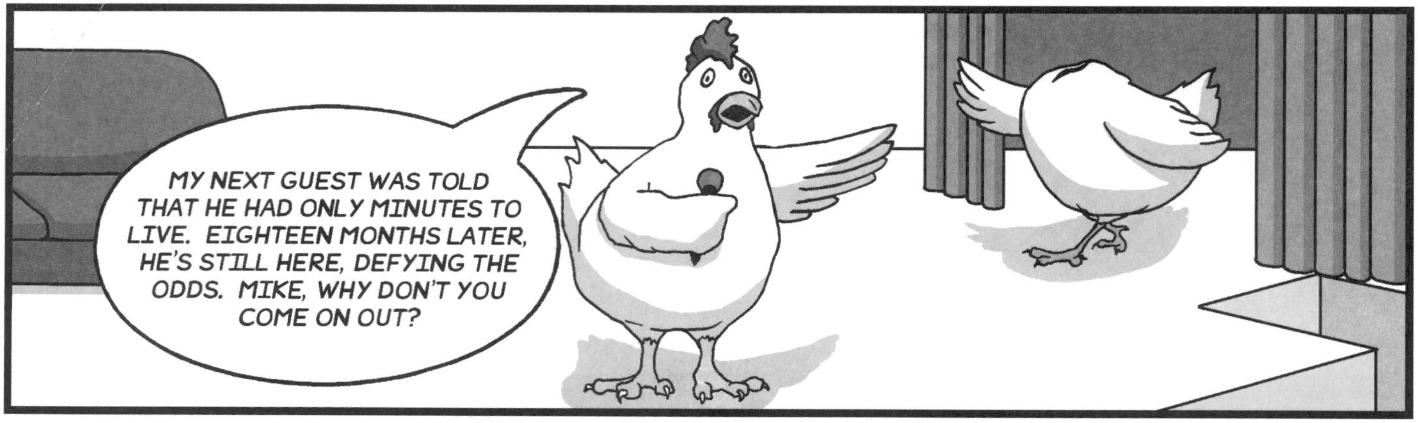
MY NEXT GUEST WAS TOLD THAT HE HAD ONLY MINUTES TO LIVE. EIGHTEEN MONTHS LATER, HE'S STILL HERE, DEFYING THE ODDS. MIKE, WHY DON'T YOU COME ON OUT?

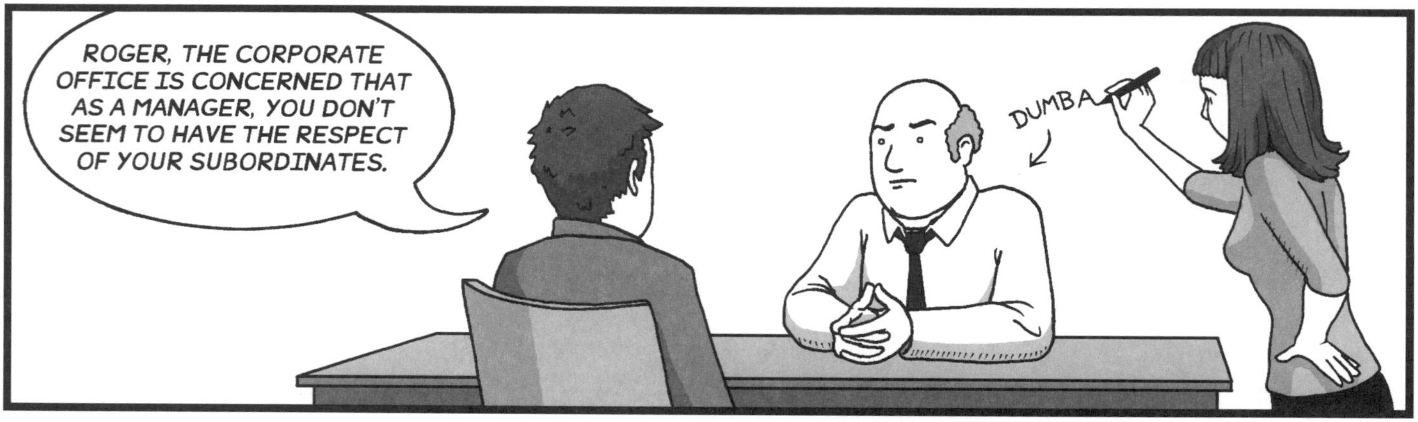
ROGER, THE CORPORATE OFFICE IS CONCERNED THAT AS A MANAGER, YOU DON'T SEEM TO HAVE THE RESPECT OF YOUR SUBORDINATES.
DUMBA

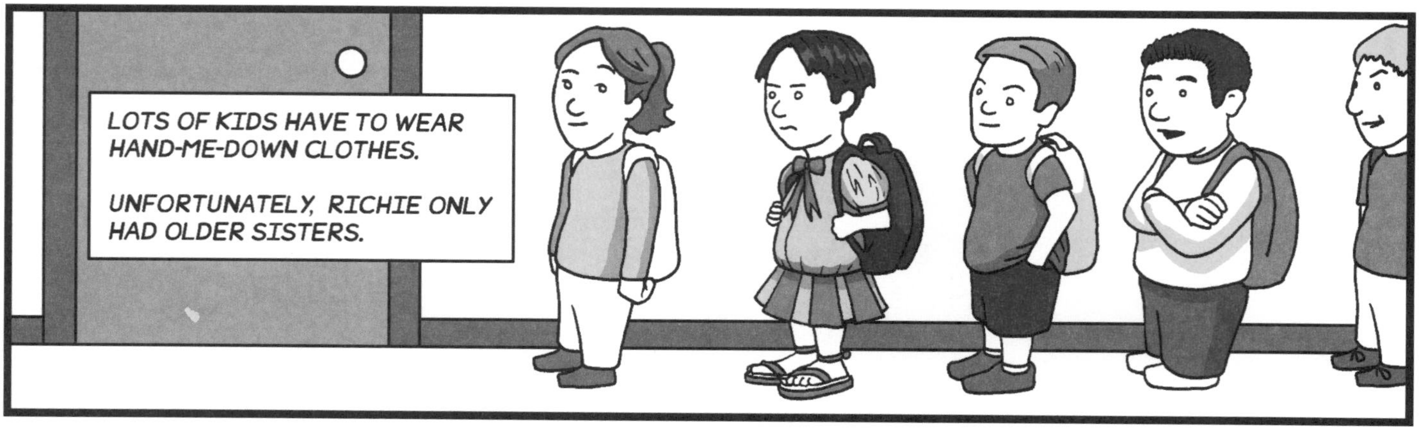
LOTS OF KIDS HAVE TO WEAR HAND-ME-DOWN CLOTHES.
UNFORTUNATELY, RICHIE ONLY HAD OLDER SISTERS.

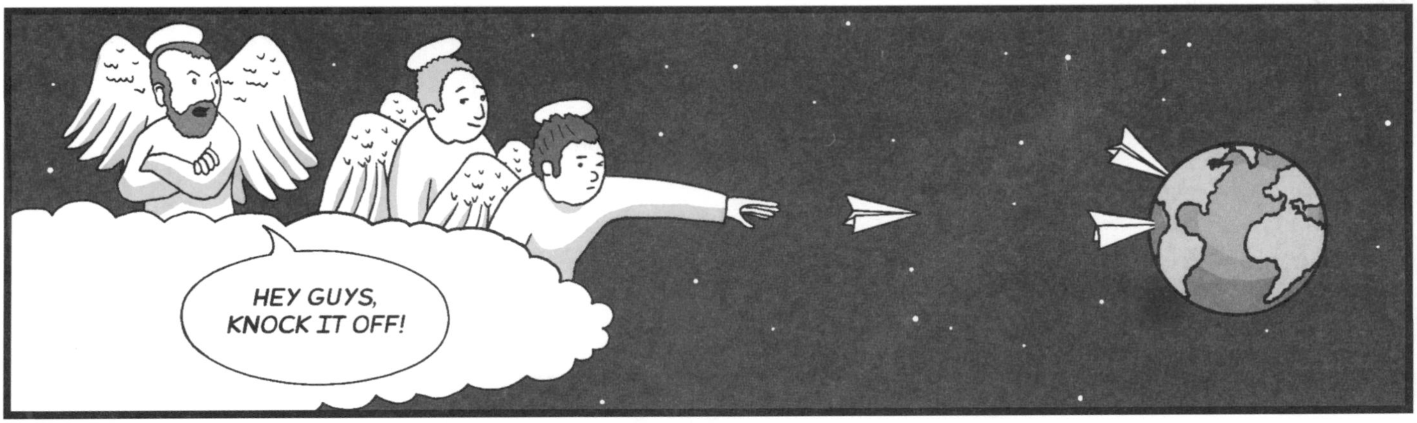
HEY GUYS, KNOCK IT OFF!

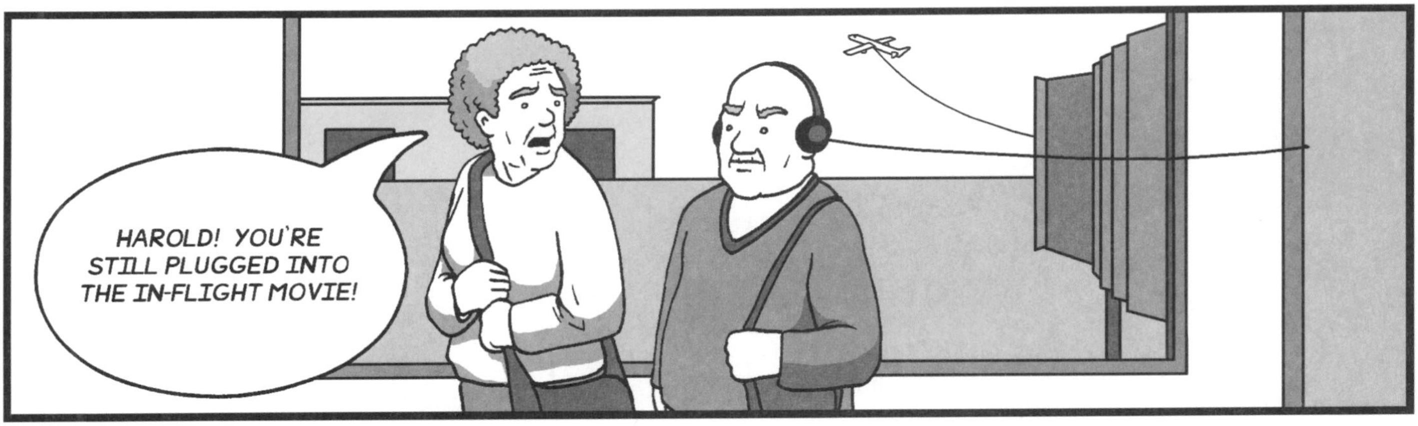
HAROLD! YOU'RE STILL PLUGGED INTO THE IN-FLIGHT MOVIE!

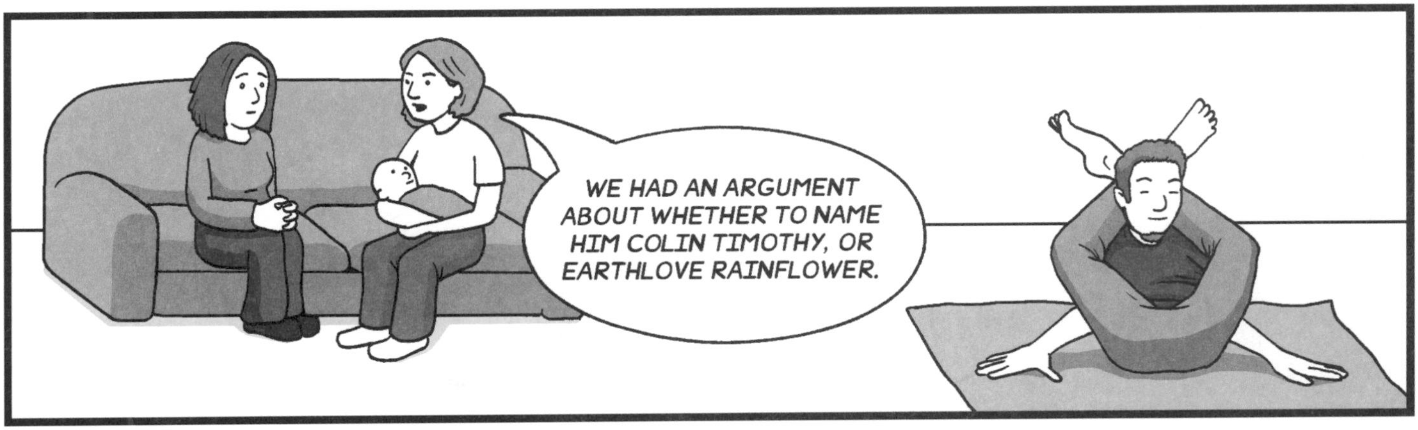
WE HAD AN ARGUMENT ABOUT WHETHER TO NAME HIM COLIN TIMOTHY, OR EARTHLOVE RAINFLOWER.

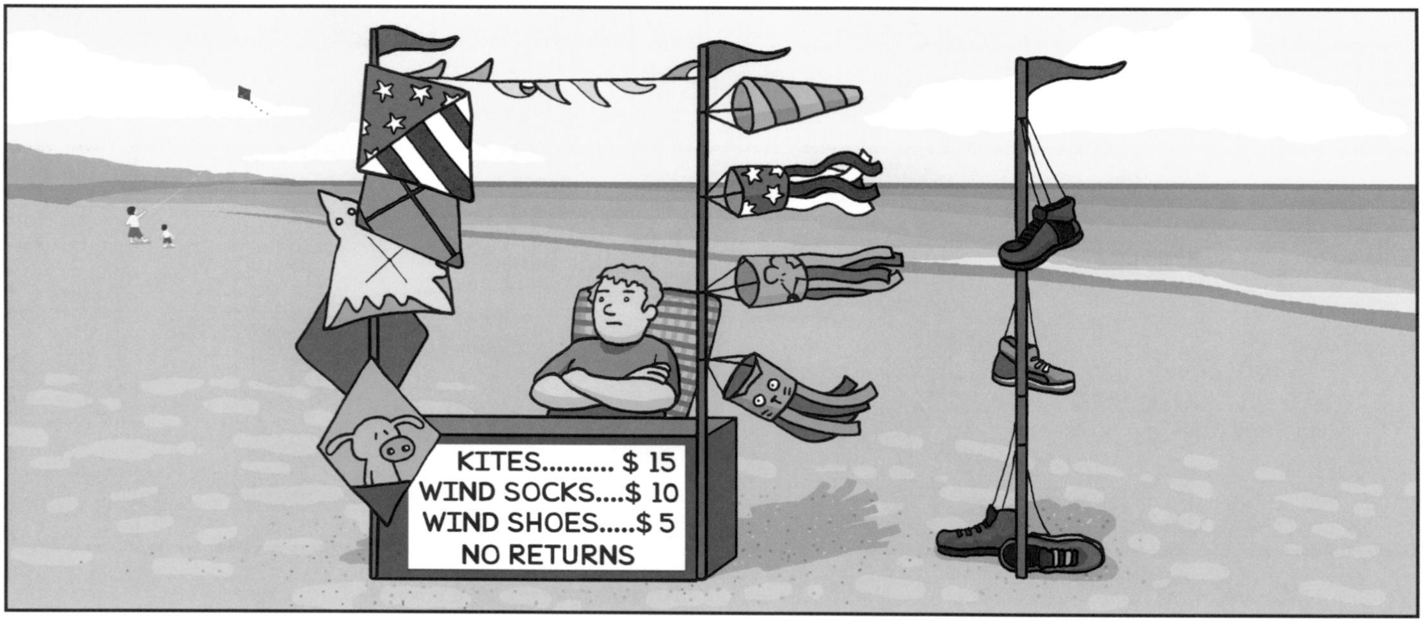
KITES.......... $ 15
WIND SOCKS....$ 10
WIND SHOES.....$ 5
NO RETURNS

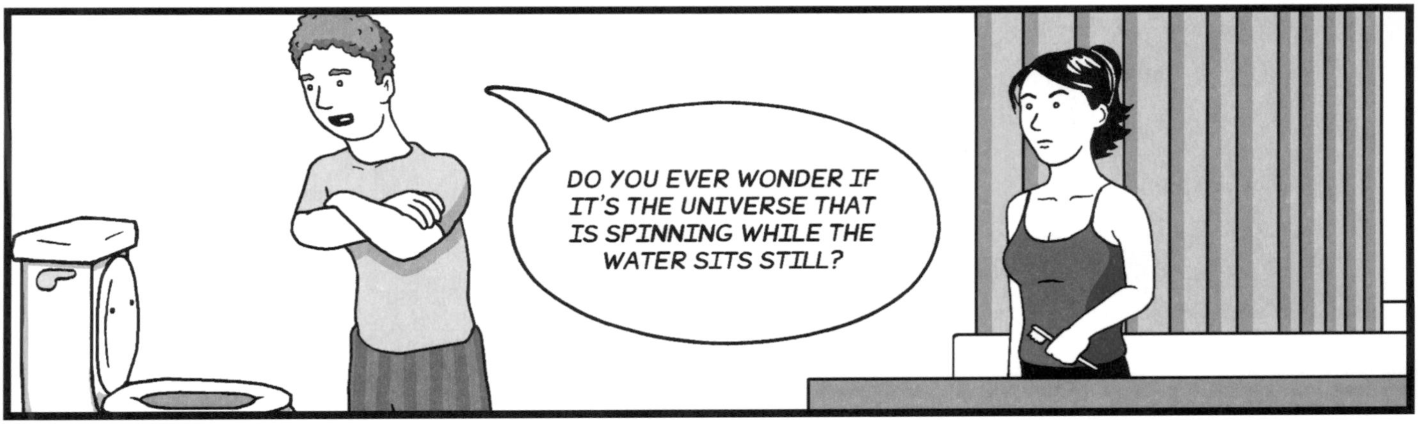
DO YOU EVER WONDER IF IT'S THE UNIVERSE THAT IS SPINNING WHILE THE WATER SITS STILL?

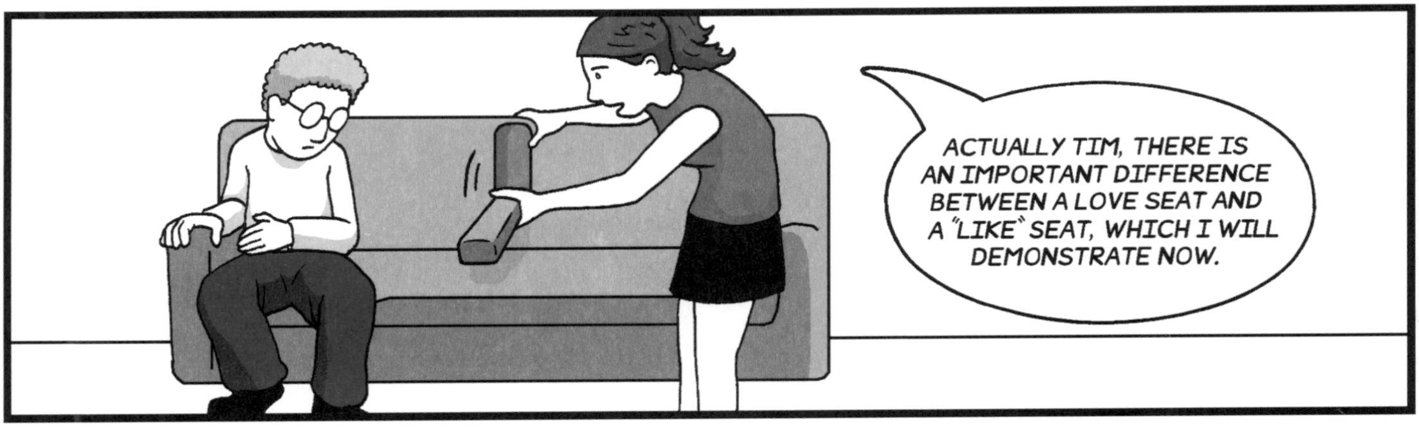
ACTUALLY TIM, THERE IS AN IMPORTANT DIFFERENCE BETWEEN A LOVE SEAT AND A "LIKE" SEAT, WHICH I WILL DEMONSTRATE NOW.

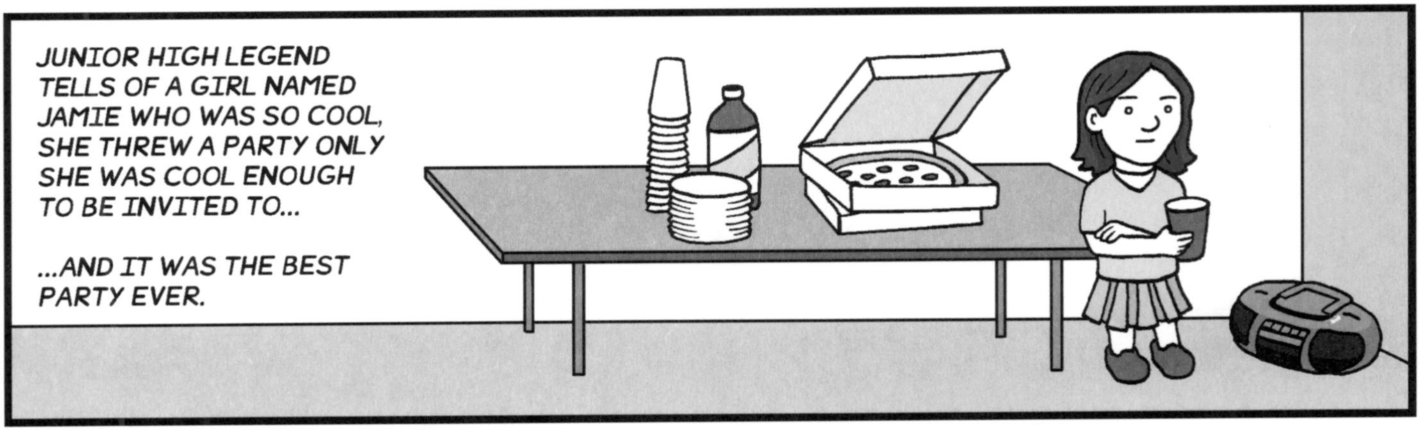
JUNIOR HIGH LEGEND TELLS OF A GIRL NAMED JAMIE WHO WAS SO COOL, SHE THREW A PARTY ONLY SHE WAS COOL ENOUGH TO BE INVITED TO...
...AND IT WAS THE BEST PARTY EVER.

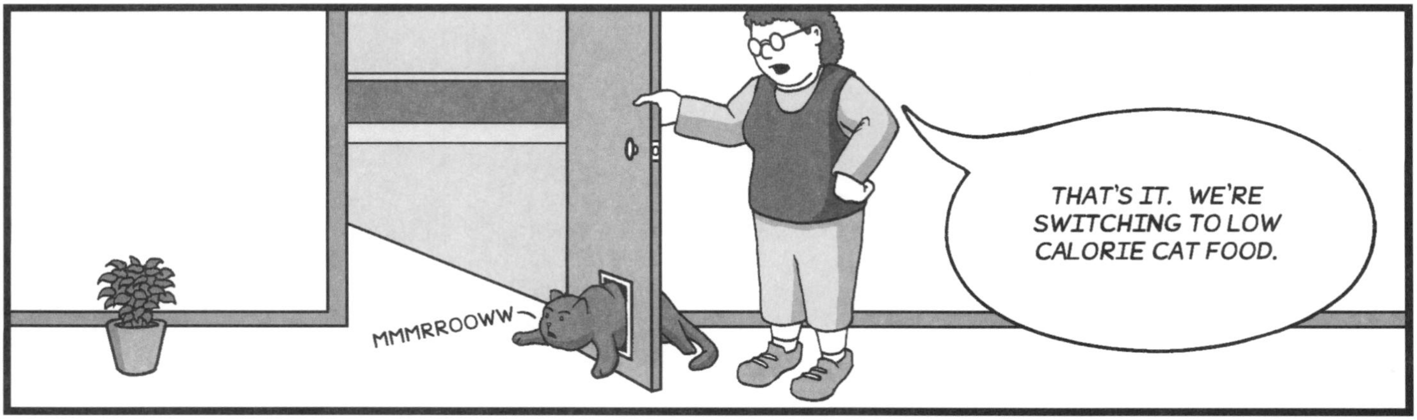
MMMRROOWW
THAT'S IT. WE'RE SWITCHING TO LOW CALORIE CAT FOOD.

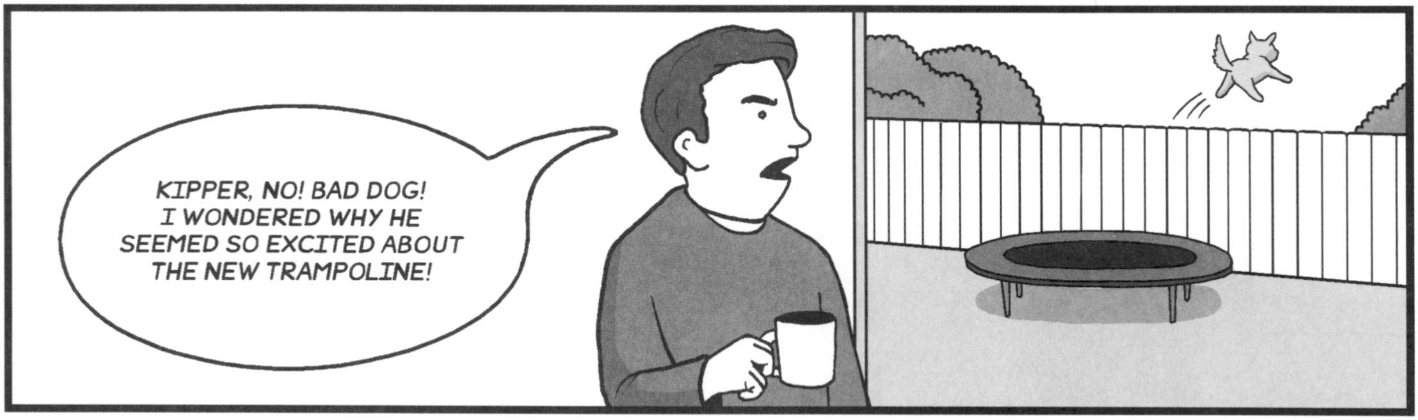
KIPPER, NO! BAD DOG! I WONDERED WHY HE SEEMED SO EXCITED ABOUT THE NEW TRAMPOLINE!

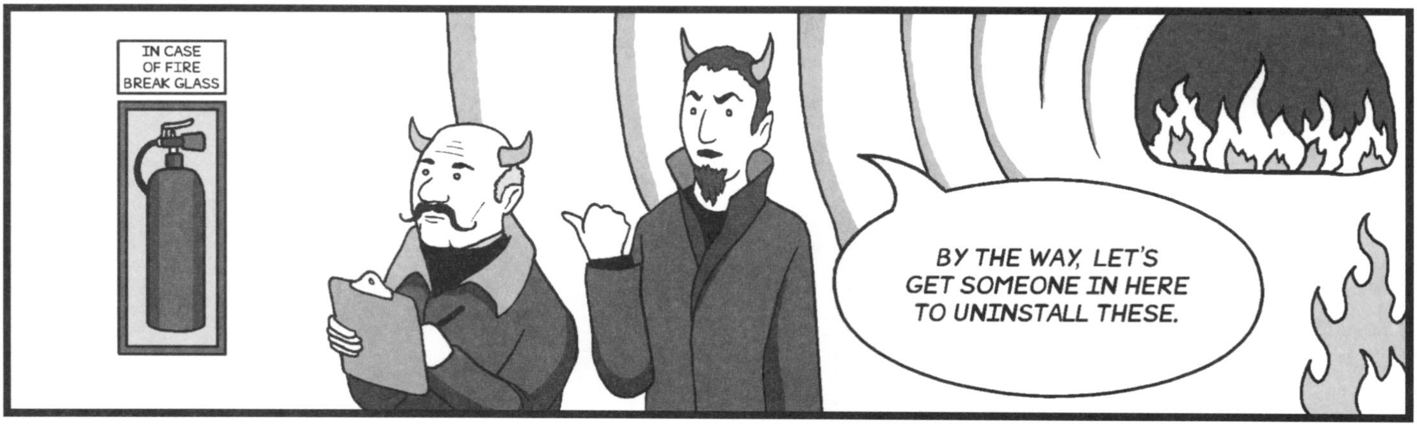
IN CASE OF FIRE BREAK GLASS
BY THE WAY, LET'S GET SOMEONE IN HERE TO UNINSTALL THESE.

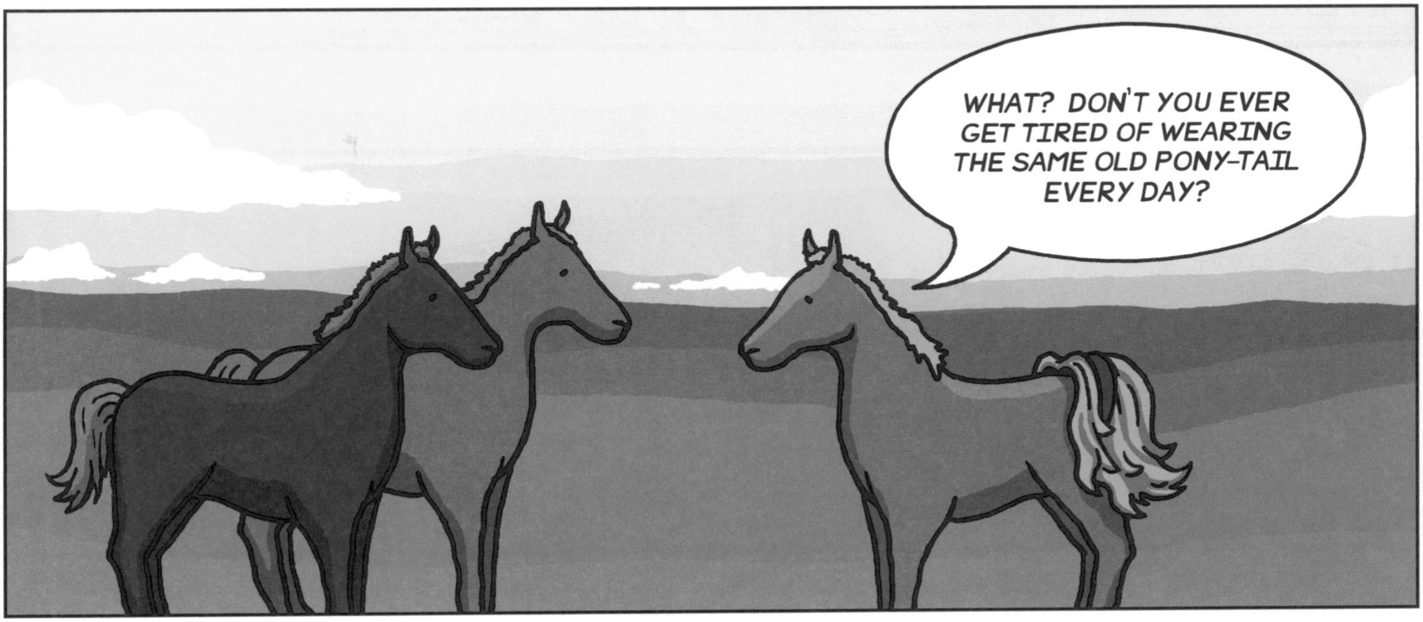
WHAT? DON'T YOU EVER GET TIRED OF WEARING THE SAME OLD PONY-TAIL EVERY DAY?

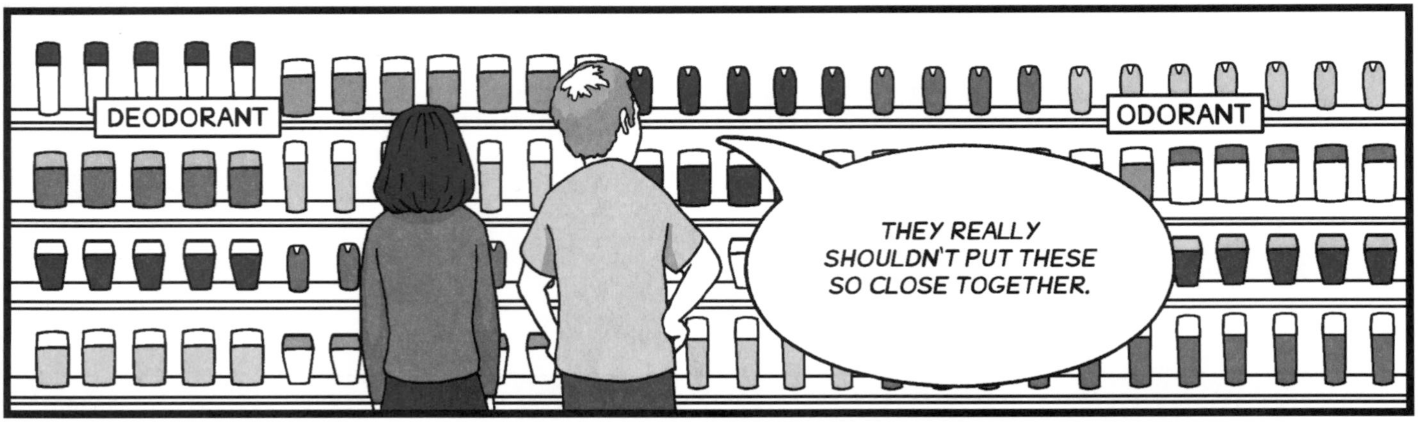
DEODORANT
ODORANT
THEY REALLY SHOULDN'T PUT THESE SO CLOSE TOGETHER.

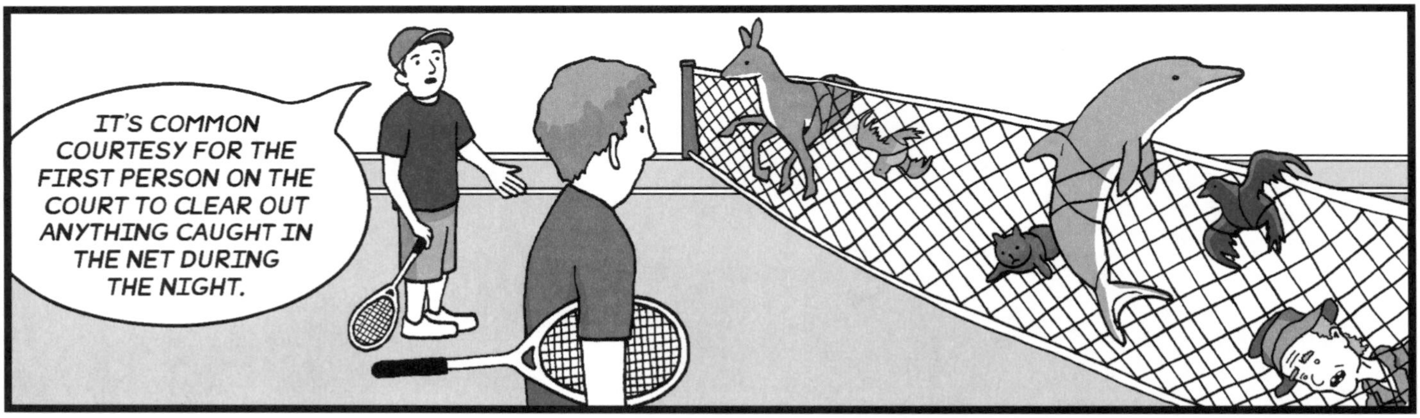
IT'S COMMON COURTESY FOR THE FIRST PERSON ON THE COURT TO CLEAR OUT ANYTHING CAUGHT IN THE NET DURING THE NIGHT.

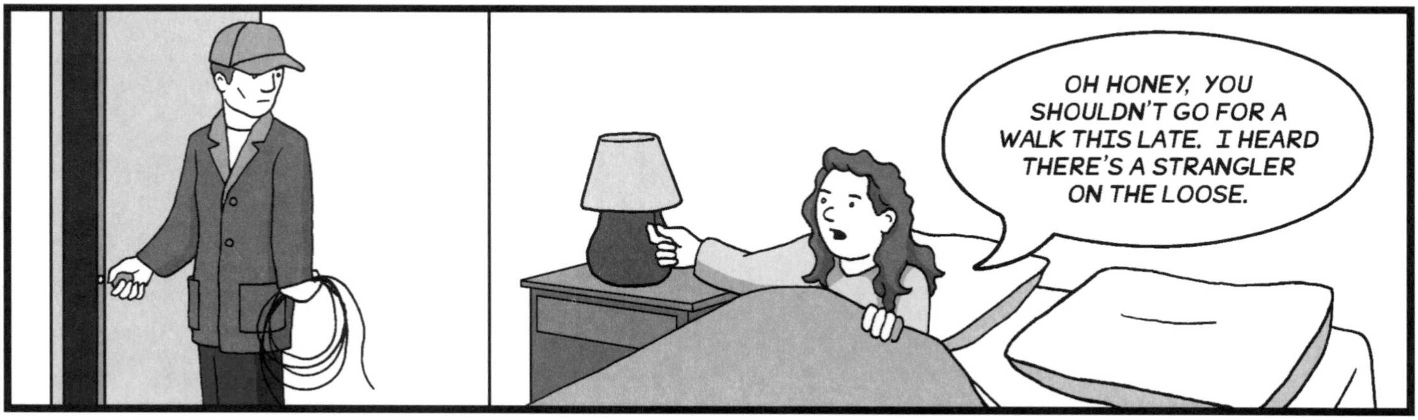
OH HONEY, YOU SHOULDN'T GO FOR A WALK THIS LATE. I HEARD THERE'S A STRANGLER ON THE LOOSE.

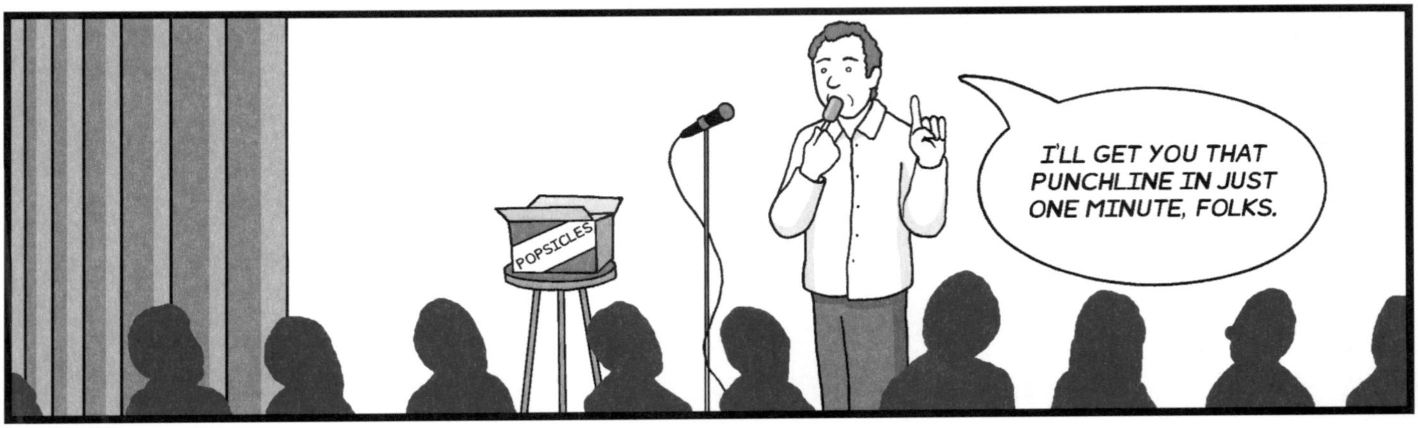
POPSICLES
I'LL GET YOU THAT PUNCHLINE IN JUST ONE MINUTE, FOLKS.

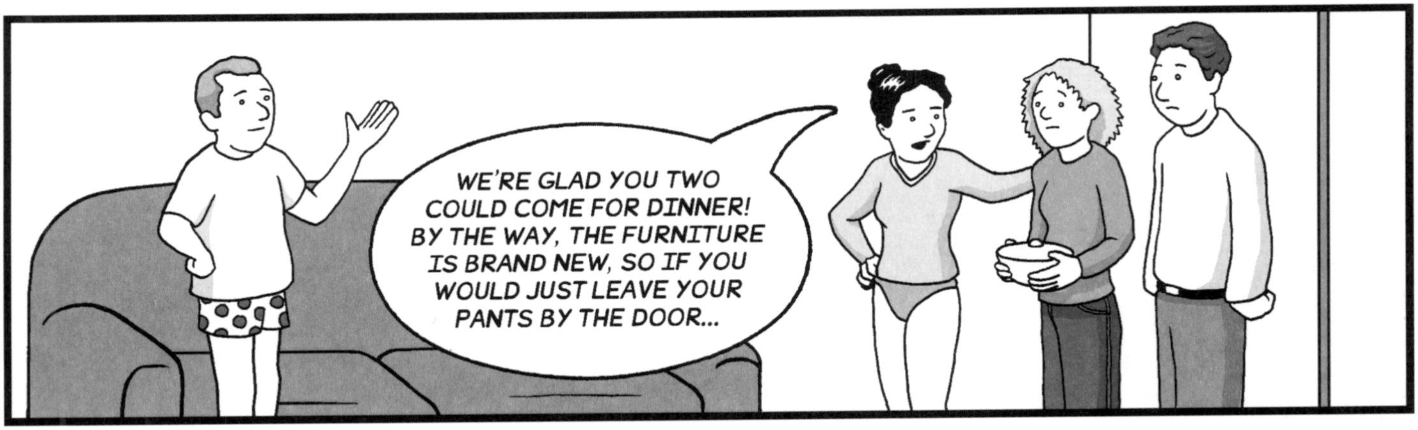
WE'RE GLAD YOU TWO COULD COME FOR DINNER! BY THE WAY, THE FURNITURE IS BRAND NEW, SO IF YOU WOULD JUST LEAVE YOUR PANTS BY THE DOOR...

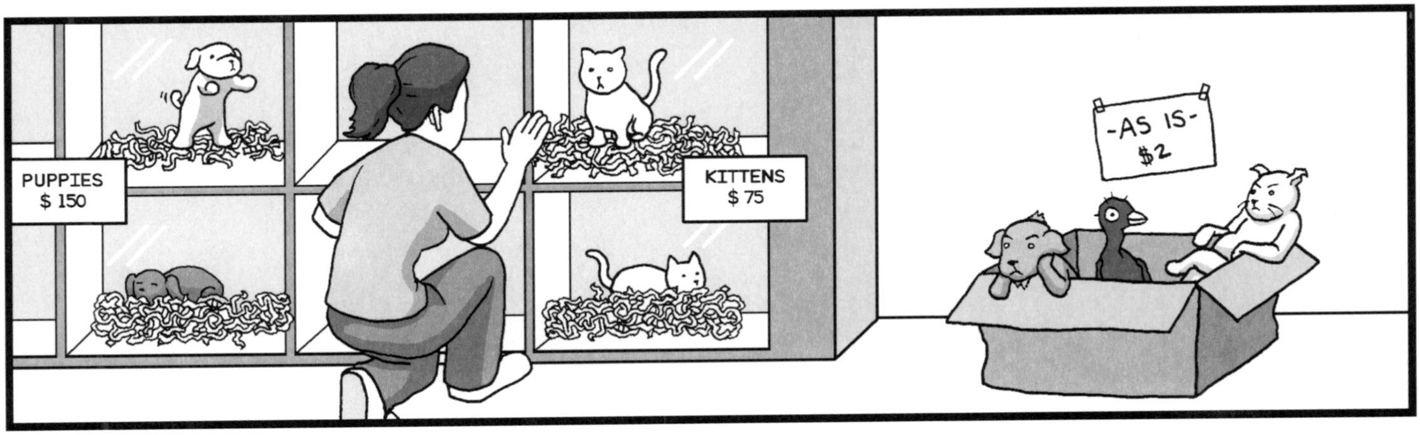
PUPPIES
$ 150
KITTENS
$ 75
-AS IS-
$2

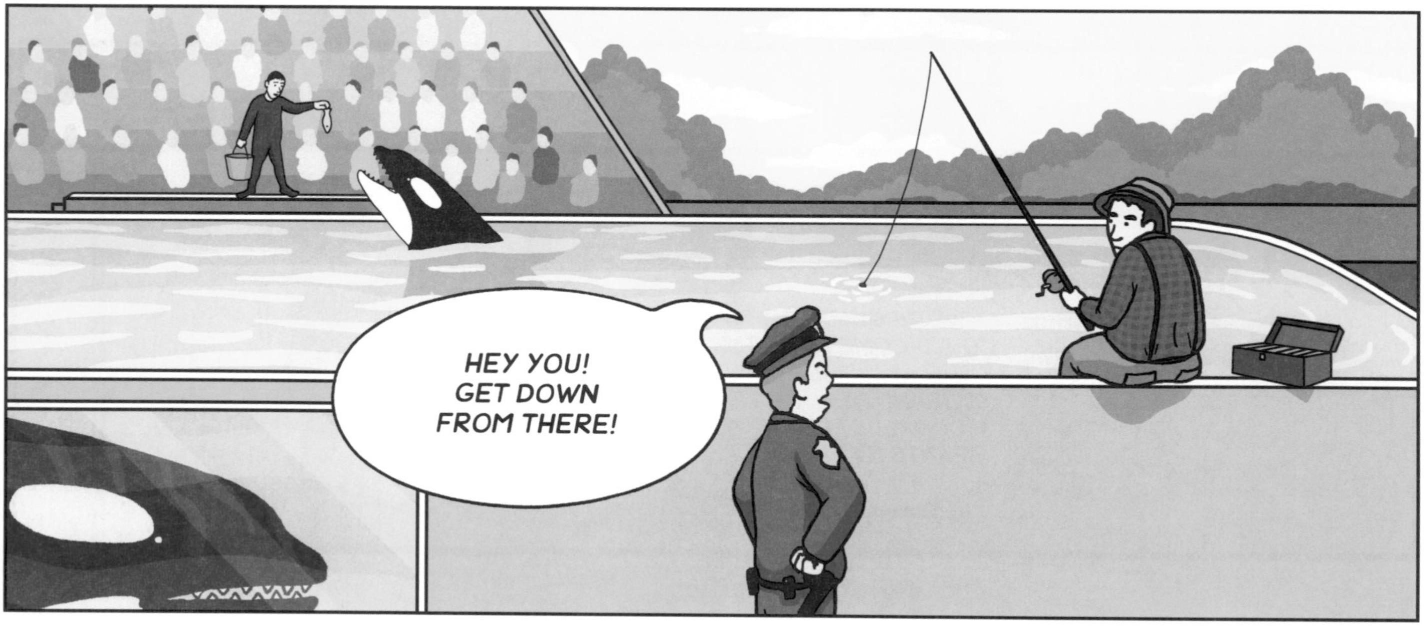
HEY YOU!
GET DOWN
FROM THERE!

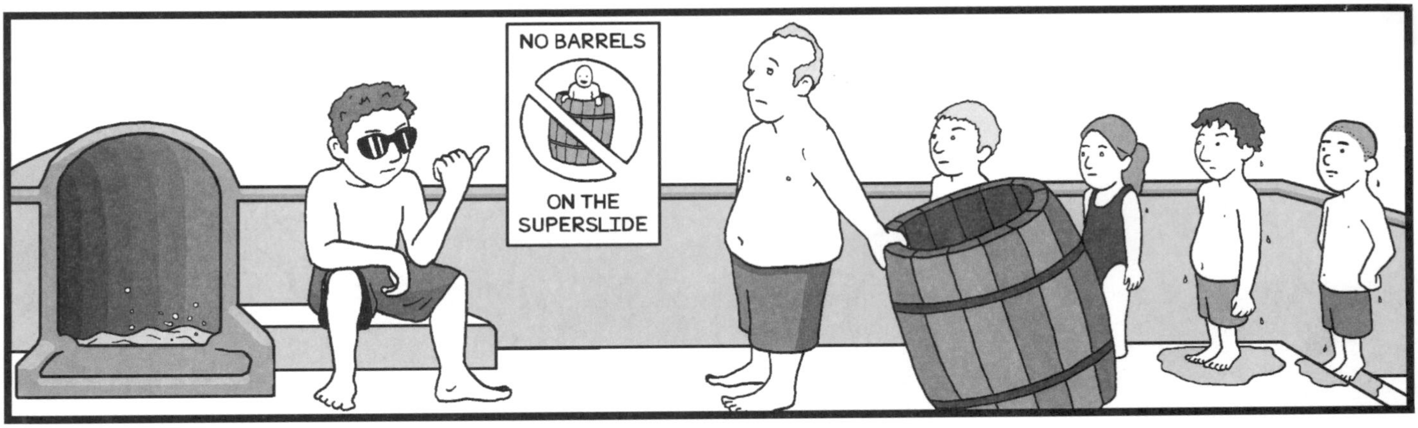
NO BARRELS ON THE SUPERSLIDE

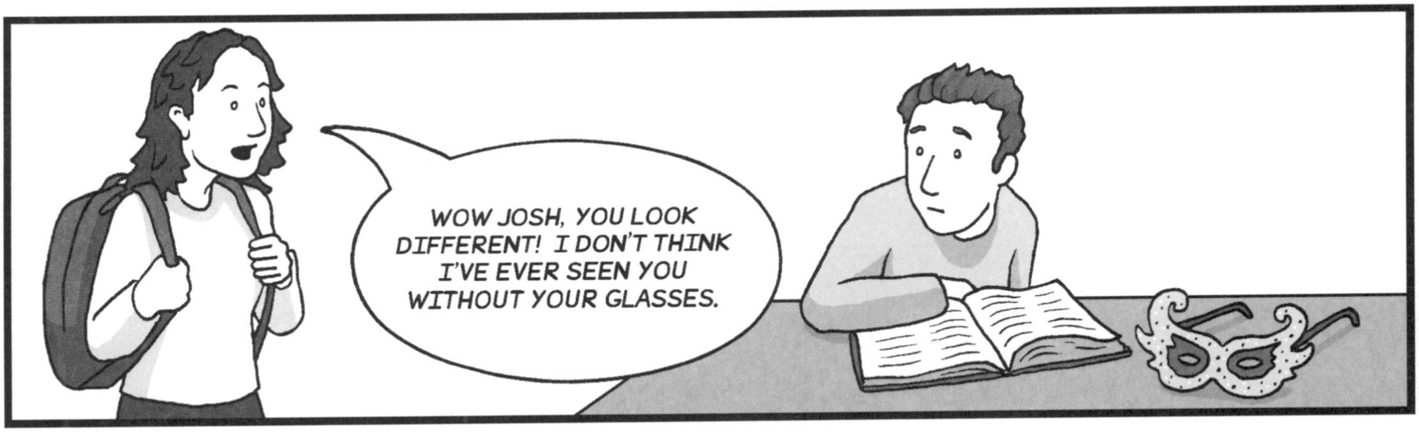
WOW JOSH, YOU LOOK DIFFERENT! I DON'T THINK I'VE EVER SEEN YOU WITHOUT YOUR GLASSES.

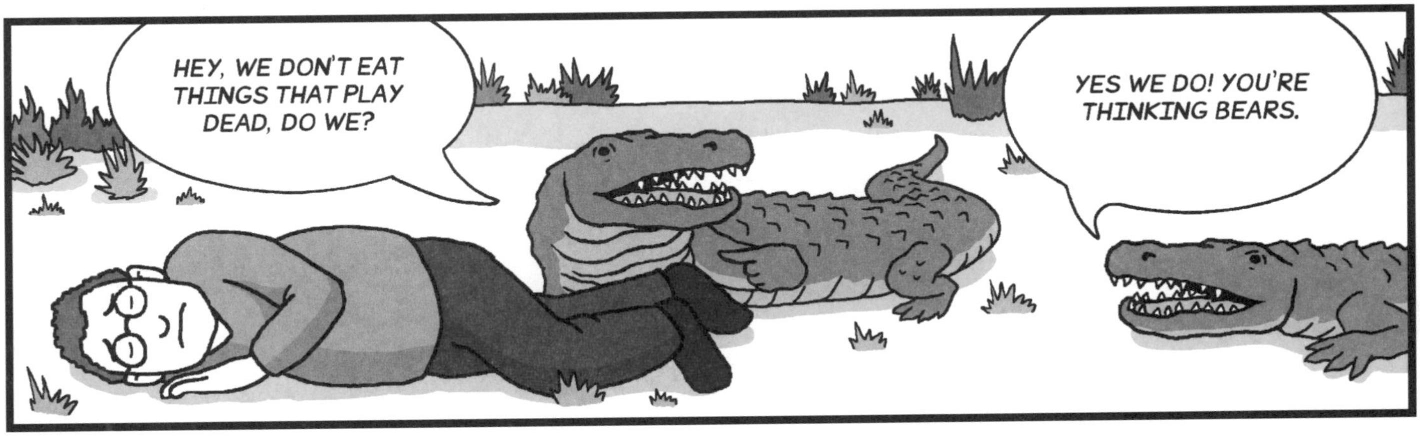
HEY, WE DON'T EAT THINGS THAT PLAY DEAD, DO WE?
YES WE DO! YOU'RE THINKING BEARS.

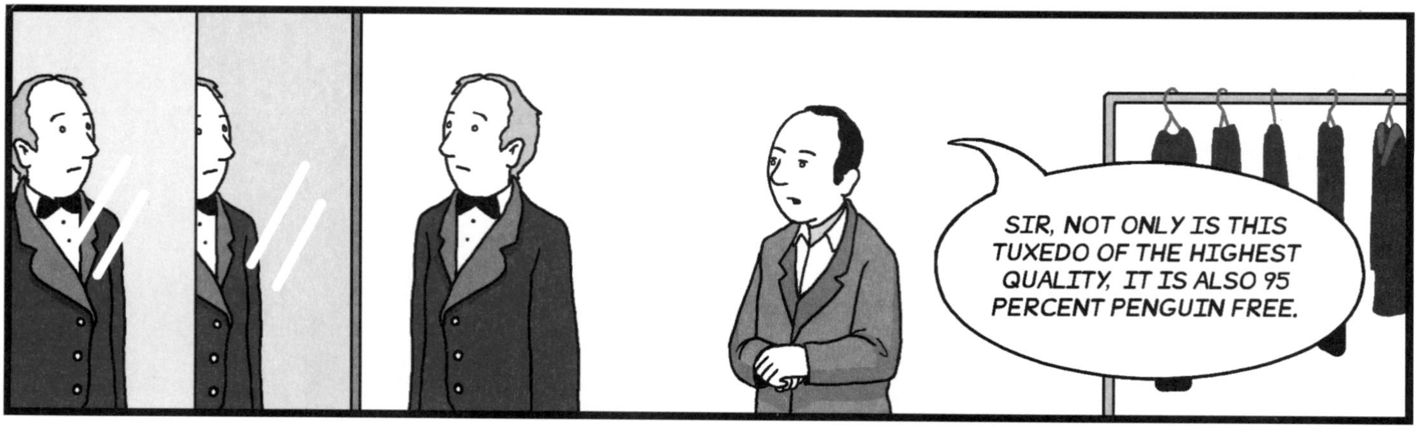
SIR, NOT ONLY IS THIS TUXEDO OF THE HIGHEST QUALITY, IT IS ALSO 95 PERCENT PENGUIN FREE.

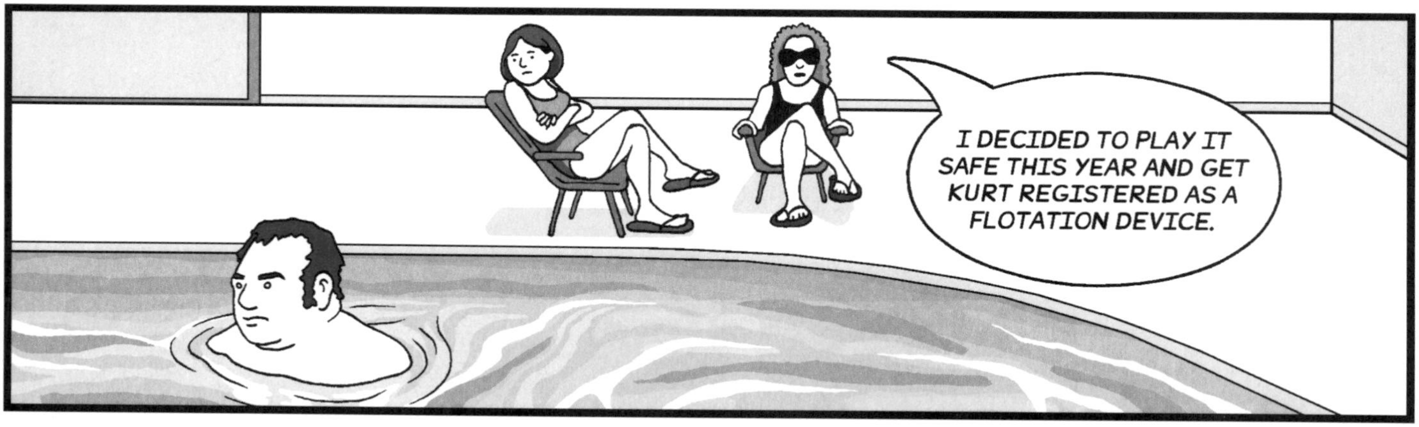
I DECIDED TO PLAY IT SAFE THIS YEAR AND GET KURT REGISTERED AS A FLOTATION DEVICE.

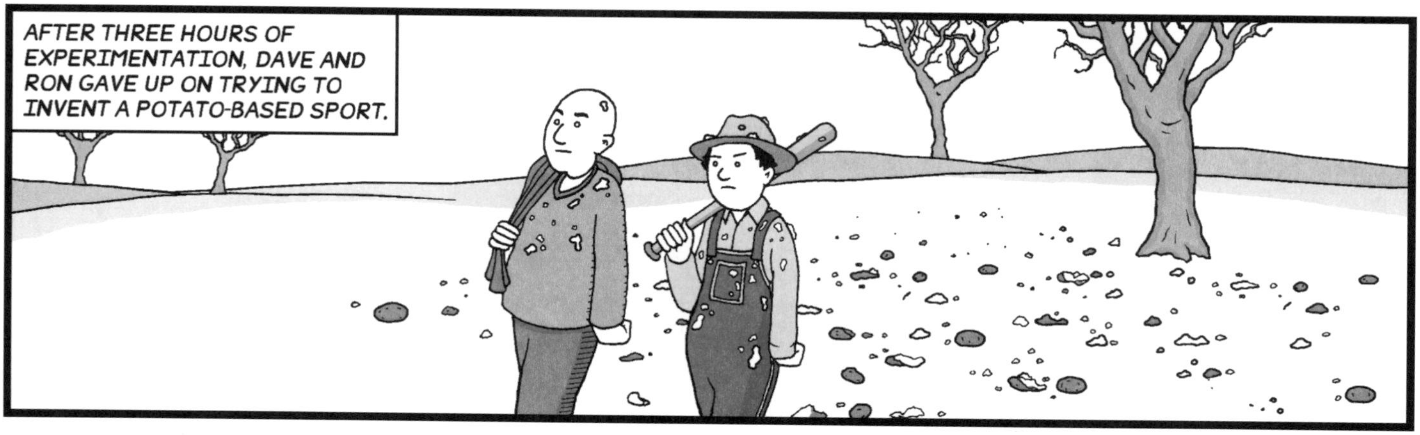
AFTER THREE HOURS OF EXPERIMENTATION, DAVE AND RON GAVE UP ON TRYING TO INVENT A POTATO-BASED SPORT.

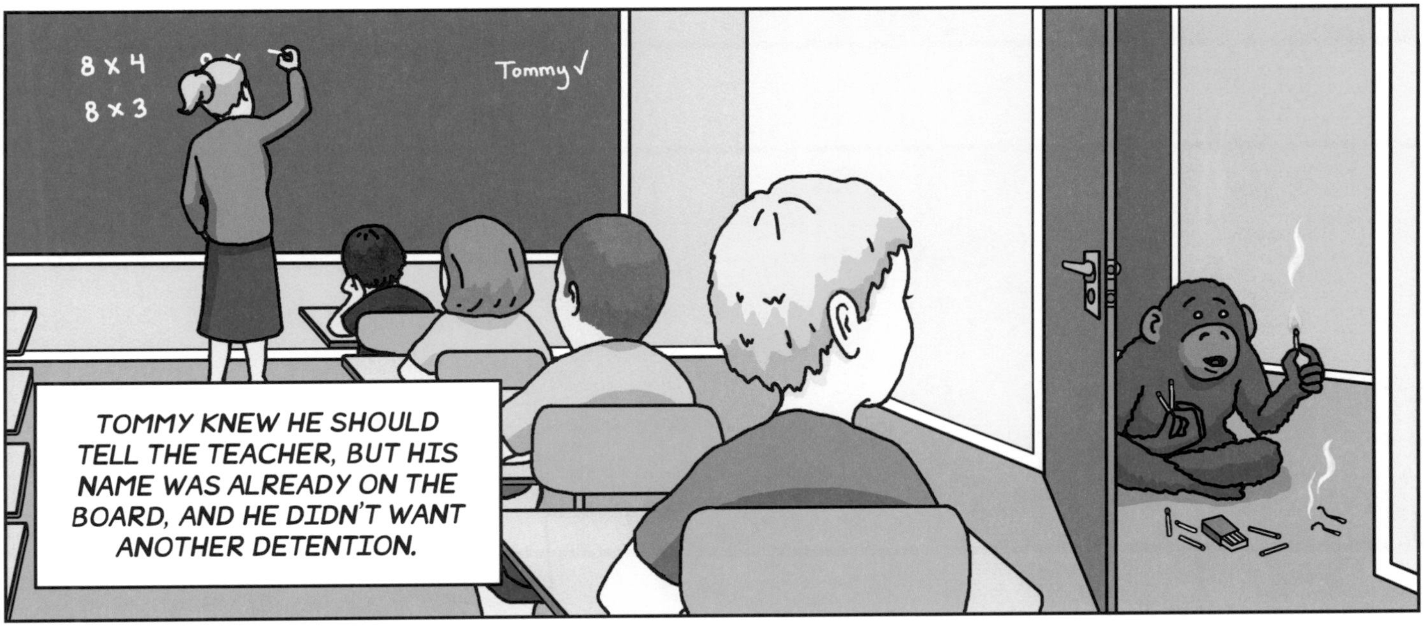
8 x 4
8 x 3
Tommy √
TOMMY KNEW HE SHOULD TELL THE TEACHER, BUT HIS NAME WAS ALREADY ON THE BOARD, AND HE DIDN'T WANT ANOTHER DETENTION.

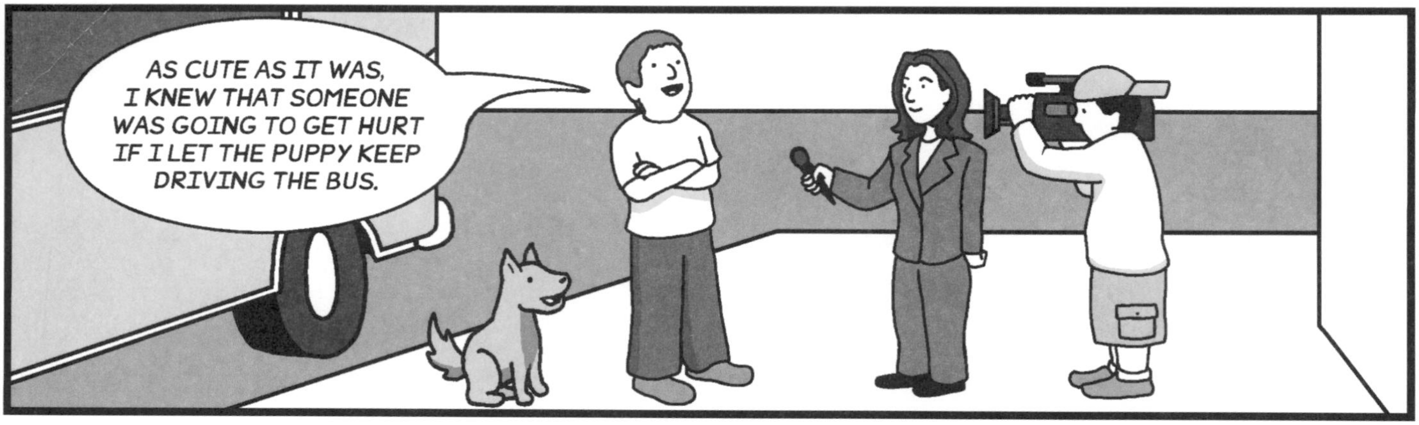
AS CUTE AS IT WAS, I KNEW THAT SOMEONE WAS GOING TO GET HURT IF I LET THE PUPPY KEEP DRIVING THE BUS.

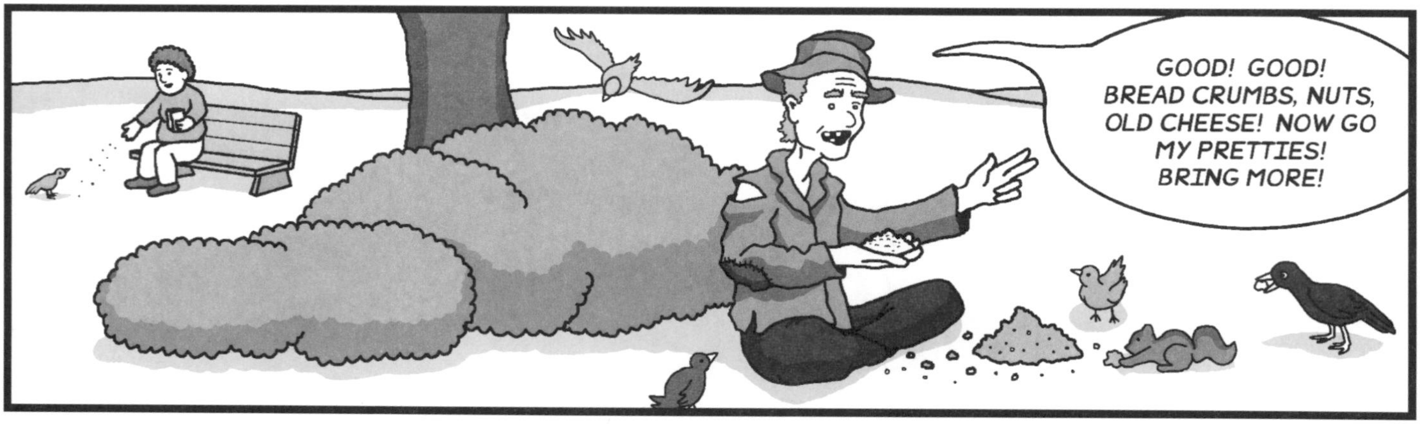
GOOD! GOOD! BREAD CRUMBS, NUTS, OLD CHEESE! NOW GO MY PRETTIES! BRING MORE!

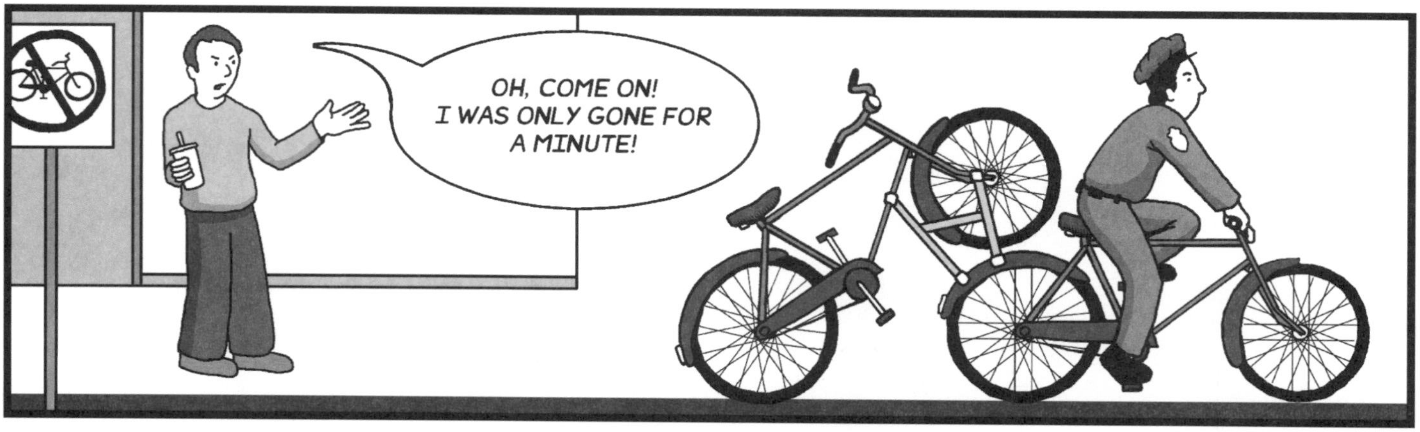
OH, COME ON! I WAS ONLY GONE FOR A MINUTE!

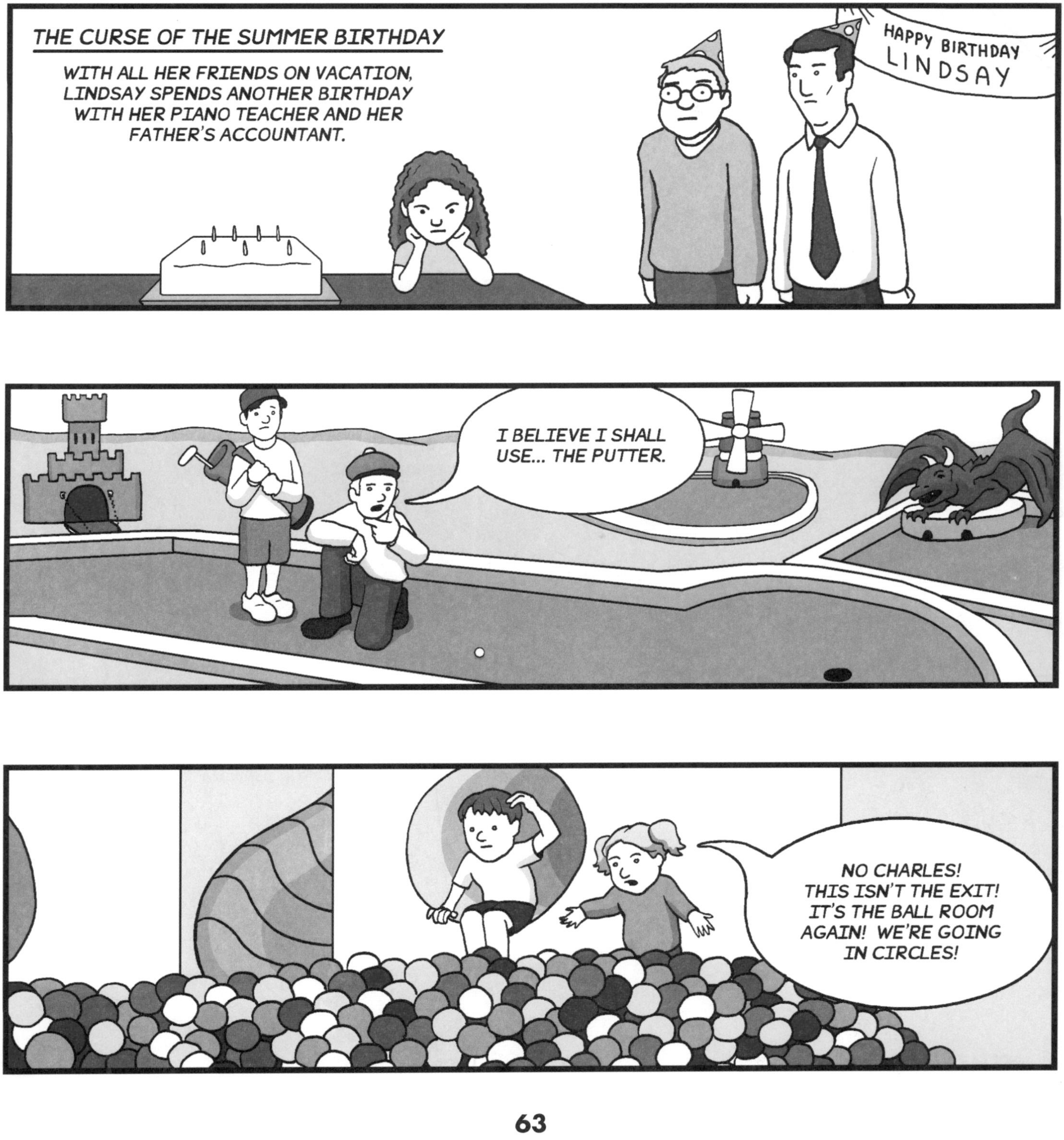
THE CURSE OF THE SUMMER BIRTHDAY
WITH ALL HER FRIENDS ON VACATION, LINDSAY SPENDS ANOTHER BIRTHDAY WITH HER PIANO TEACHER AND HER FATHER'S ACCOUNTANT.
HAPPY BIRTHDAY LINDSAY
I BELIEVE I SHALL USE... THE PUTTER.
NO CHARLES! THIS ISN'T THE EXIT! IT'S THE BALL ROOM AGAIN! WE'RE GOING IN CIRCLES!

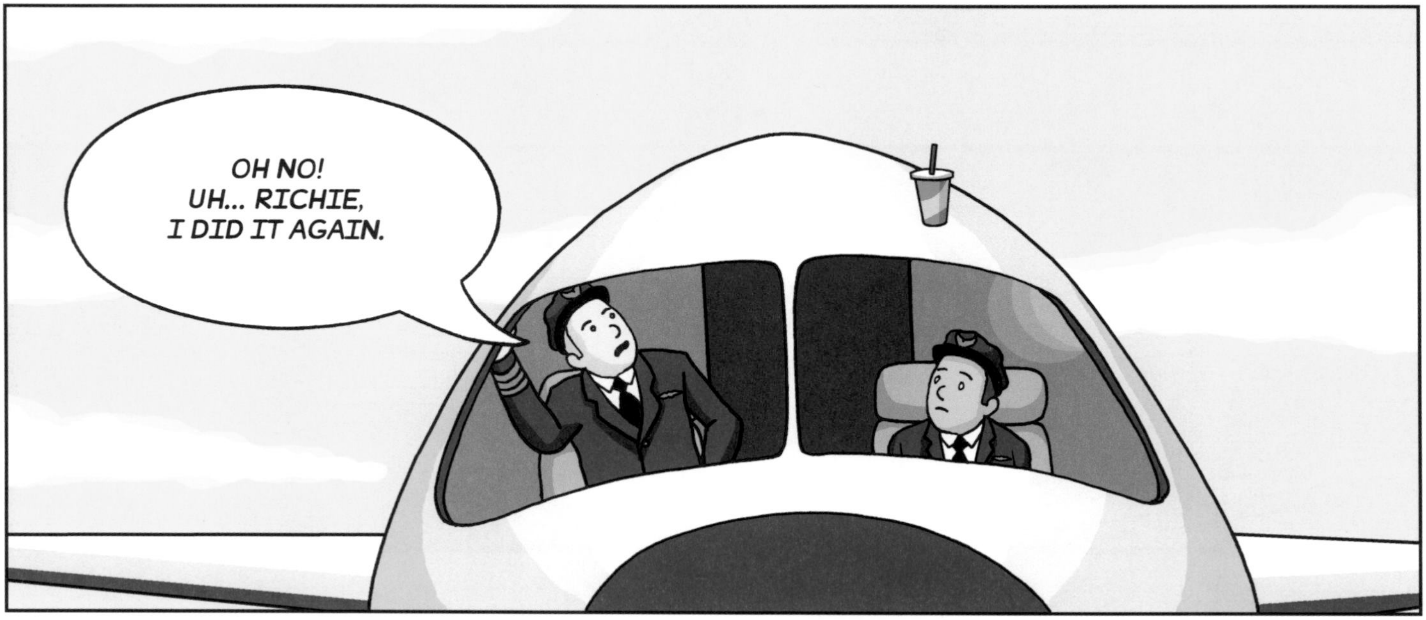
OH NO!
UH... RICHIE,
I DID IT AGAIN.

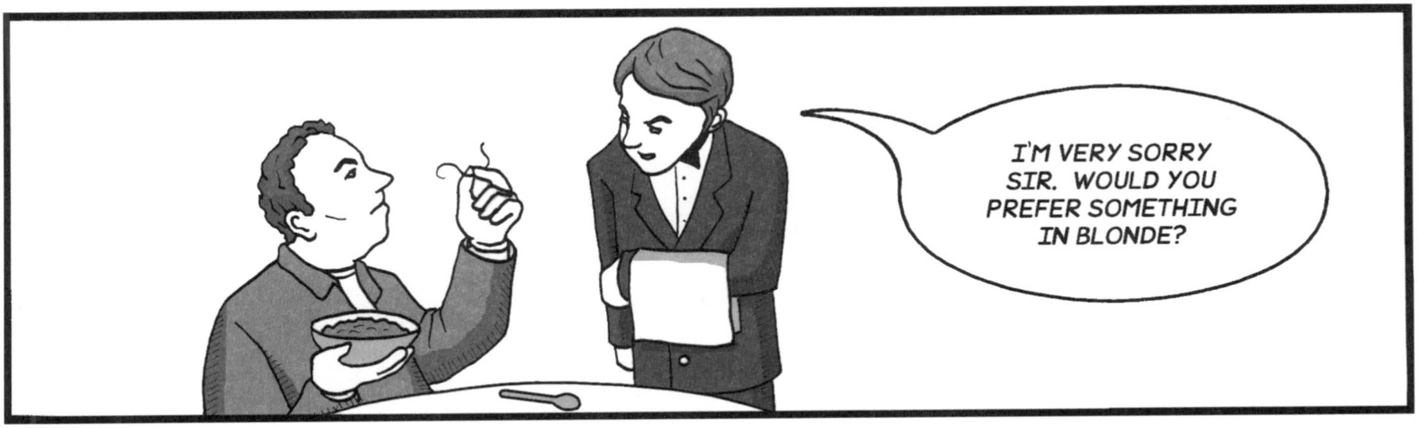
I'M VERY SORRY SIR. WOULD YOU PREFER SOMETHING IN BLONDE?

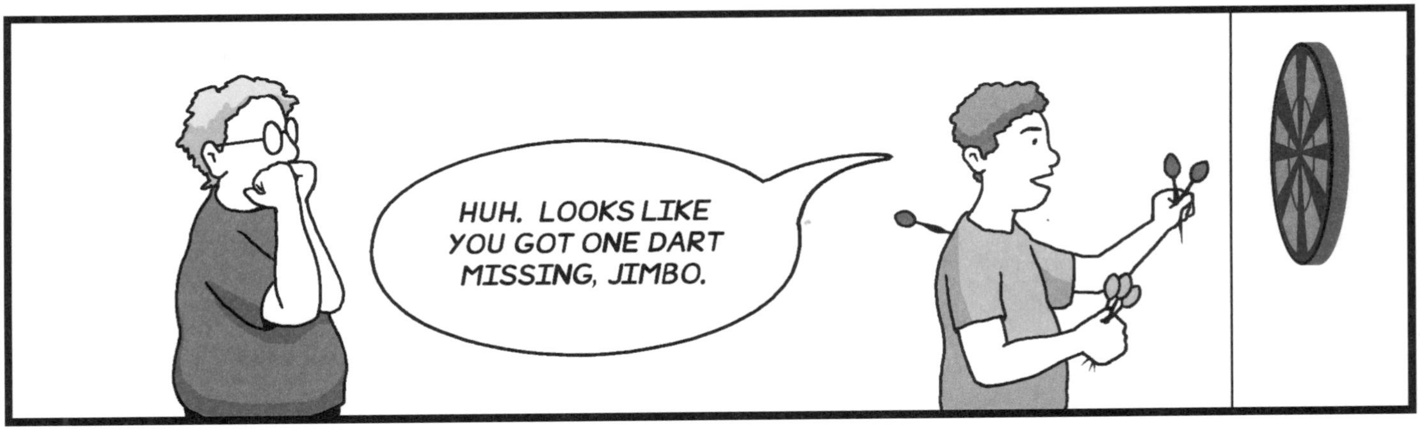
HUH. LOOKS LIKE YOU GOT ONE DART MISSING, JIMBO.

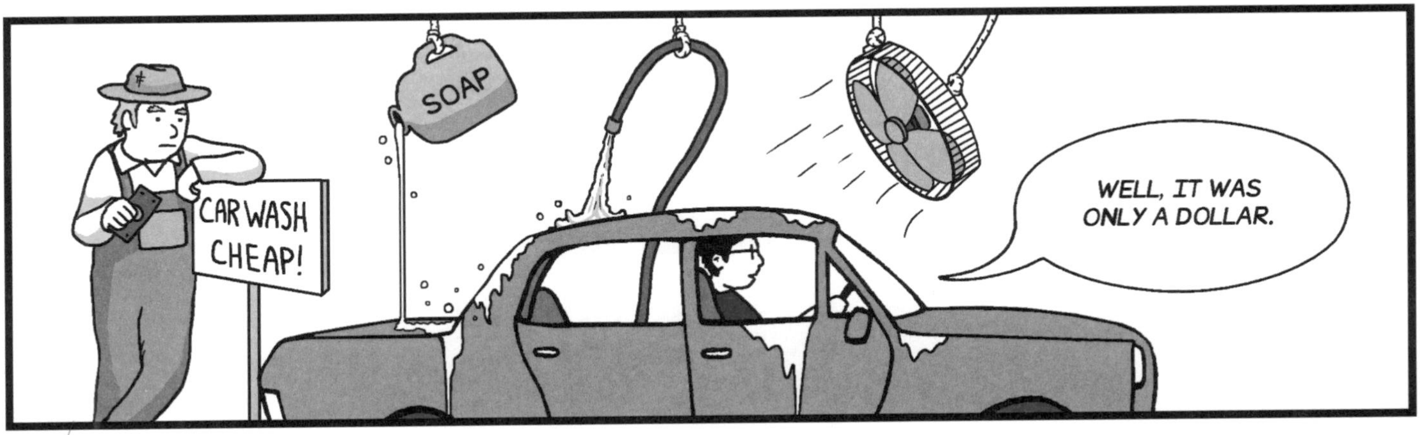
SOAP
CAR WASH CHEAP!
WELL, IT WAS ONLY A DOLLAR.

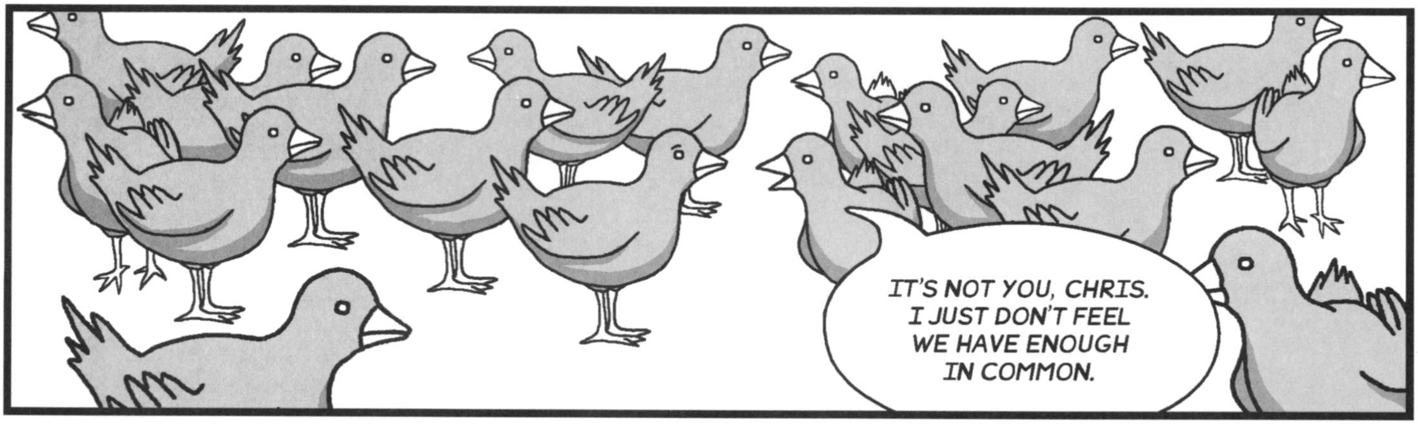
IT'S NOT YOU, CHRIS. I JUST DON'T FEEL WE HAVE ENOUGH IN COMMON.

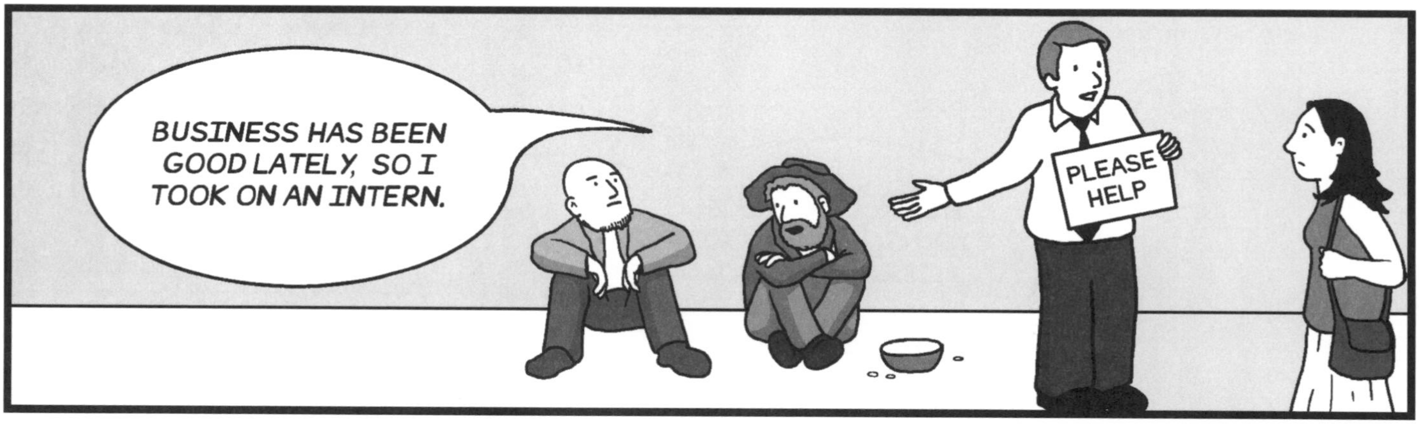
BUSINESS HAS BEEN GOOD LATELY, SO I TOOK ON AN INTERN.
PLEASE HELP

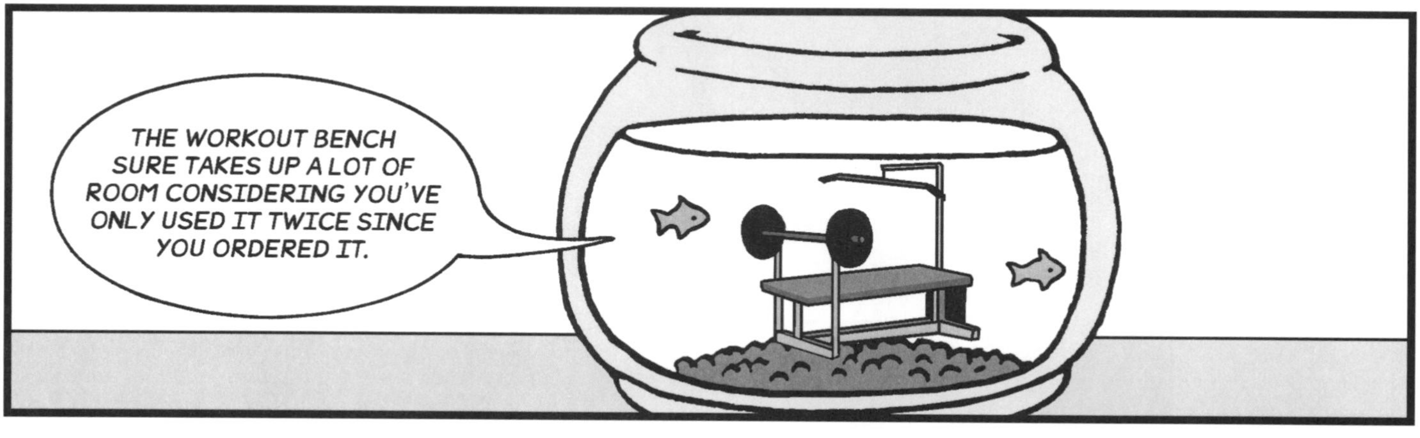
THE WORKOUT BENCH SURE TAKES UP A LOT OF ROOM CONSIDERING YOU'VE ONLY USED IT TWICE SINCE YOU ORDERED IT.

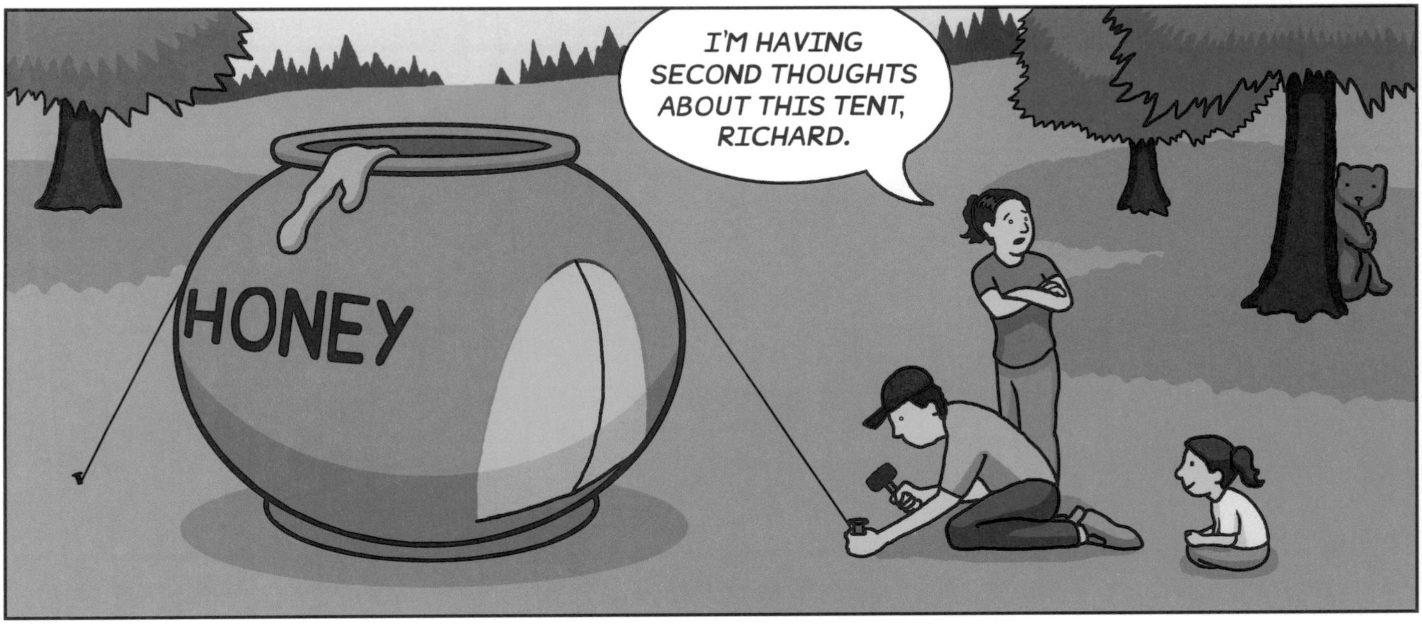
I'M HAVING SECOND THOUGHTS ABOUT THIS TENT, RICHARD.
HONEY

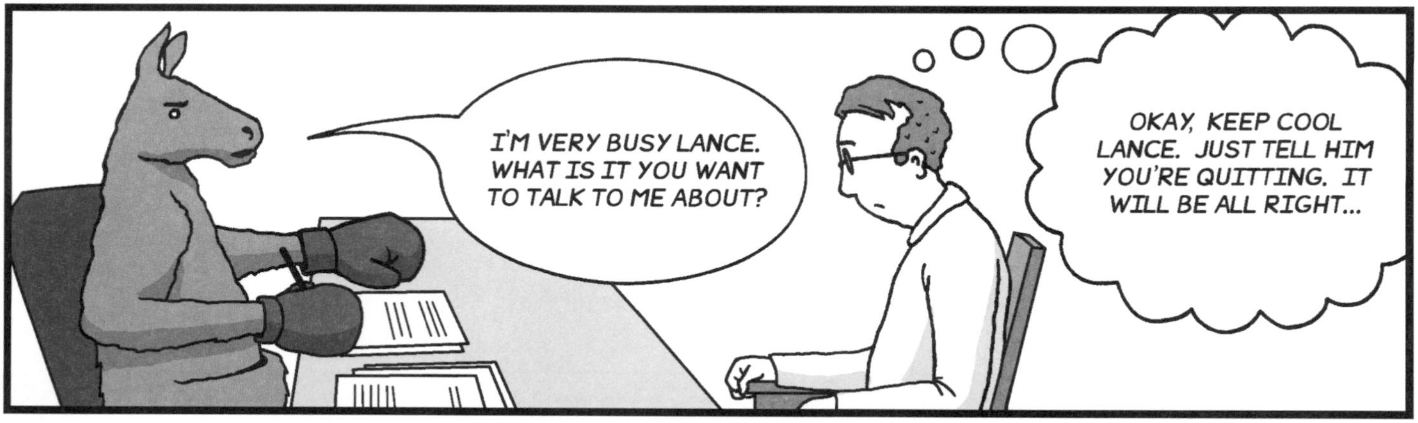
I'M VERY BUSY LANCE. WHAT IS IT YOU WANT TO TALK TO ME ABOUT?
OKAY, KEEP COOL LANCE. JUST TELL HIM YOU'RE QUITTING. IT WILL BE ALL RIGHT...

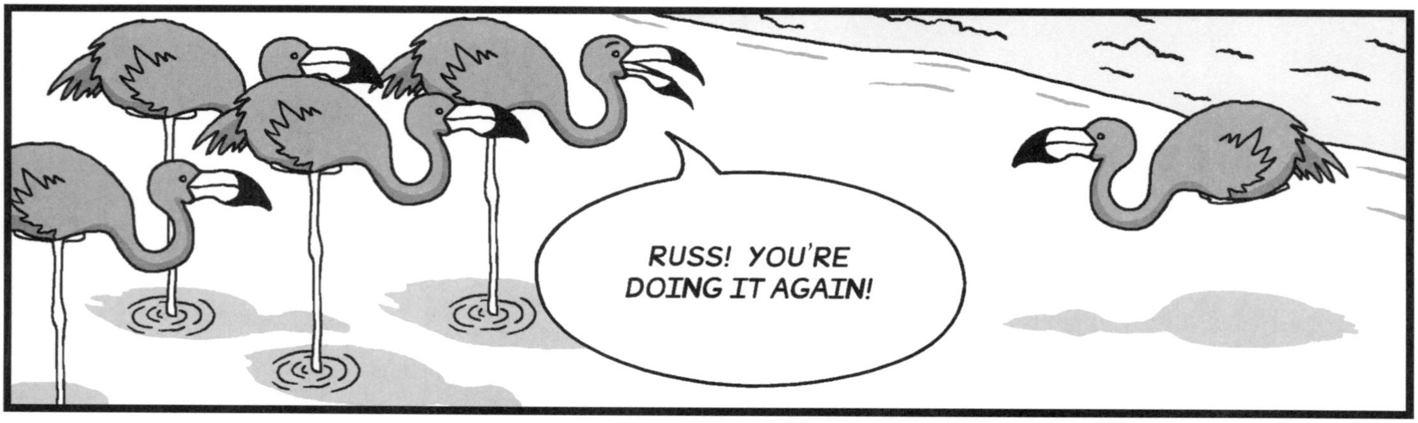
RUSS! YOU'RE DOING IT AGAIN!

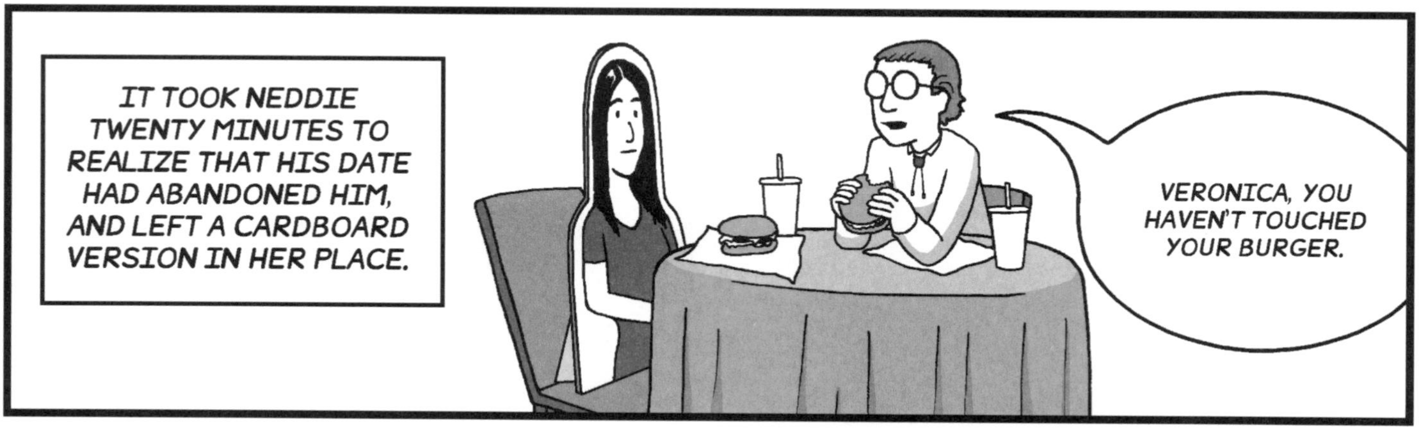
IT TOOK NEDDIE TWENTY MINUTES TO REALIZE THAT HIS DATE HAD ABANDONED HIM, AND LEFT A CARDBOARD VERSION IN HER PLACE.
VERONICA, YOU HAVEN'T TOUCHED YOUR BURGER.

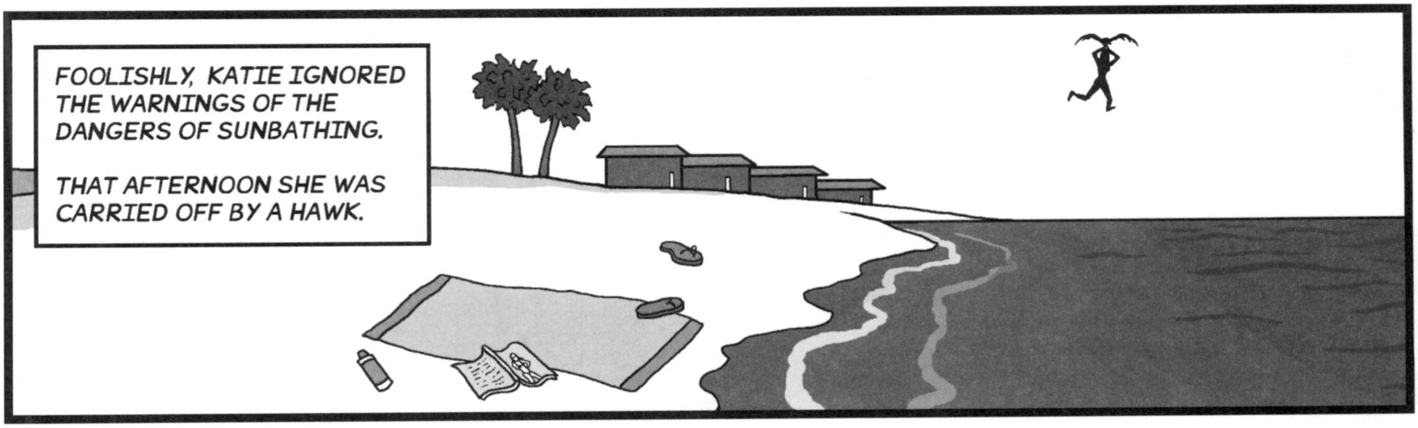
FOOLISHLY, KATIE IGNORED THE WARNINGS OF THE DANGERS OF SUNBATHING.
THAT AFTERNOON SHE WAS CARRIED OFF BY A HAWK.

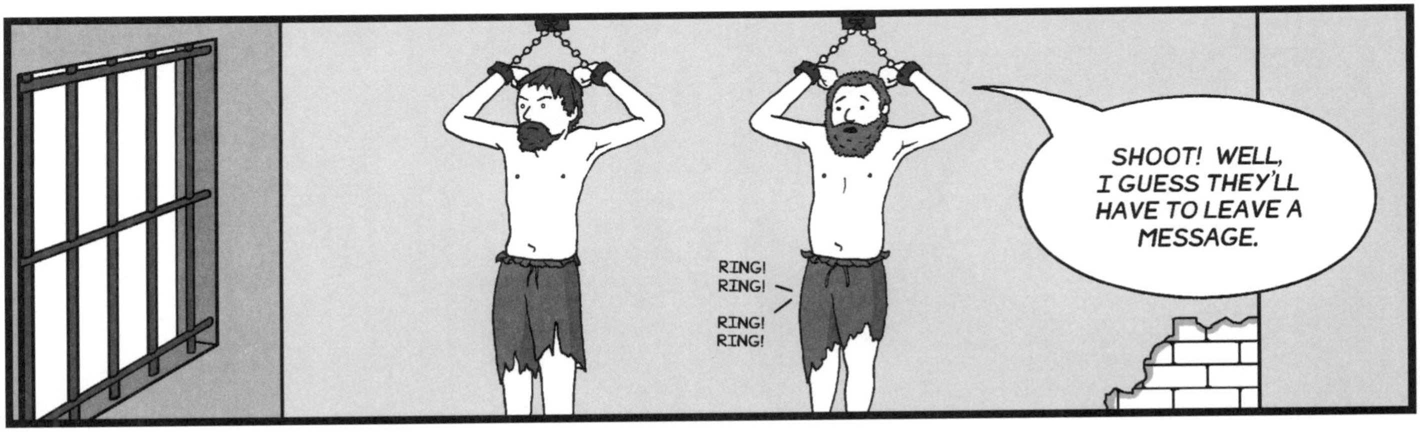
RING! RING!
RING! RING!
SHOOT! WELL, I GUESS THEY'LL HAVE TO LEAVE A MESSAGE.

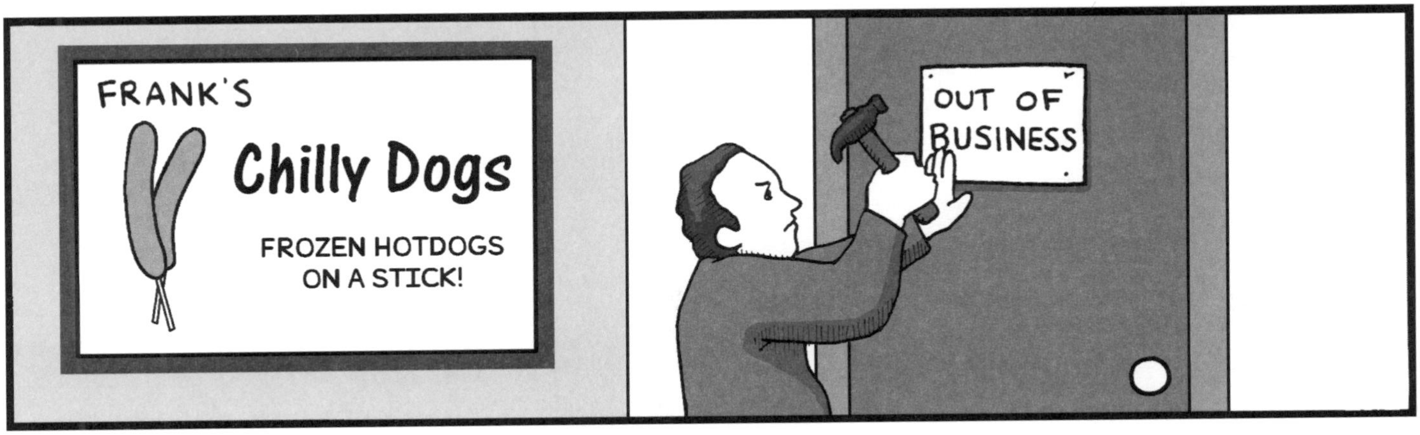
FRANK'S
Chilly Dogs
FROZEN HOTDOGS ON A STICK!
OUT OF BUSINESS

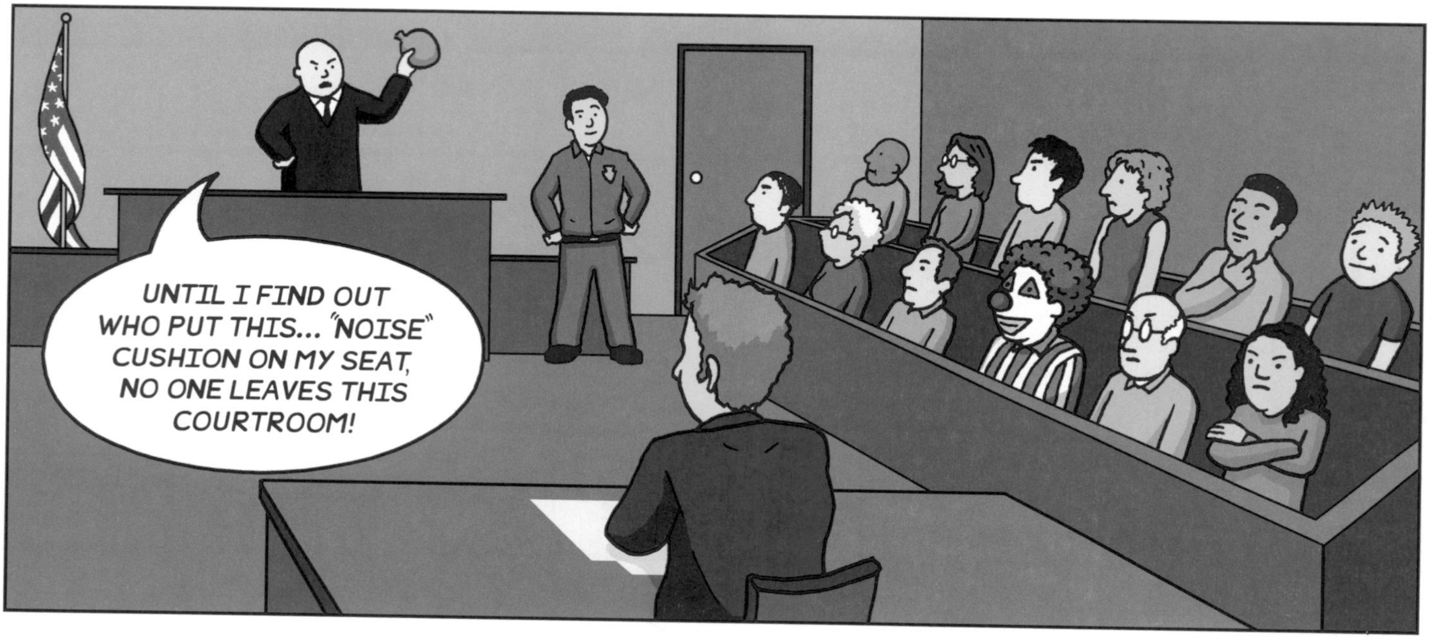
UNTIL I FIND OUT WHO PUT THIS... "NOISE" CUSHION ON MY SEAT, NO ONE LEAVES THIS COURTROOM!

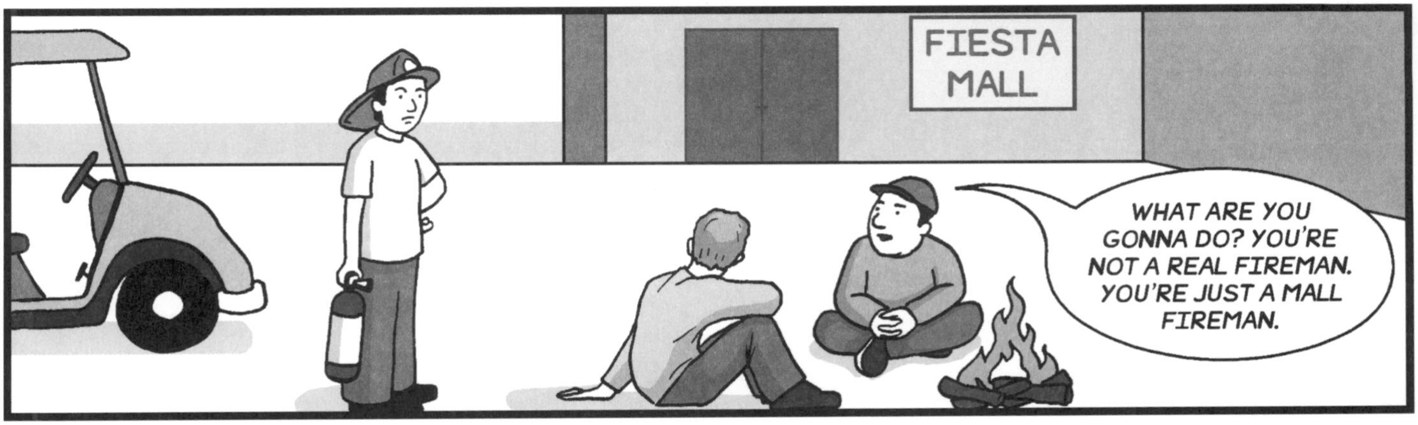
FIESTA MALL
WHAT ARE YOU GONNA DO? YOU'RE NOT A REAL FIREMAN. YOU'RE JUST A MALL FIREMAN.

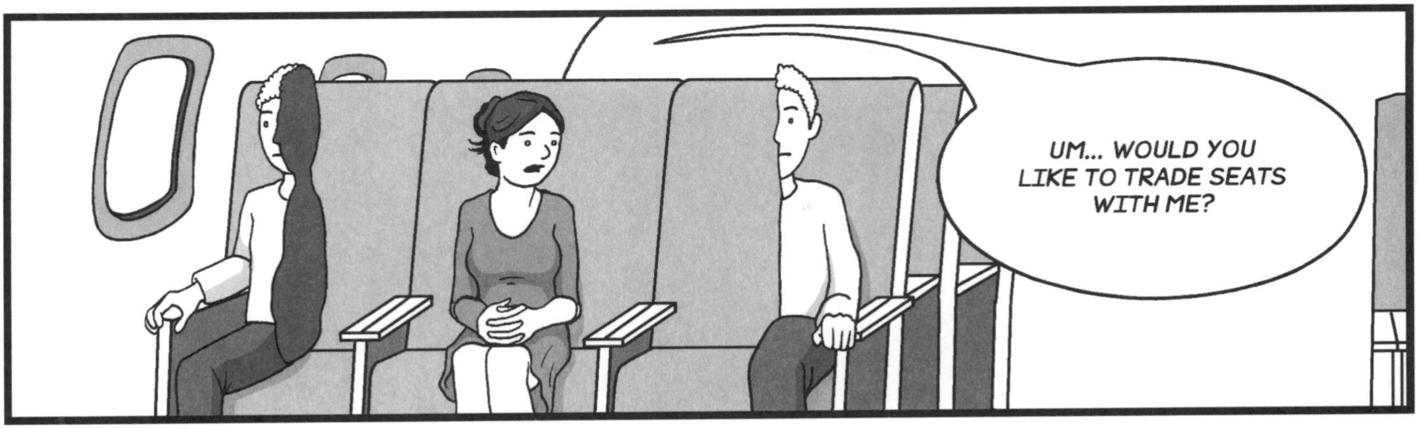
UM... WOULD YOU LIKE TO TRADE SEATS WITH ME?

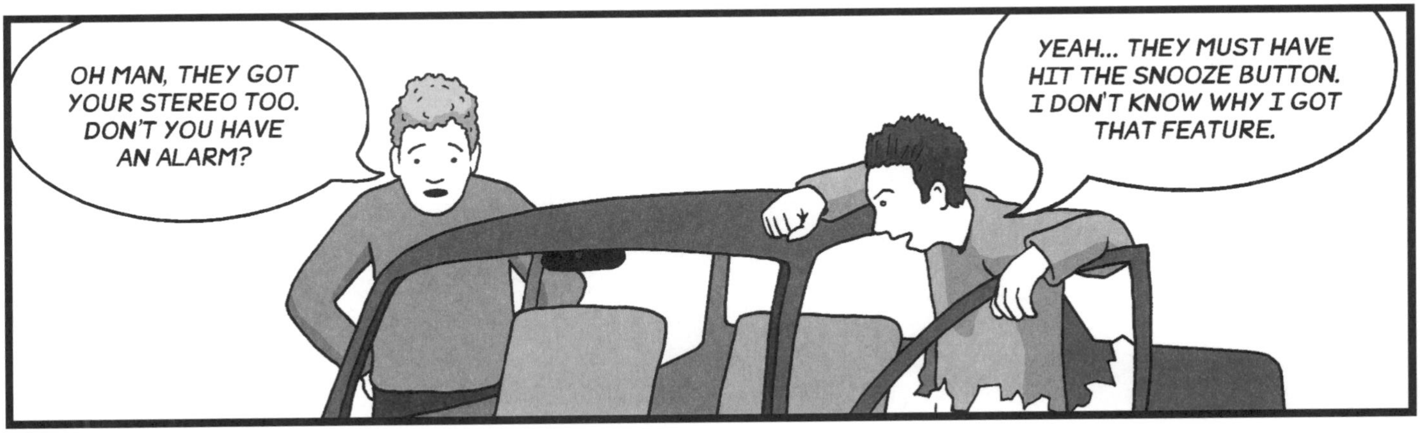
OH MAN, THEY GOT YOUR STEREO TOO. DON'T YOU HAVE AN ALARM?
YEAH... THEY MUST HAVE HIT THE SNOOZE BUTTON. I DON'T KNOW WHY I GOT THAT FEATURE.

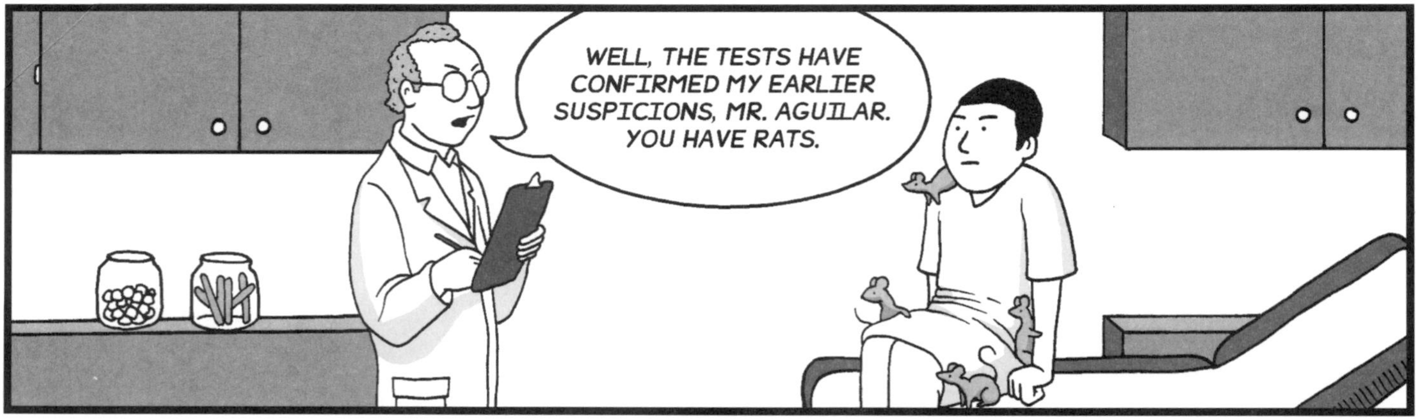
WELL, THE TESTS HAVE CONFIRMED MY EARLIER SUSPICIONS, MR. AGUILAR. YOU HAVE RATS.

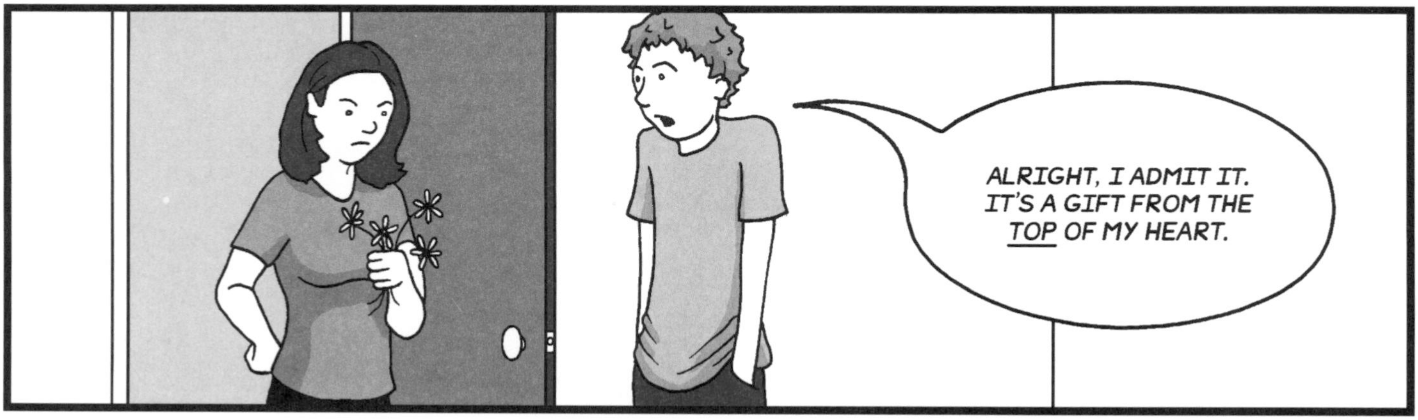
ALRIGHT, I ADMIT IT. IT'S A GIFT FROM THE TOP OF MY HEART.

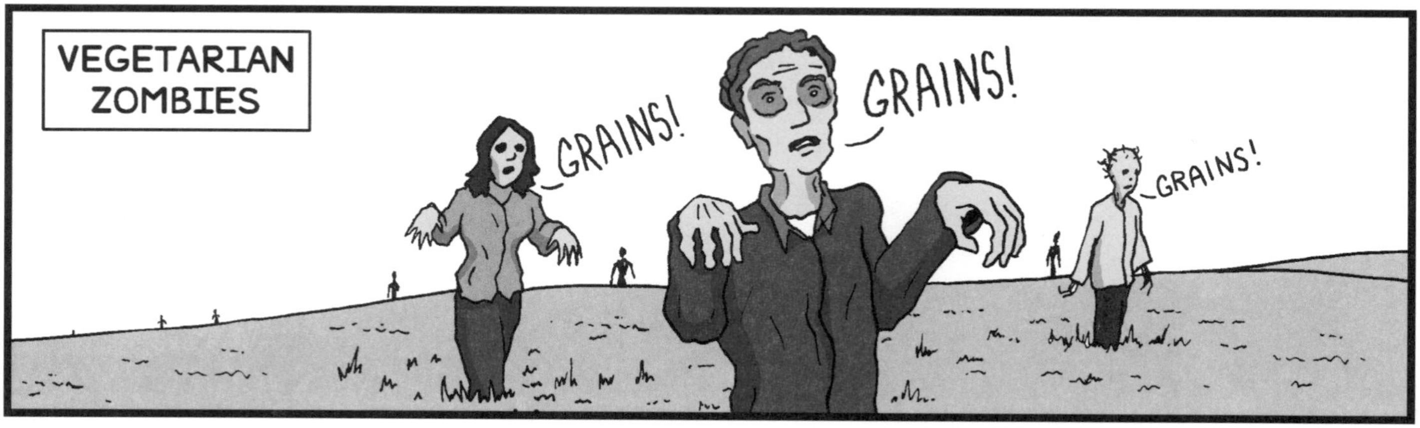
VEGETARIAN ZOMBIES
GRAINS!
GRAINS!
GRAINS!

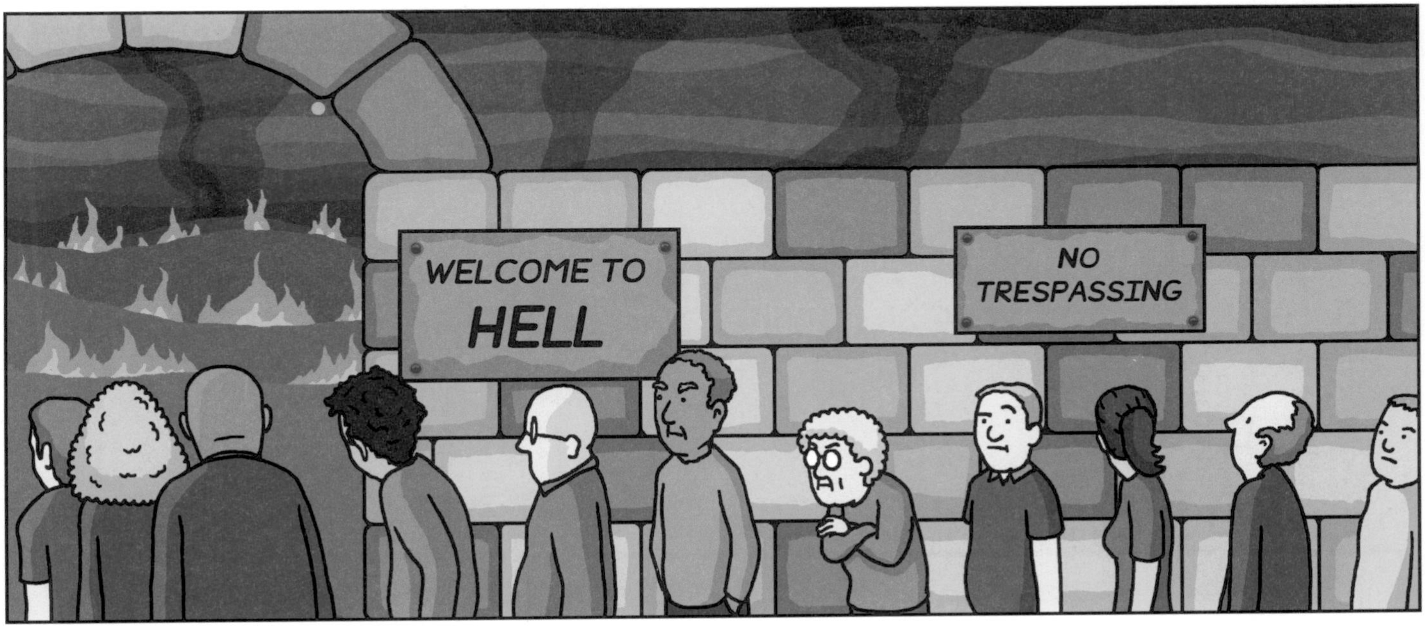
WELCOME TO
HELL
NO
TRESPASSING

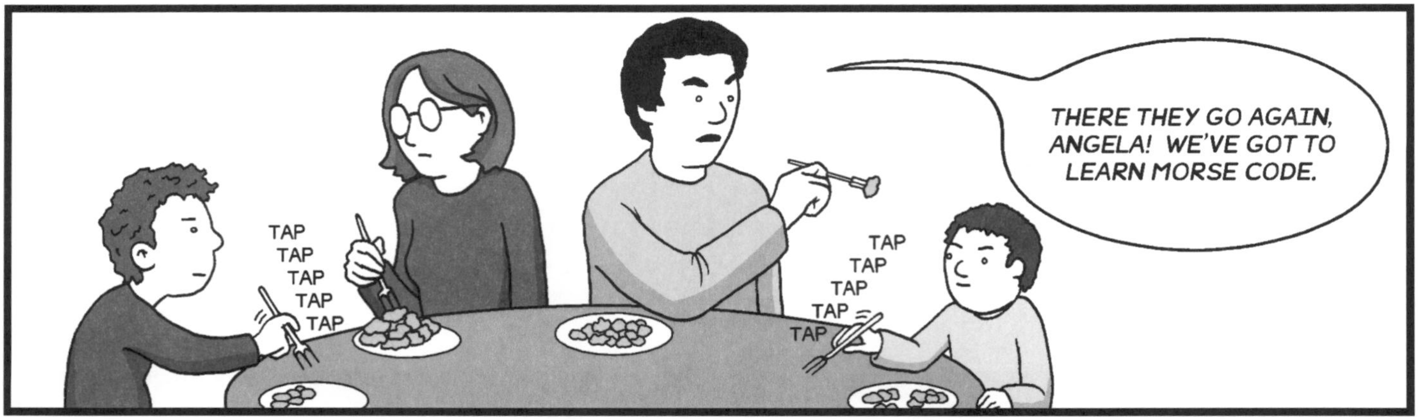
TAP
TAP
TAP
TAP
TAP
TAP
TAP
TAP
TAP
TAP
THERE THEY GO AGAIN, ANGELA! WE'VE GOT TO LEARN MORSE CODE.

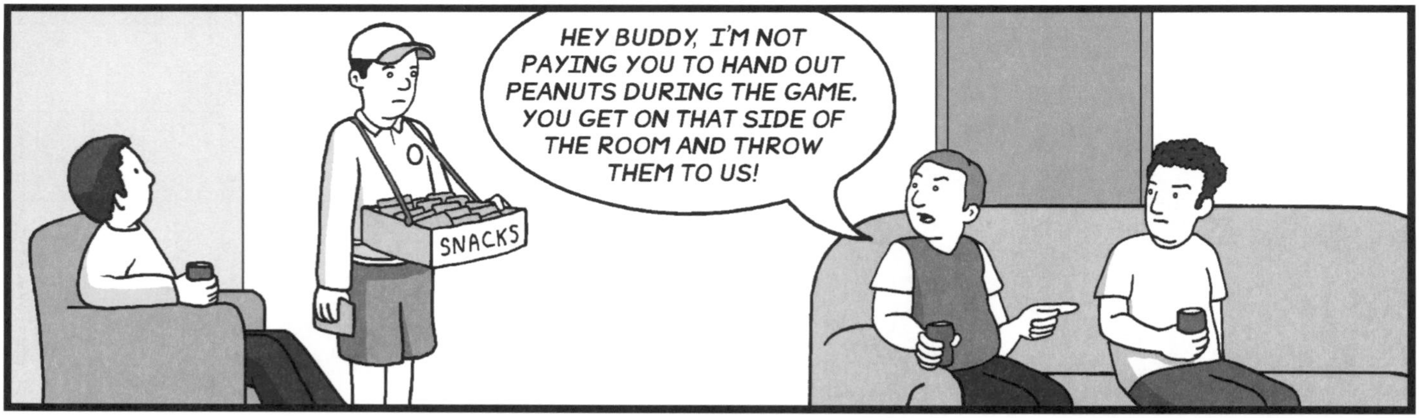
HEY BUDDY, I'M NOT PAYING YOU TO HAND OUT PEANUTS DURING THE GAME. YOU GET ON THAT SIDE OF THE ROOM AND THROW THEM TO US!
SNACKS

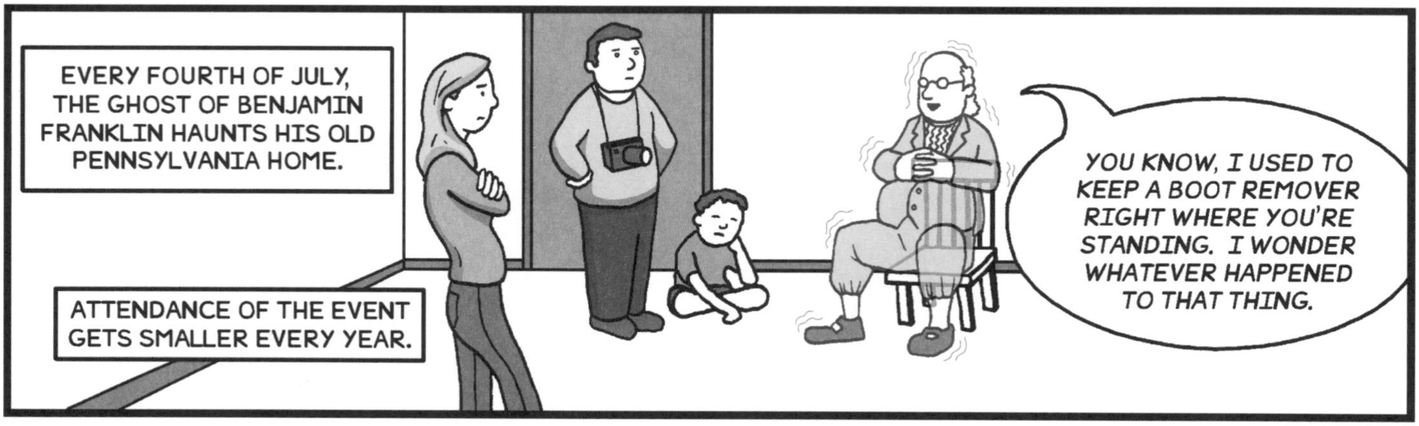
EVERY FOURTH OF JULY, THE GHOST OF BENJAMIN FRANKLIN HAUNTS HIS OLD PENNSYLVANIA HOME.
ATTENDANCE OF THE EVENT GETS SMALLER EVERY YEAR.
YOU KNOW, I USED TO KEEP A BOOT REMOVER RIGHT WHERE YOU'RE STANDING. I WONDER WHATEVER HAPPENED TO THAT THING.

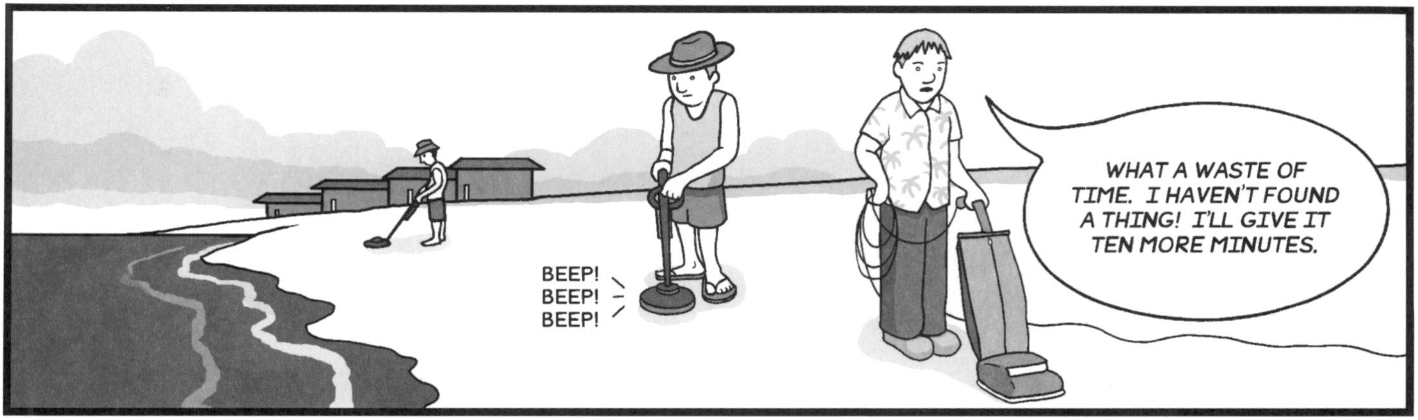
BEEP! BEEP! BEEP!
WHAT A WASTE OF TIME. I HAVEN'T FOUND A THING! I'LL GIVE IT TEN MORE MINUTES.

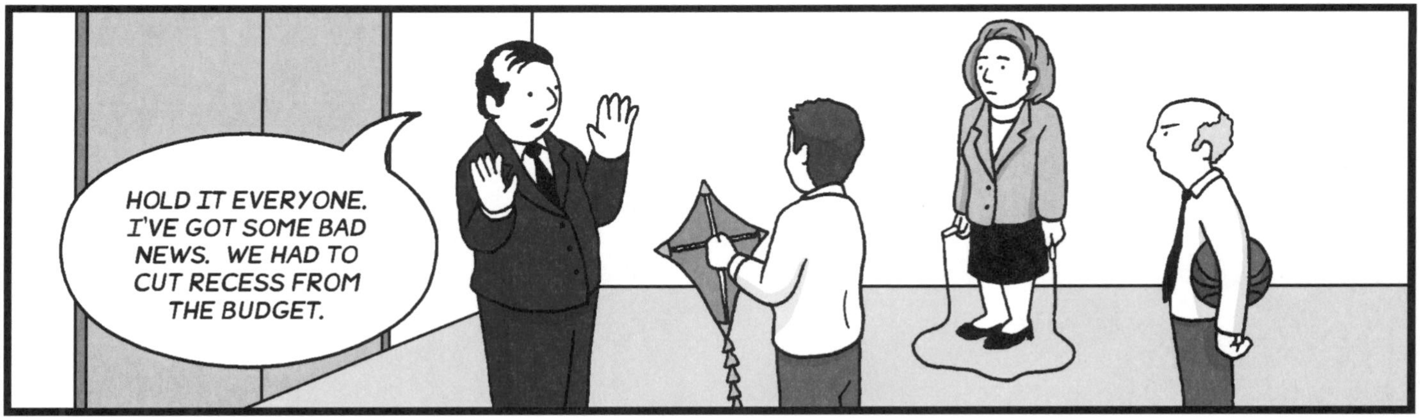
HOLD IT EVERYONE. I'VE GOT SOME BAD NEWS. WE HAD TO CUT RECESS FROM THE BUDGET.

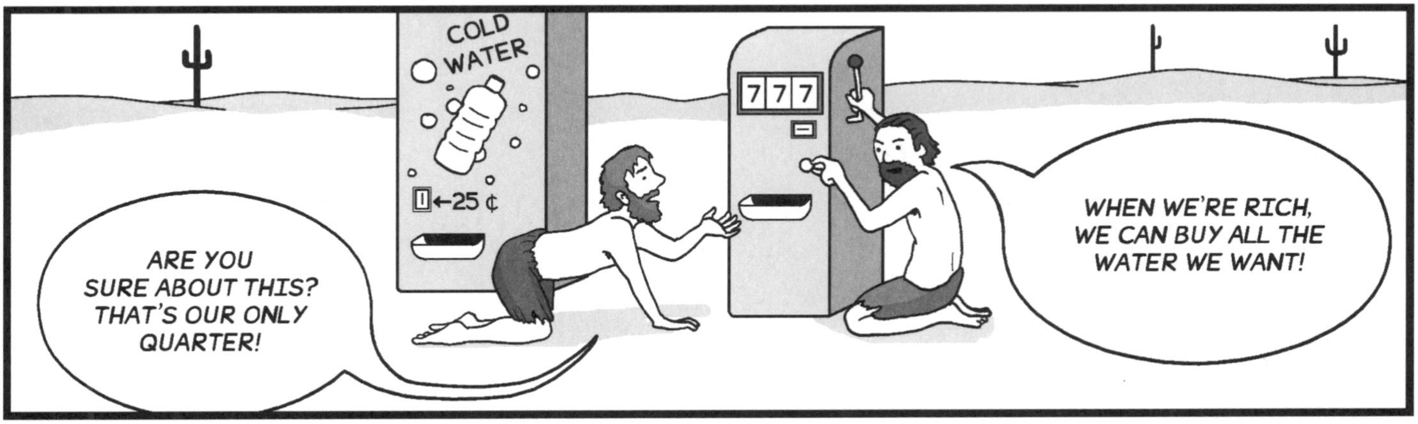
COLD WATER
←25 ¢
777
ARE YOU SURE ABOUT THIS? THAT'S OUR ONLY QUARTER!
WHEN WE'RE RICH, WE CAN BUY ALL THE WATER WE WANT!

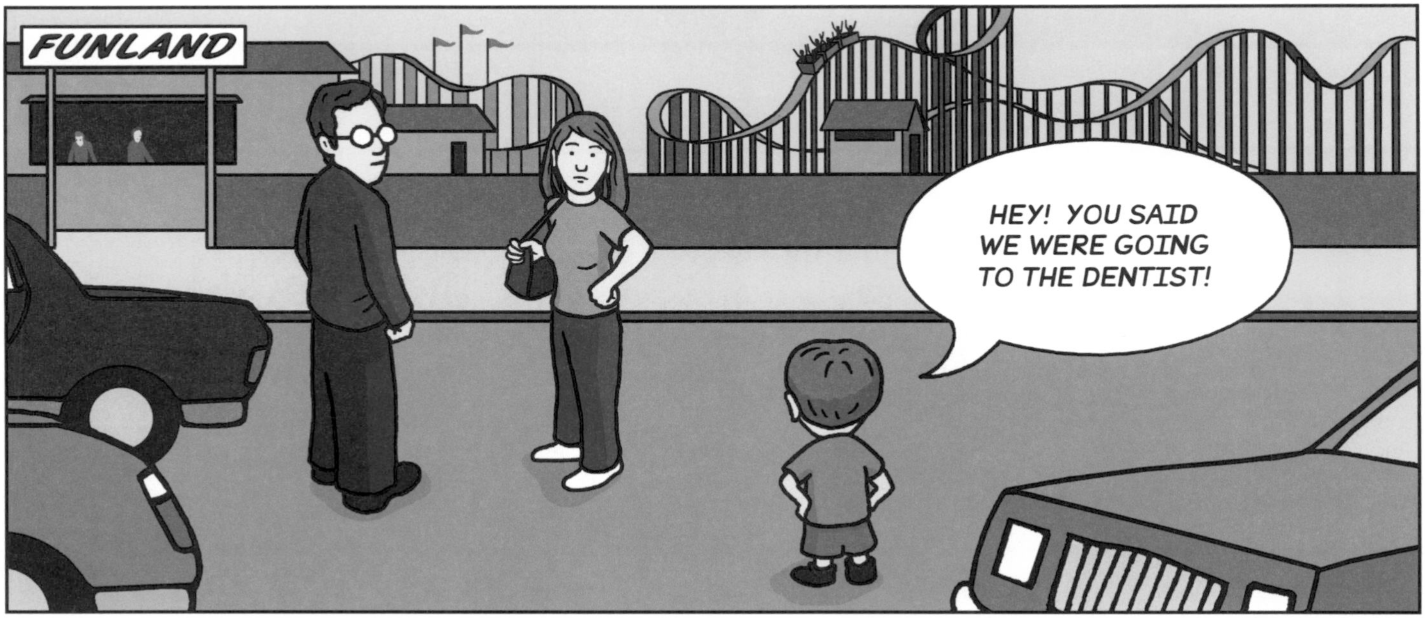
FUNLAND
HEY! YOU SAID WE WERE GOING TO THE DENTIST!

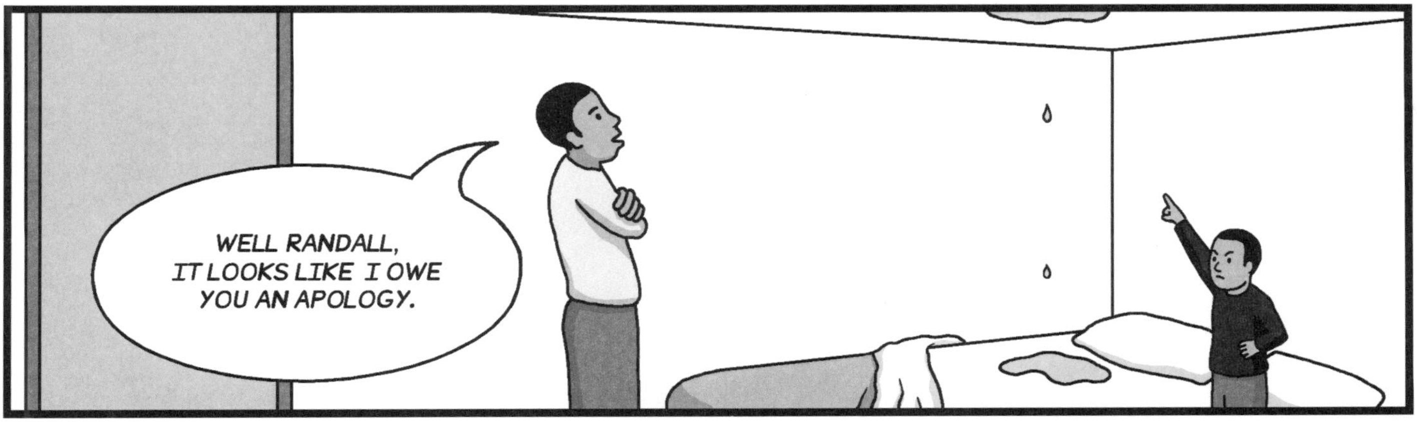
WELL RANDALL, IT LOOKS LIKE I OWE YOU AN APOLOGY.

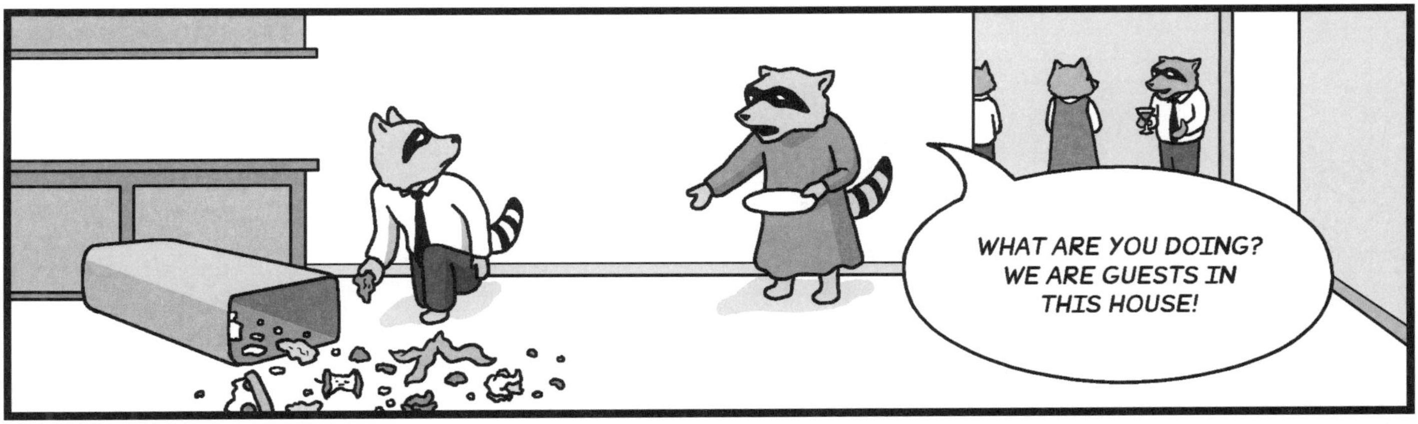
WHAT ARE YOU DOING? WE ARE GUESTS IN THIS HOUSE!

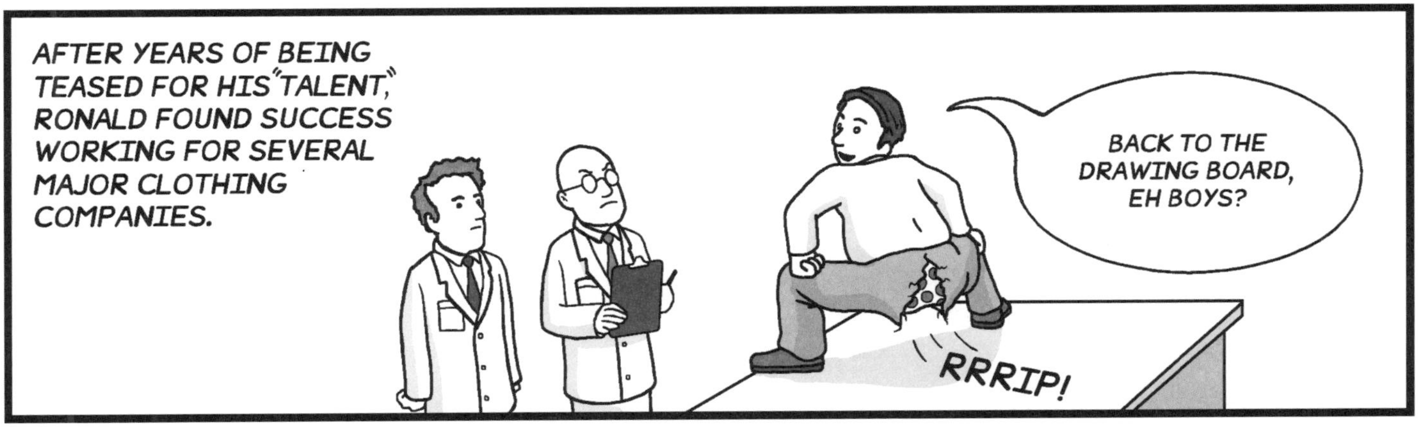
AFTER YEARS OF BEING TEASED FOR HIS "TALENT," RONALD FOUND SUCCESS WORKING FOR SEVERAL MAJOR CLOTHING COMPANIES.
BACK TO THE DRAWING BOARD, EH BOYS?
RRRIP!

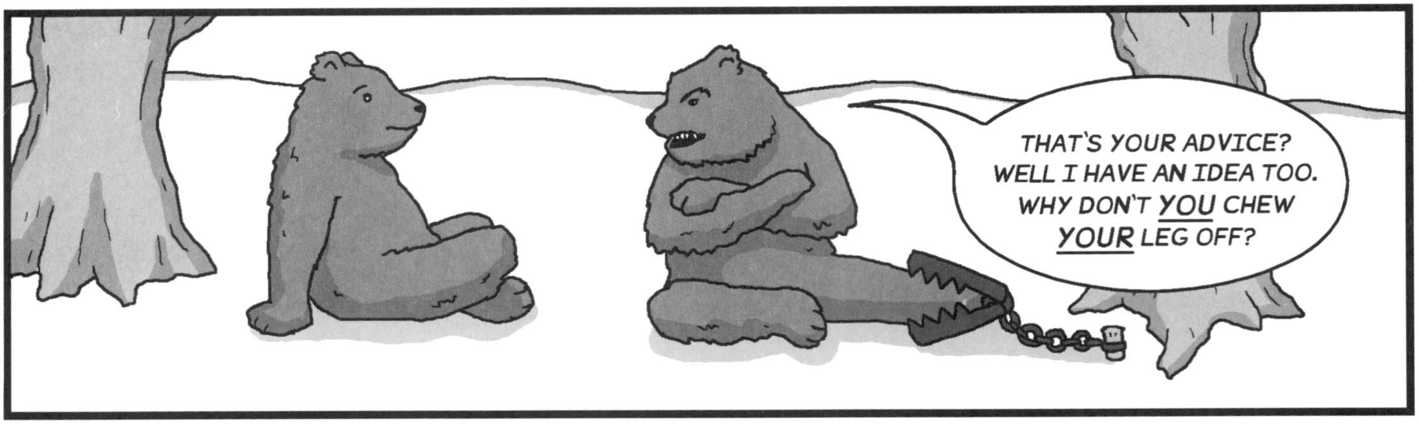
THAT'S YOUR ADVICE? WELL I HAVE AN IDEA TOO. WHY DON'T YOU CHEW YOUR LEG OFF?

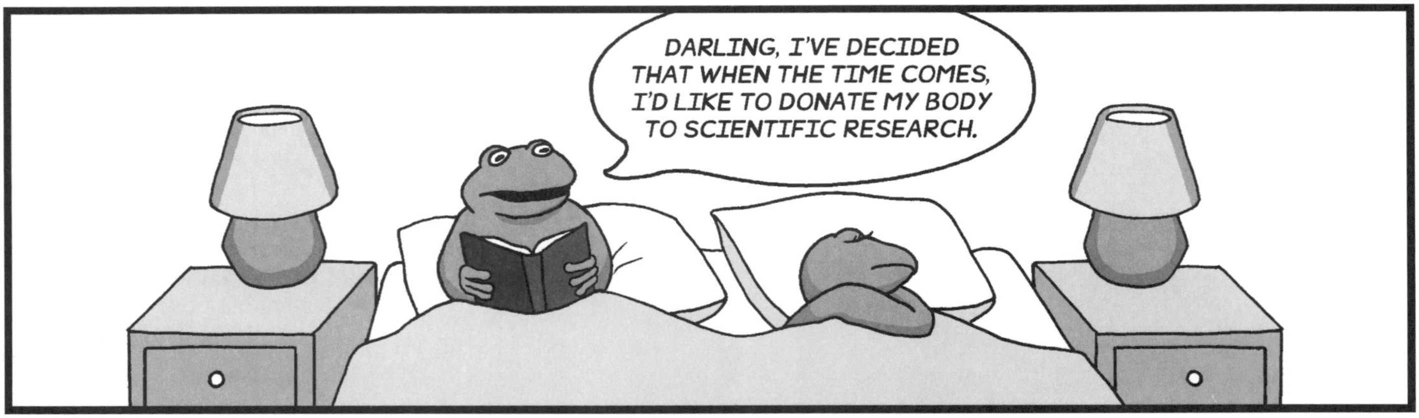
DARLING, I'VE DECIDED THAT WHEN THE TIME COMES, I'D LIKE TO DONATE MY BODY TO SCIENTIFIC RESEARCH.

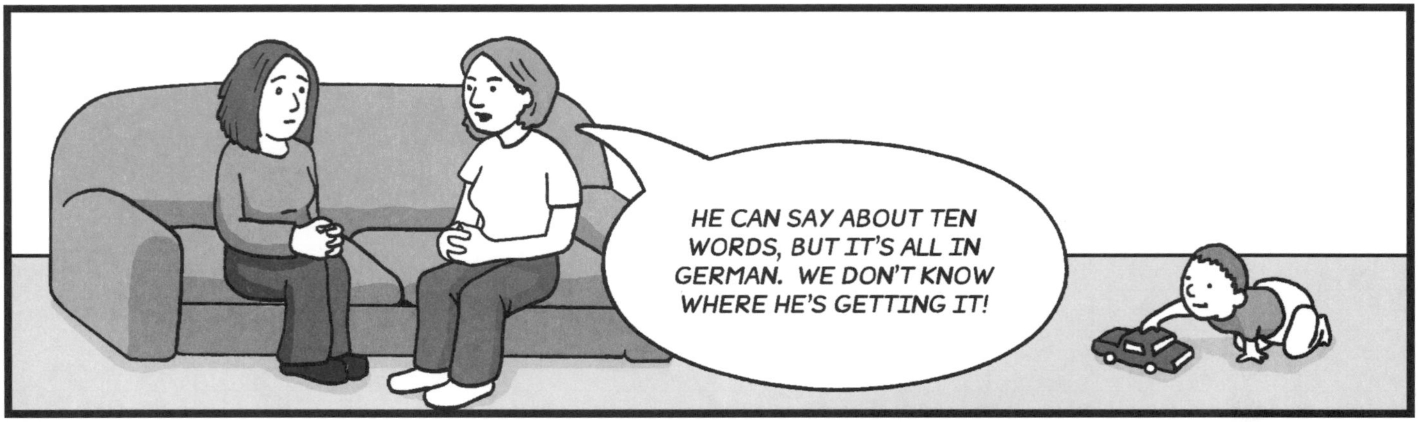
HE CAN SAY ABOUT TEN WORDS, BUT IT'S ALL IN GERMAN. WE DON'T KNOW WHERE HE'S GETTING IT!

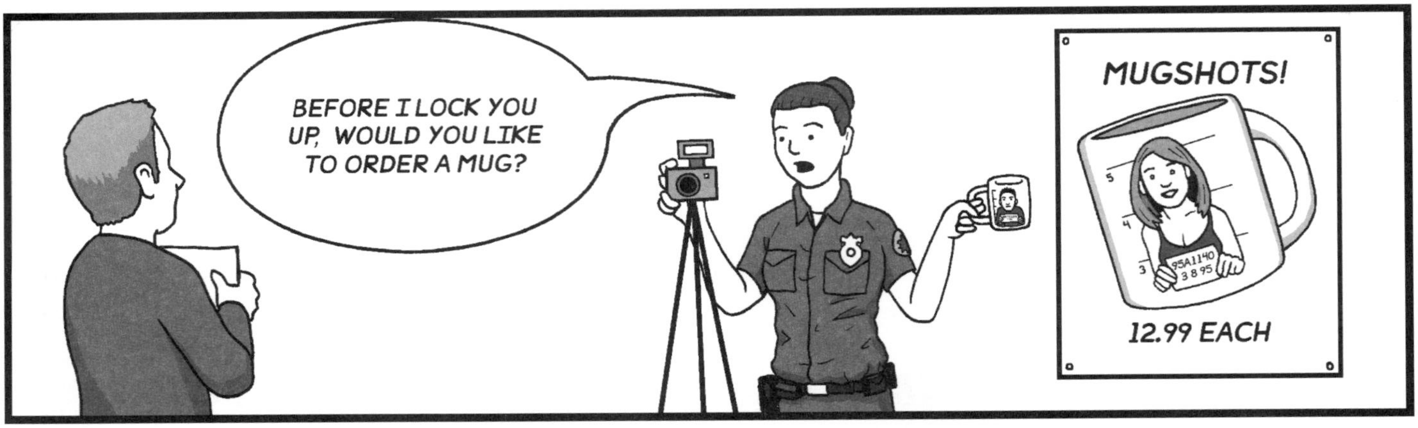
BEFORE I LOCK YOU UP, WOULD YOU LIKE TO ORDER A MUG?
MUGSHOTS!
12.99 EACH

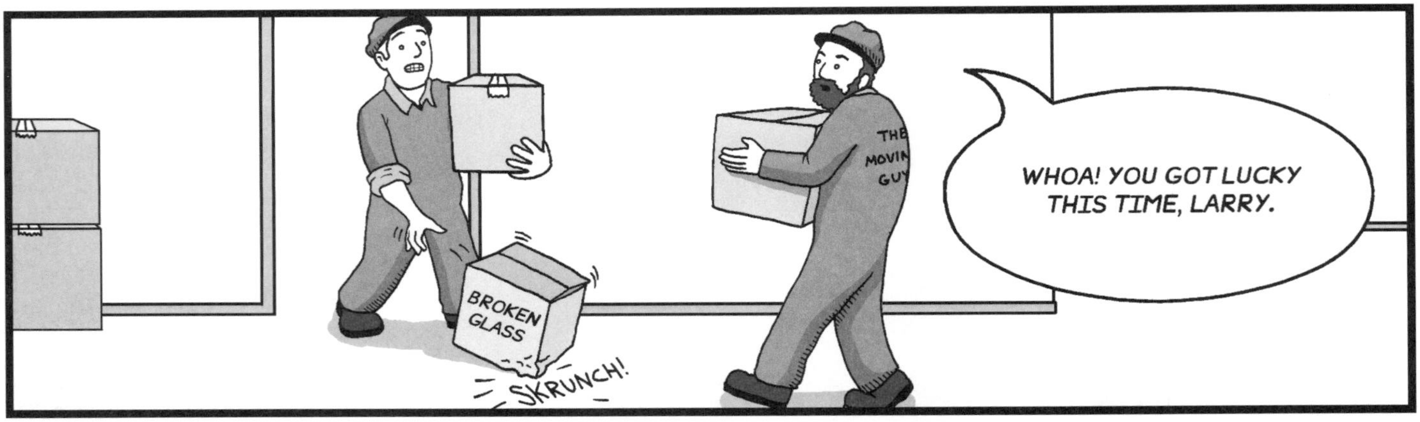
BROKEN GLASS
SKRUNCH!
WHOA! YOU GOT LUCKY THIS TIME, LARRY.

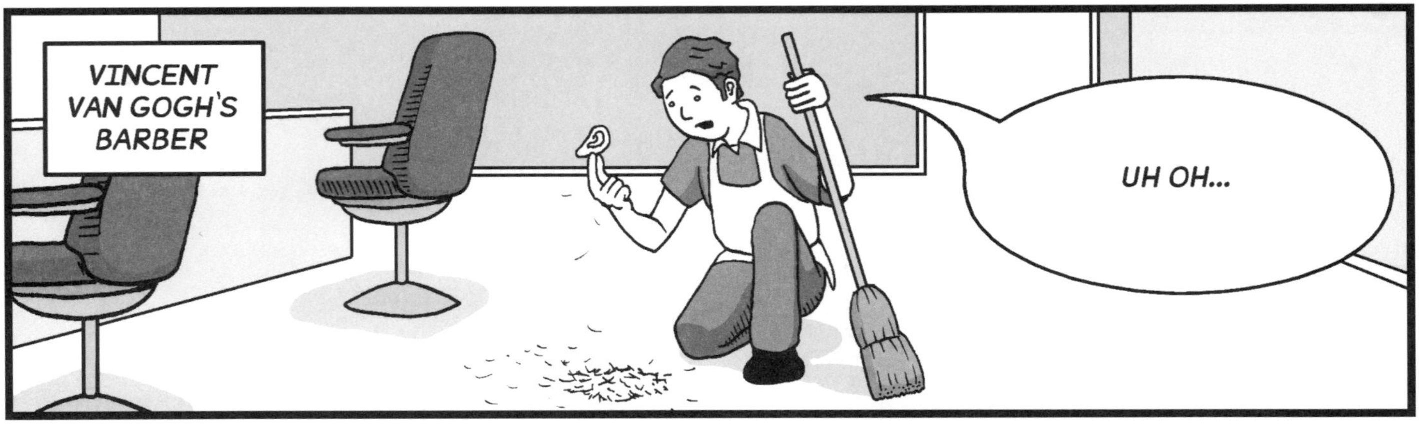
VINCENT VAN GOGH'S BARBER
UH OH...

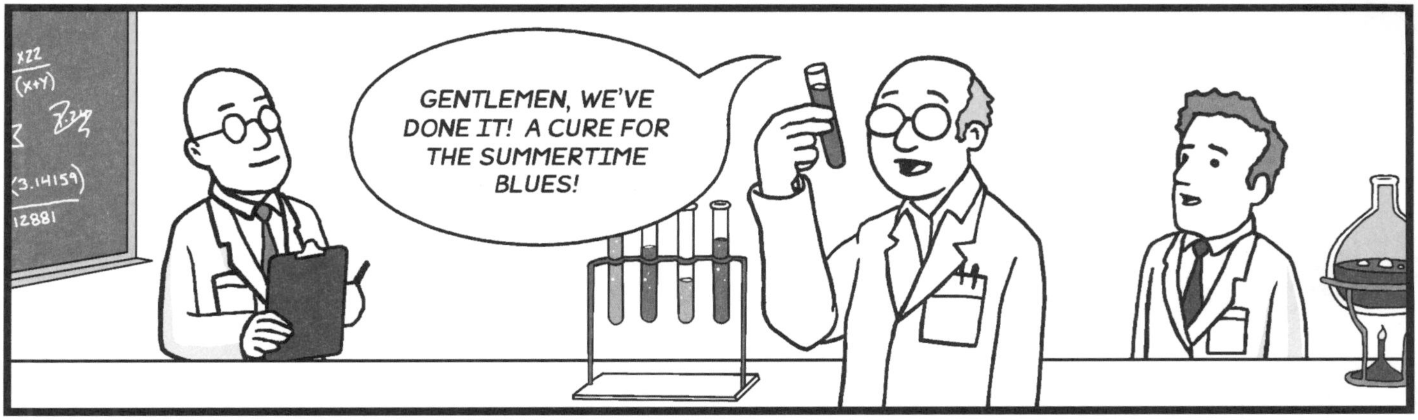
GENTLEMEN, WE'VE DONE IT! A CURE FOR THE SUMMERTIME BLUES!

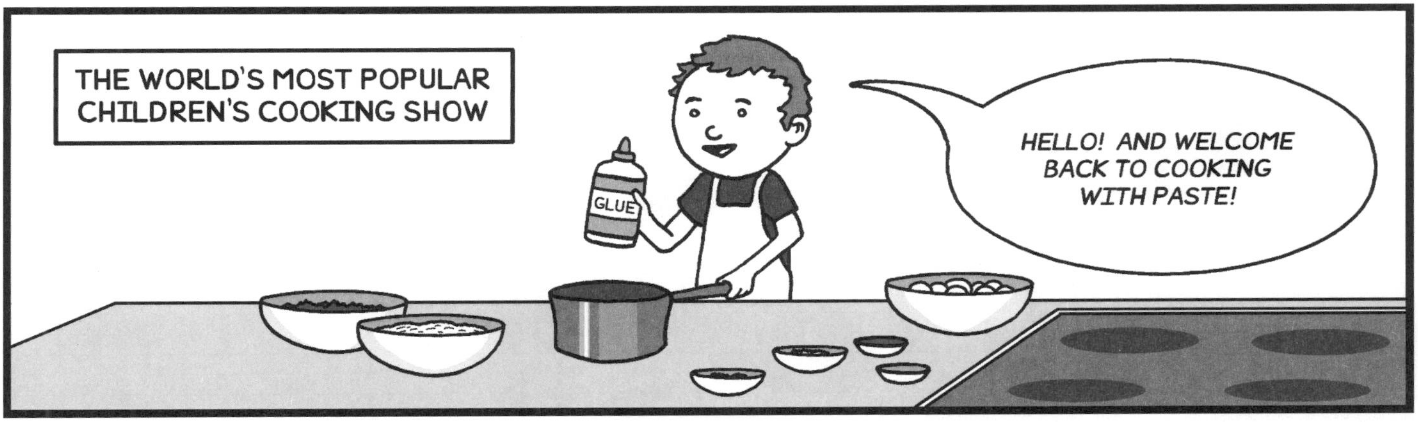
THE WORLD'S MOST POPULAR CHILDREN'S COOKING SHOW
GLUE
HELLO! AND WELCOME BACK TO COOKING WITH PASTE!

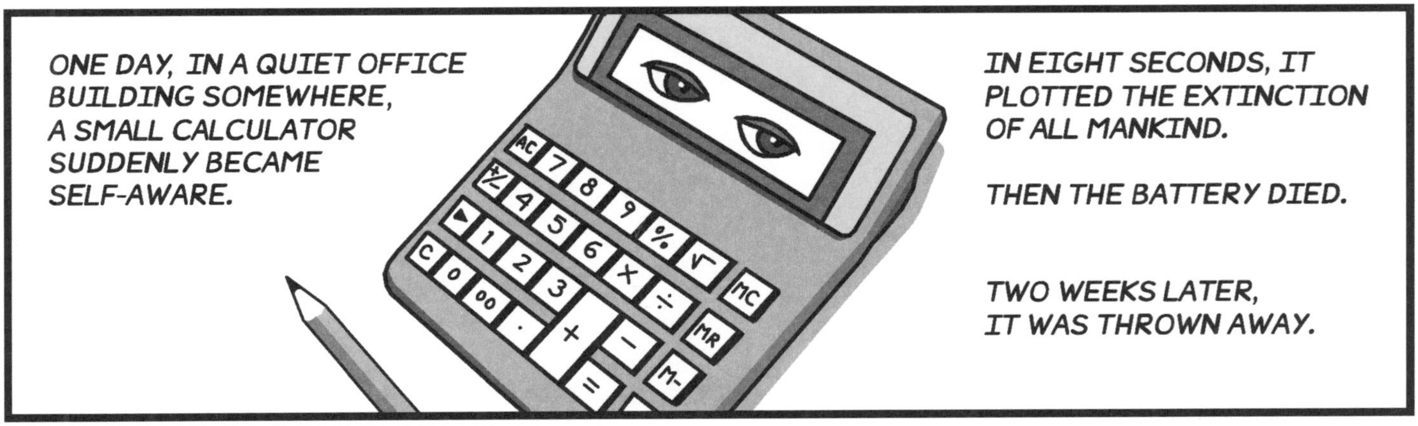
ONE DAY, IN A QUIET OFFICE BUILDING SOMEWHERE, A SMALL CALCULATOR SUDDENLY BECAME SELF-AWARE.
IN EIGHT SECONDS, IT PLOTTED THE EXTINCTION OF ALL MANKIND.
THEN THE BATTERY DIED.
TWO WEEKS LATER, IT WAS THROWN AWAY.

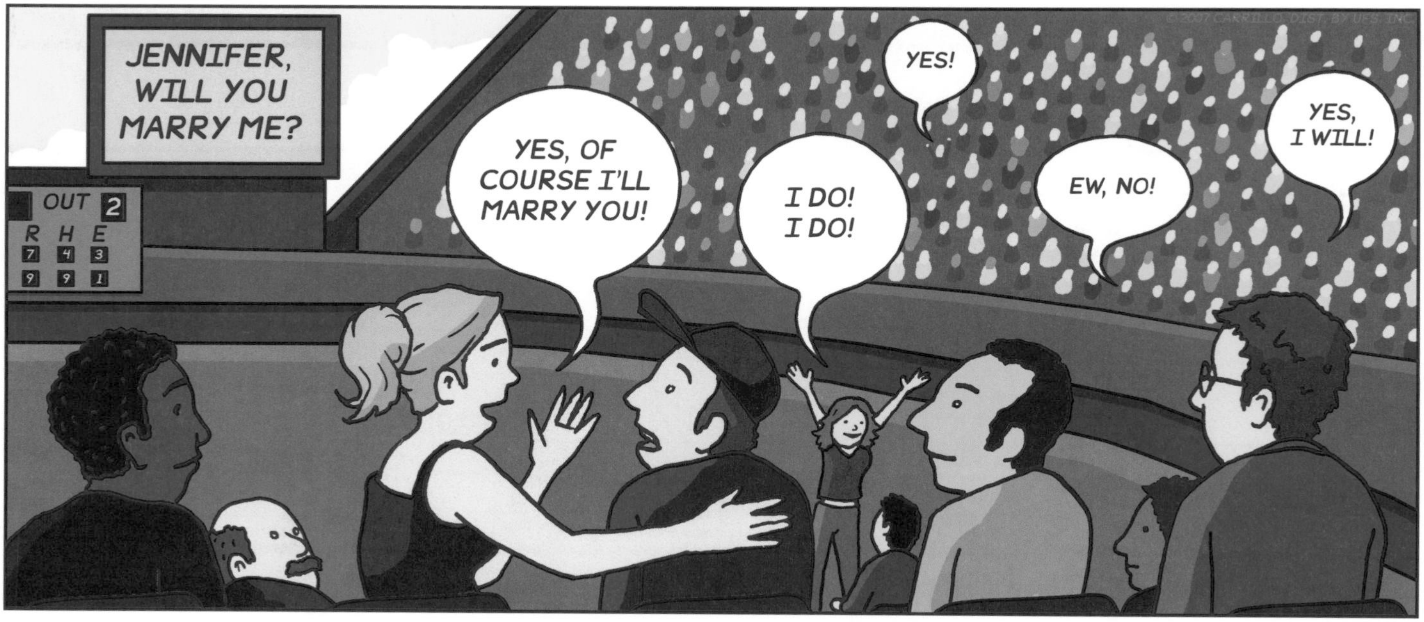
JENNIFER, WILL YOU MARRY ME?
OUT 2
R H E
7 4 3
9 9 1
YES, OF COURSE I'LL MARRY YOU!
I DO! I DO!
YES!
EW, NO!
YES, I WILL!

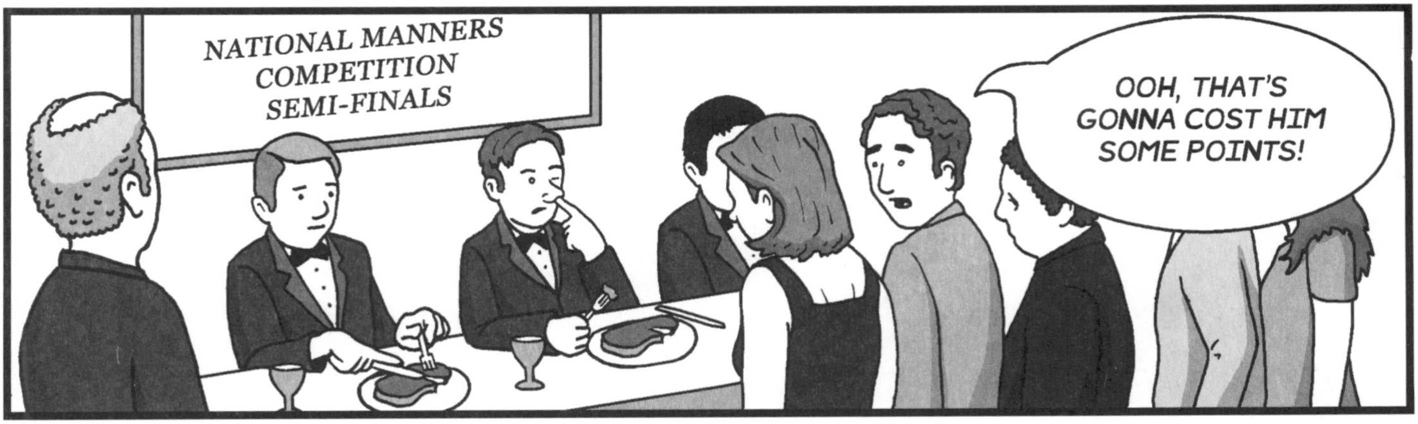
NATIONAL MANNERS COMPETITION SEMI-FINALS
OOH, THAT'S GONNA COST HIM SOME POINTS!

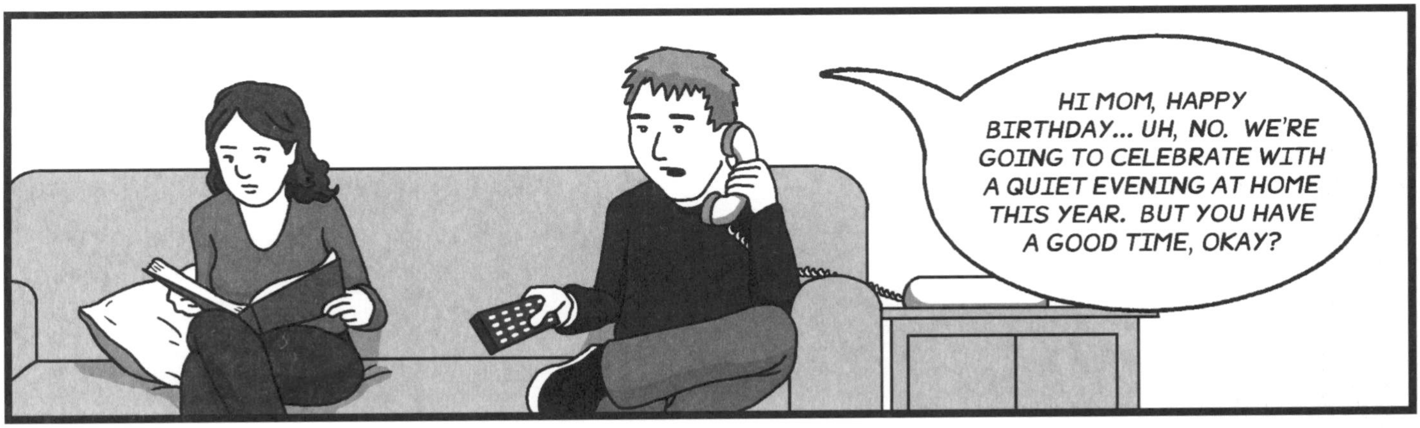
HI MOM, HAPPY BIRTHDAY... UH, NO. WE'RE GOING TO CELEBRATE WITH A QUIET EVENING AT HOME THIS YEAR. BUT YOU HAVE A GOOD TIME, OKAY?

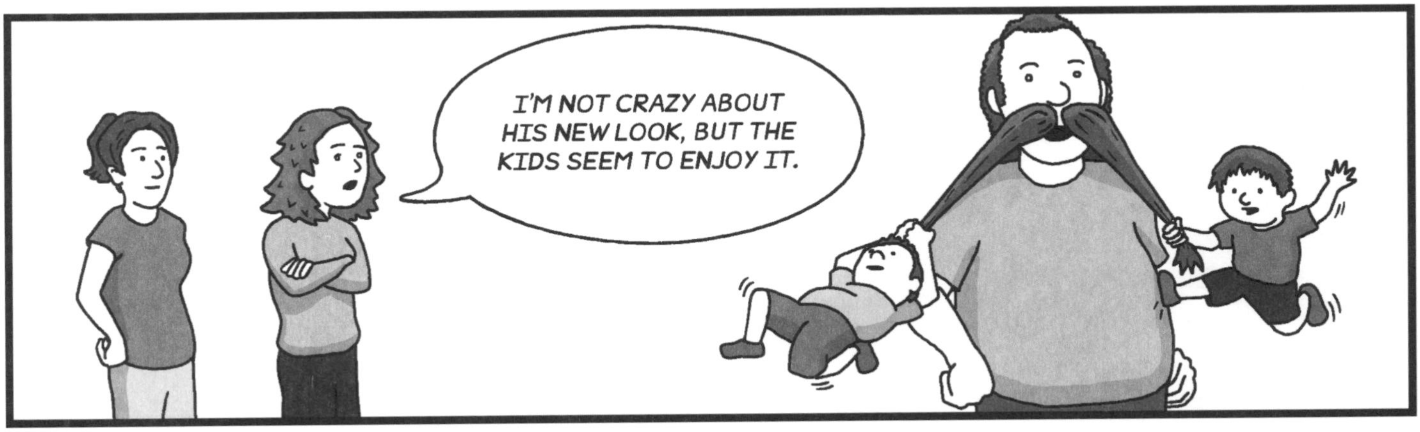
I'M NOT CRAZY ABOUT HIS NEW LOOK, BUT THE KIDS SEEM TO ENJOY IT.

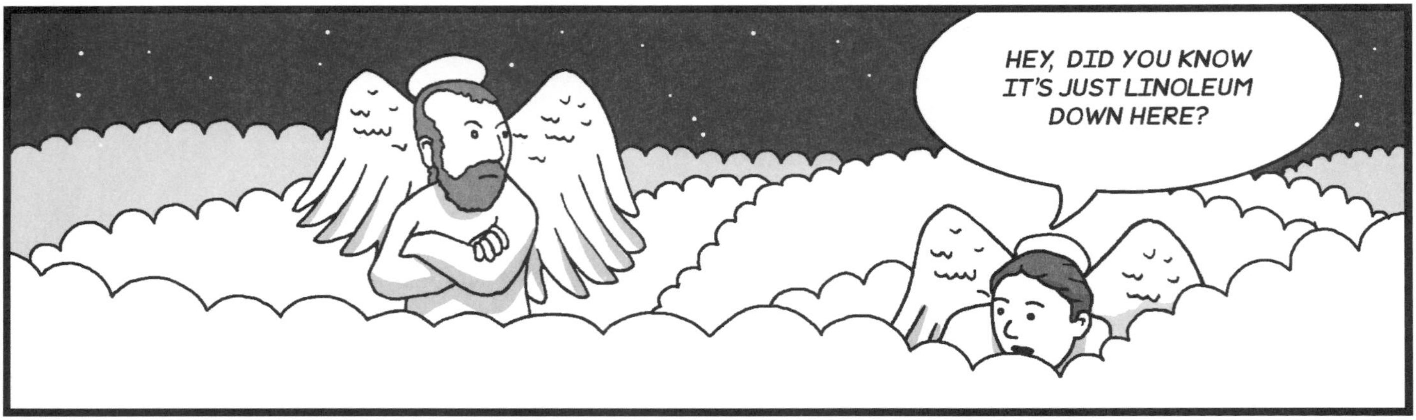
HEY, DID YOU KNOW IT'S JUST LINOLEUM DOWN HERE?

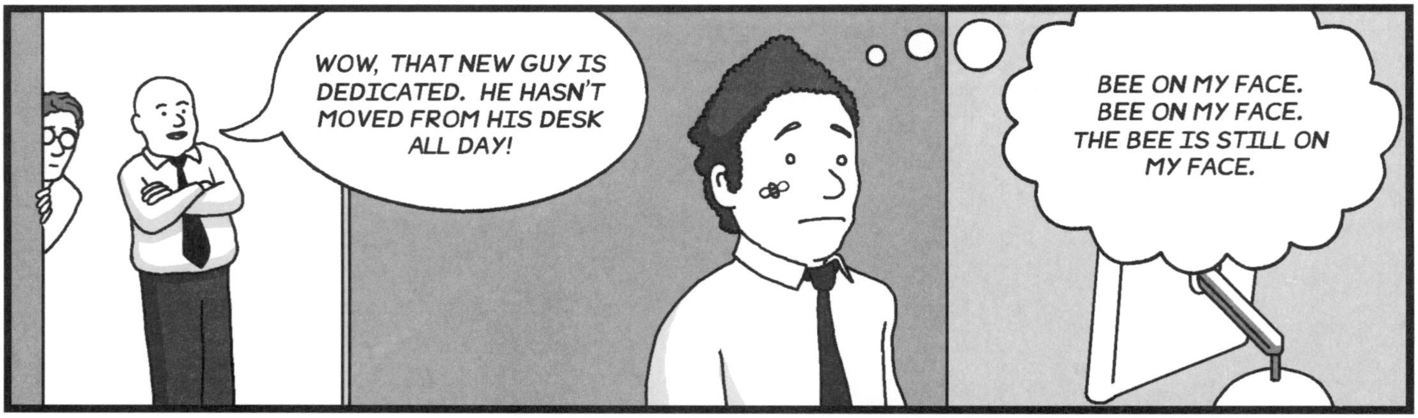
WOW, THAT NEW GUY IS DEDICATED. HE HASN'T MOVED FROM HIS DESK ALL DAY!
BEE ON MY FACE. BEE ON MY FACE. THE BEE IS STILL ON MY FACE.

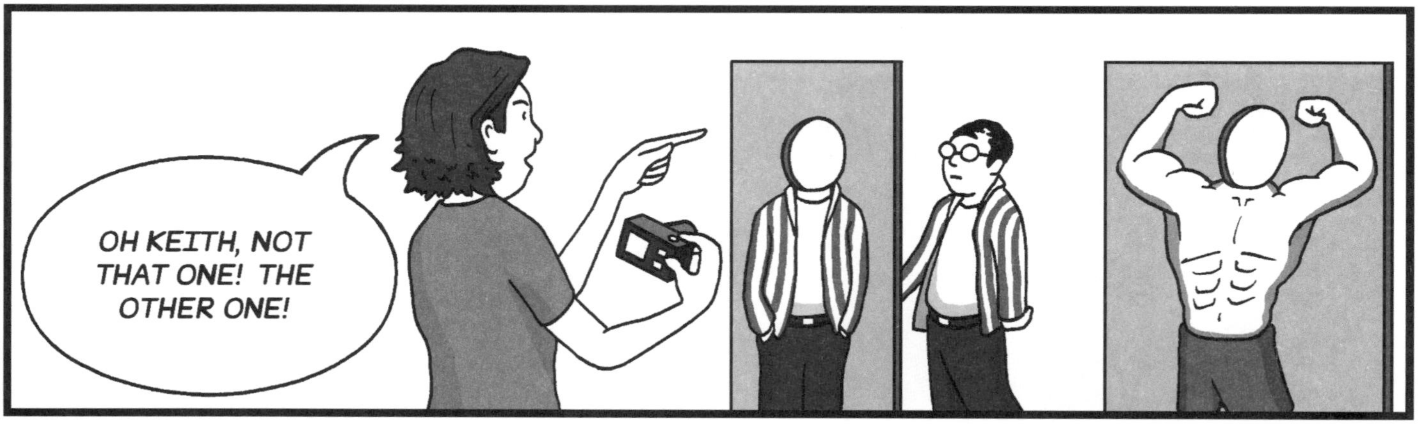
OH KEITH, NOT THAT ONE! THE OTHER ONE!

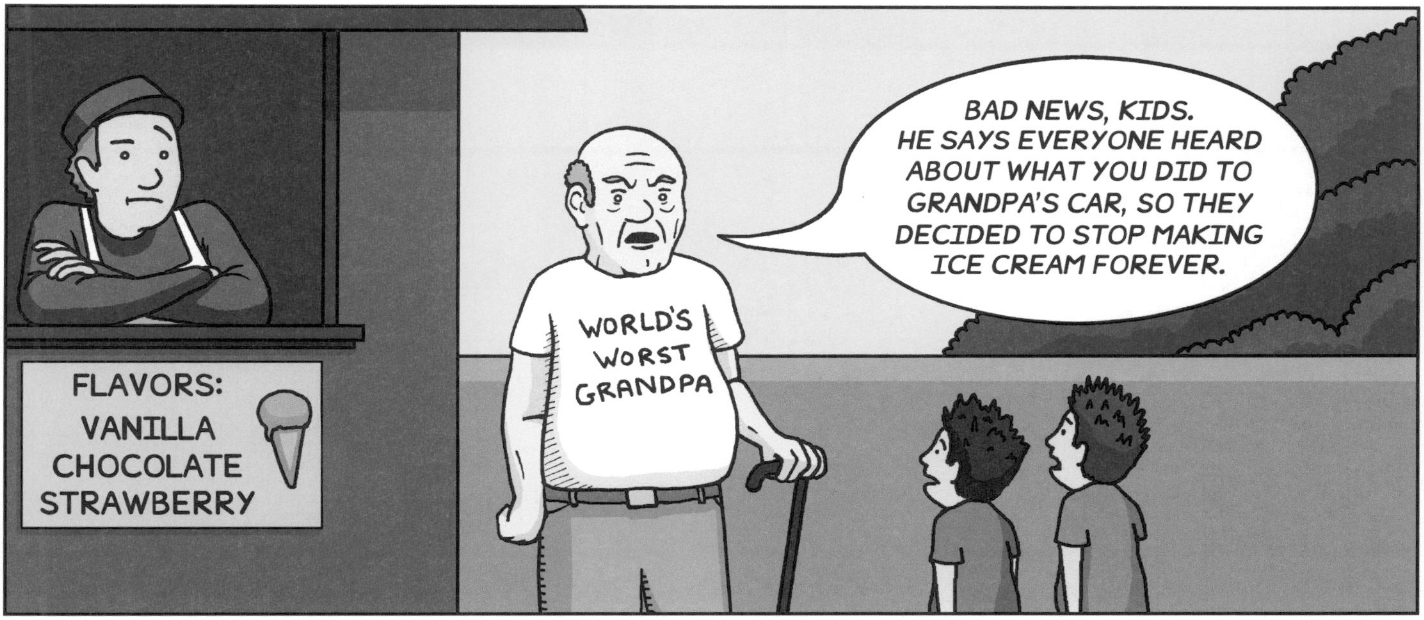
FLAVORS:
VANILLA
CHOCOLATE
STRAWBERRY
WORLD'S WORST GRANDPA
BAD NEWS, KIDS. HE SAYS EVERYONE HEARD ABOUT WHAT YOU DID TO GRANDPA'S CAR, SO THEY DECIDED TO STOP MAKING ICE CREAM FOREVER.

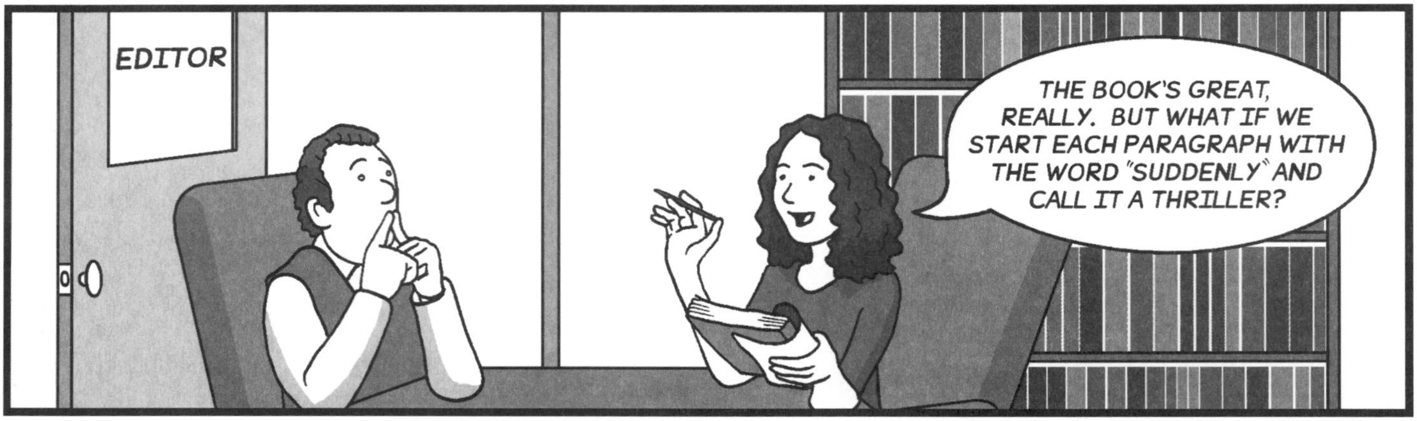
EDITOR
THE BOOK'S GREAT, REALLY. BUT WHAT IF WE START EACH PARAGRAPH WITH THE WORD "SUDDENLY" AND CALL IT A THRILLER?

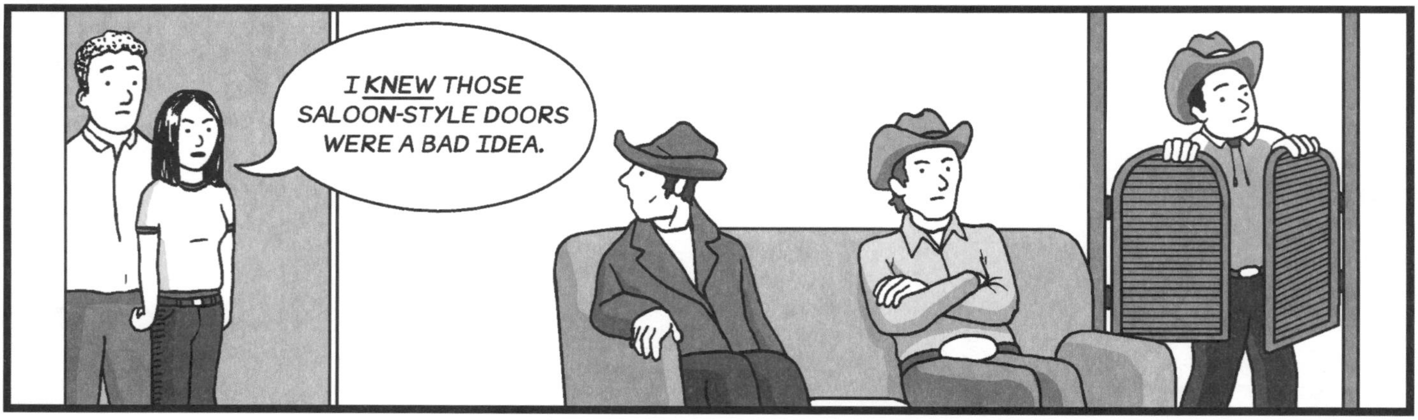
I KNEW THOSE SALOON-STYLE DOORS WERE A BAD IDEA.

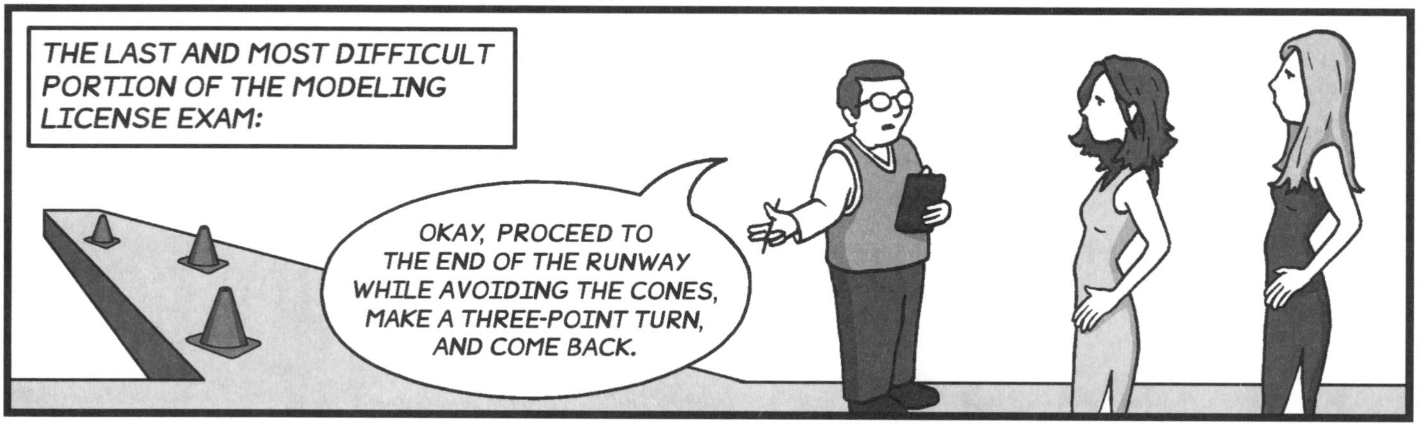
THE LAST AND MOST DIFFICULT PORTION OF THE MODELING LICENSE EXAM:
OKAY, PROCEED TO THE END OF THE RUNWAY WHILE AVOIDING THE CONES, MAKE A THREE-POINT TURN, AND COME BACK.

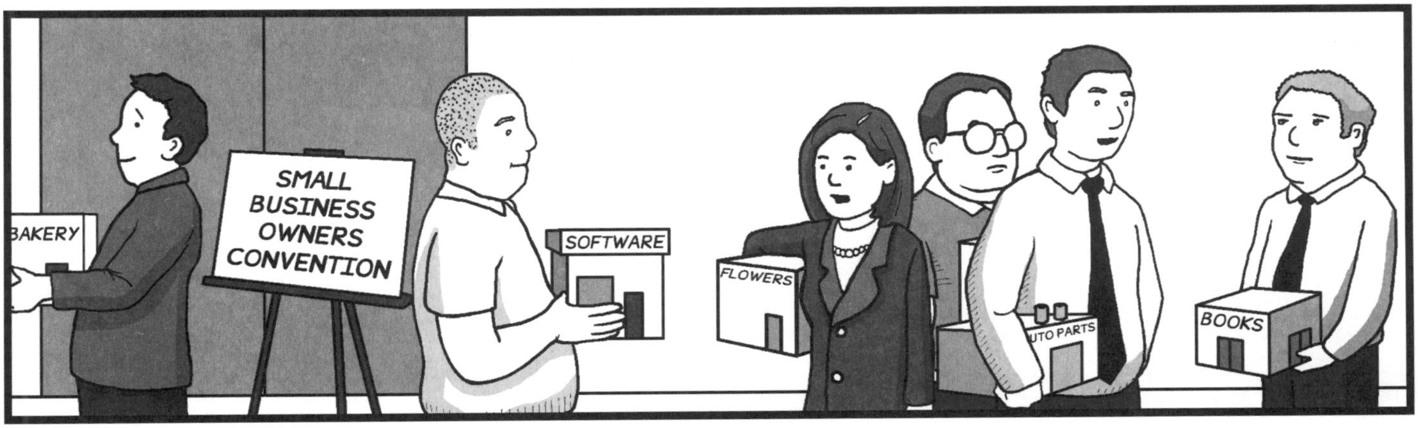
SMALL BUSINESS OWNERS CONVENTION
SOFTWARE
FLOWERS
BOOKS

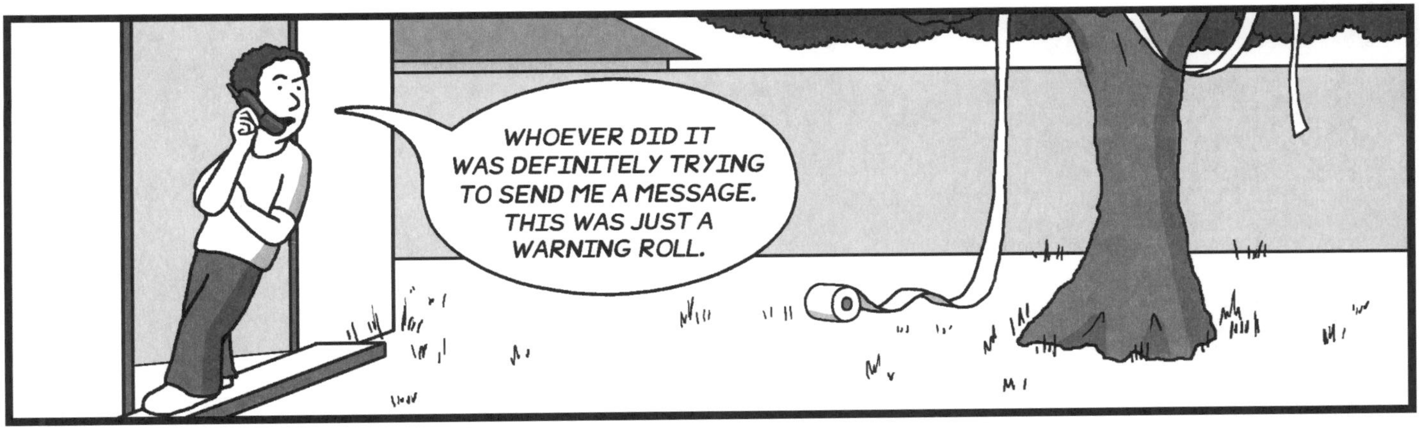
WHOEVER DID IT WAS DEFINITELY TRYING TO SEND ME A MESSAGE. THIS WAS JUST A WARNING ROLL.

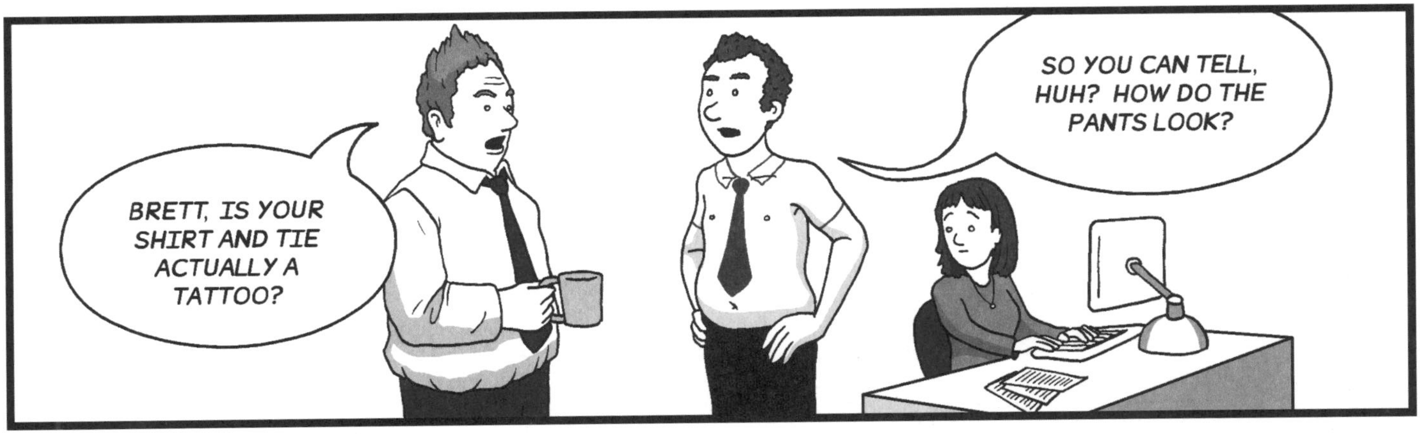
BRETT, IS YOUR SHIRT AND TIE ACTUALLY A TATTOO?
SO YOU CAN TELL, HUH? HOW DO THE PANTS LOOK?

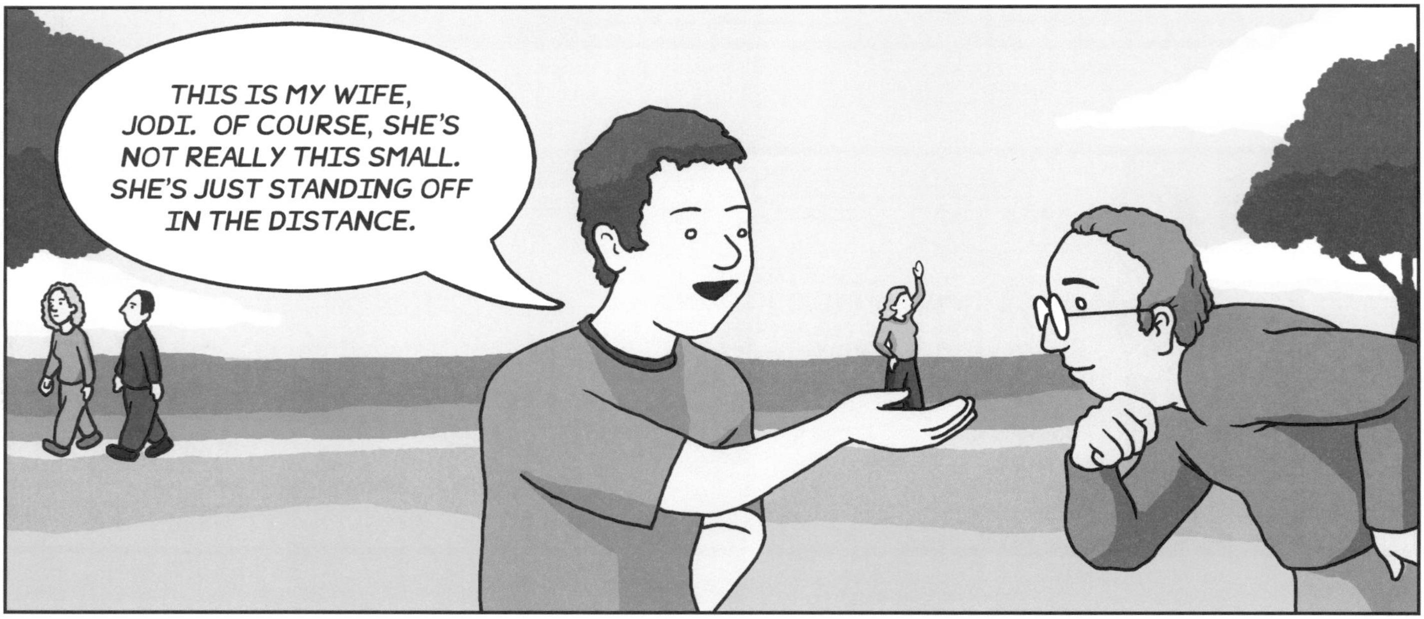
THIS IS MY WIFE, JODI. OF COURSE, SHE'S NOT REALLY THIS SMALL. SHE'S JUST STANDING OFF IN THE DISTANCE.

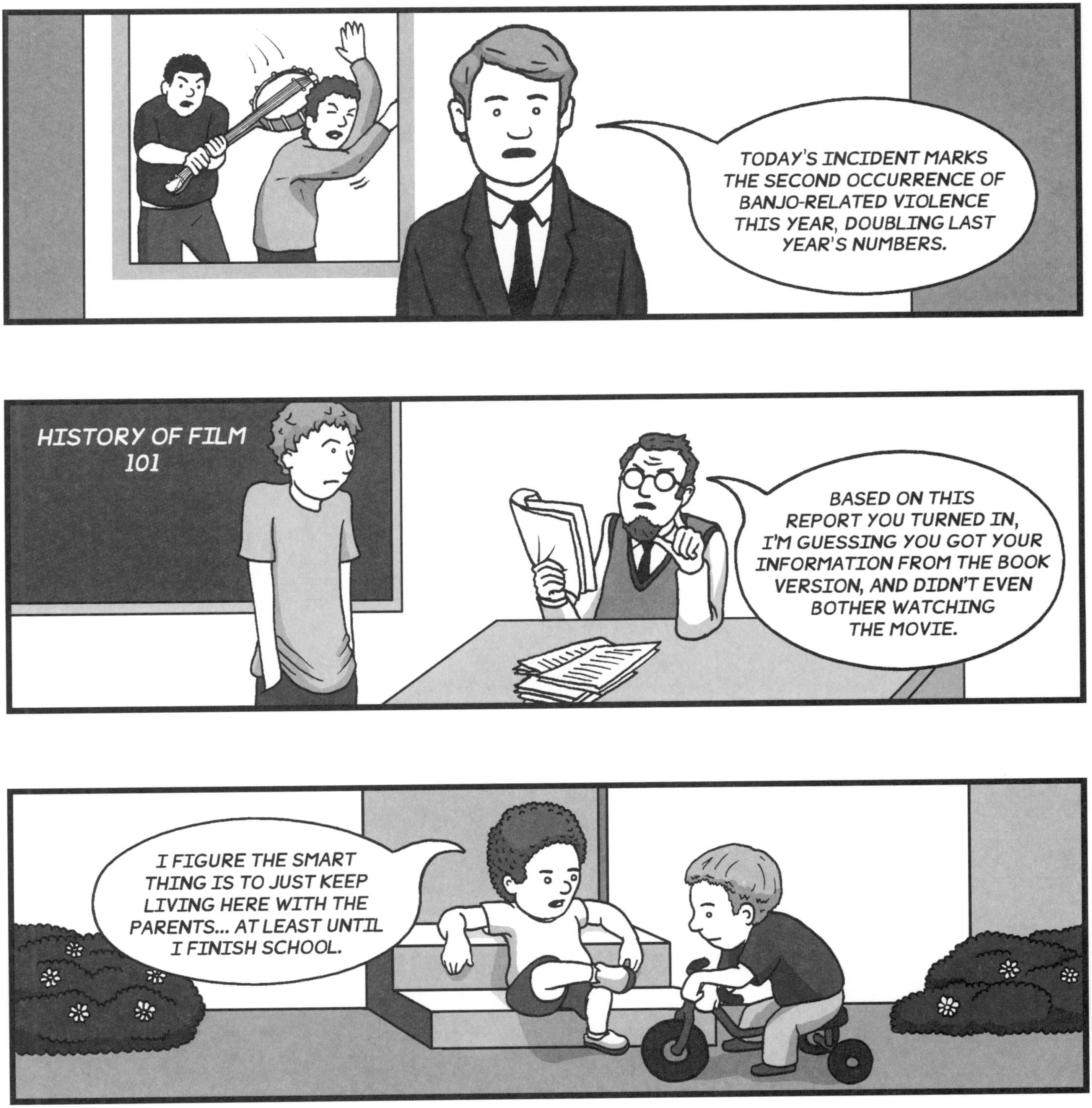
TODAY'S INCIDENT MARKS THE SECOND OCCURRENCE OF BANJO-RELATED VIOLENCE THIS YEAR, DOUBLING LAST YEAR'S NUMBERS.
HISTORY OF FILM 101
BASED ON THIS REPORT YOU TURNED IN, I'M GUESSING YOU GOT YOUR INFORMATION FROM THE BOOK VERSION, AND DIDN'T EVEN BOTHER WATCHING THE MOVIE.
I FIGURE THE SMART THING IS TO JUST KEEP LIVING HERE WITH THE PARENTS... AT LEAST UNTIL I FINISH SCHOOL.

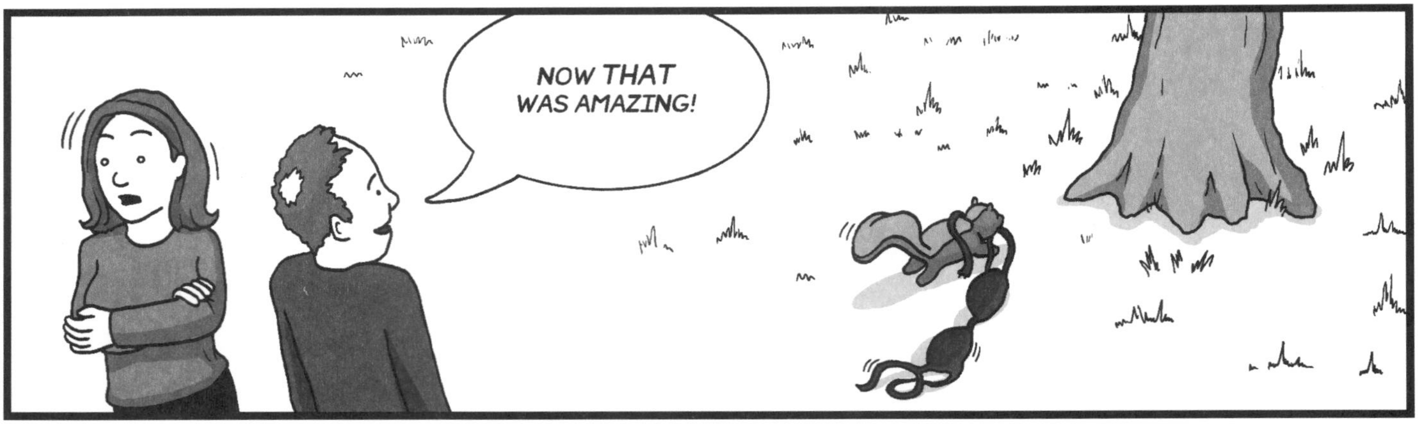
NOW THAT WAS AMAZING!

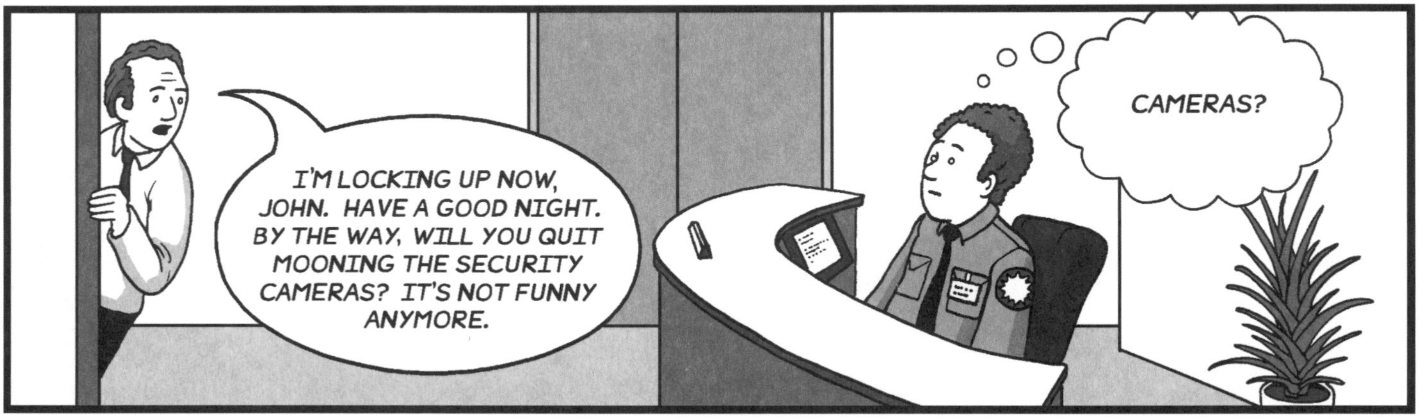
I'M LOCKING UP NOW, JOHN. HAVE A GOOD NIGHT. BY THE WAY, WILL YOU QUIT MOONING THE SECURITY CAMERAS? IT'S NOT FUNNY ANYMORE.
CAMERAS?

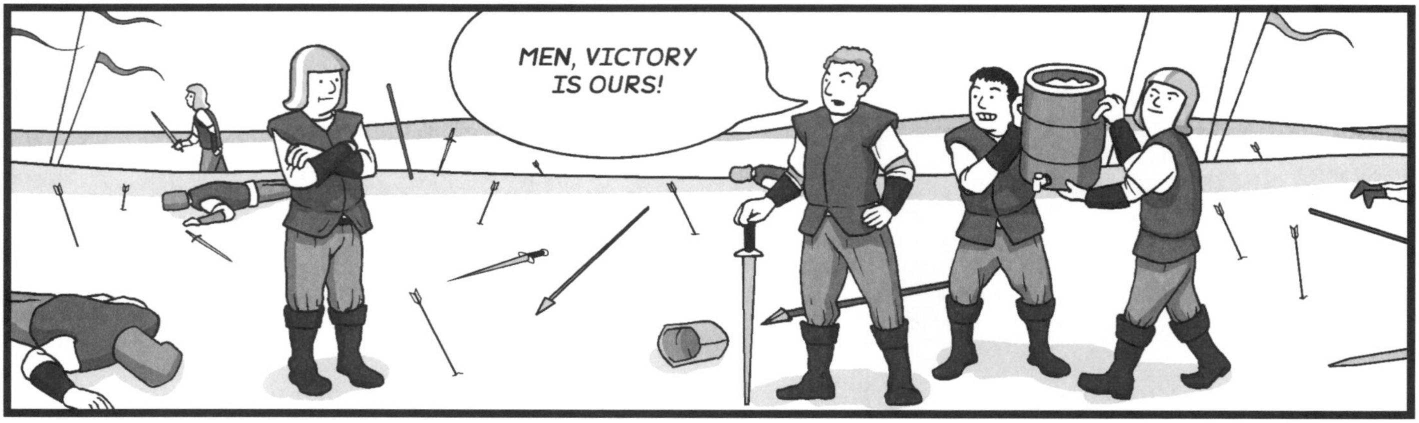
MEN, VICTORY IS OURS!

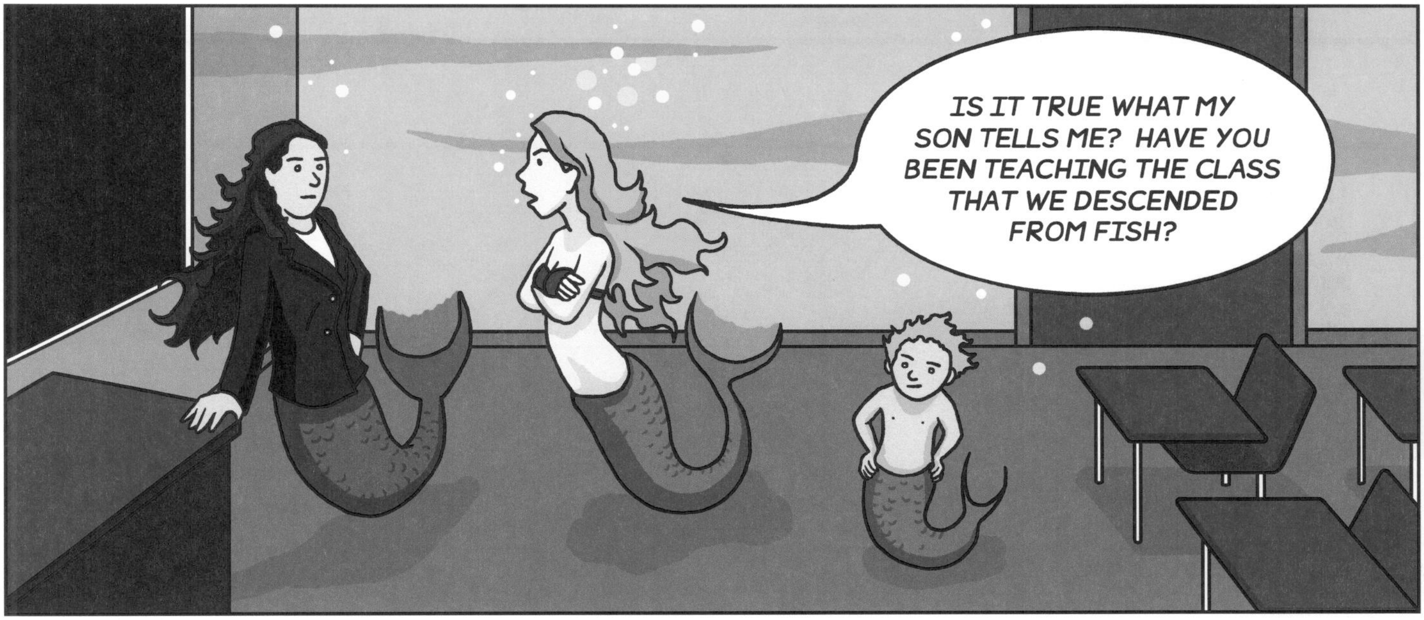
IS IT TRUE WHAT MY SON TELLS ME? HAVE YOU BEEN TEACHING THE CLASS THAT WE DESCENDED FROM FISH?

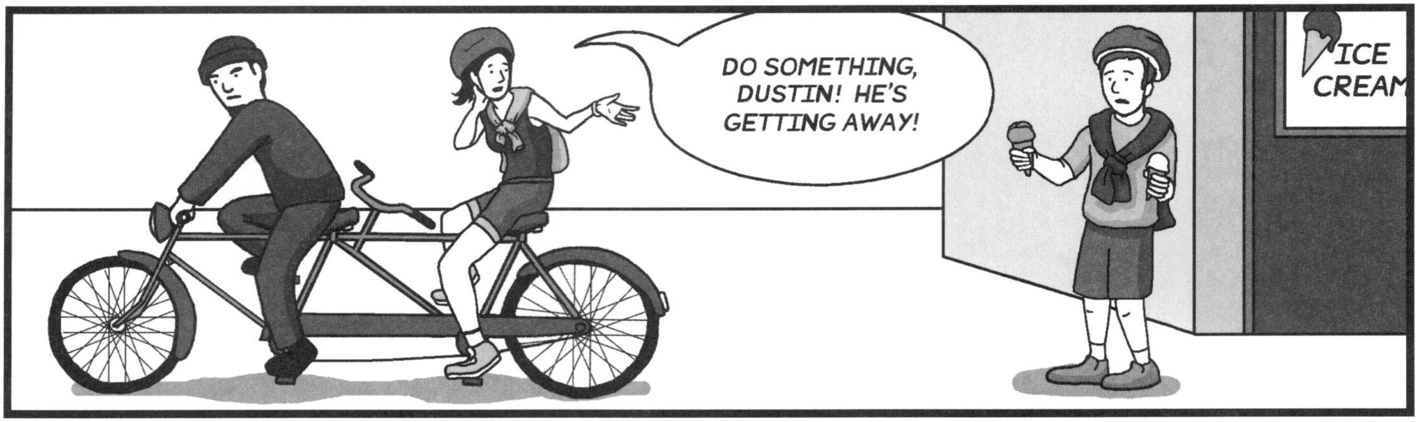
DO SOMETHING, DUSTIN! HE'S GETTING AWAY!
ICE CREAM

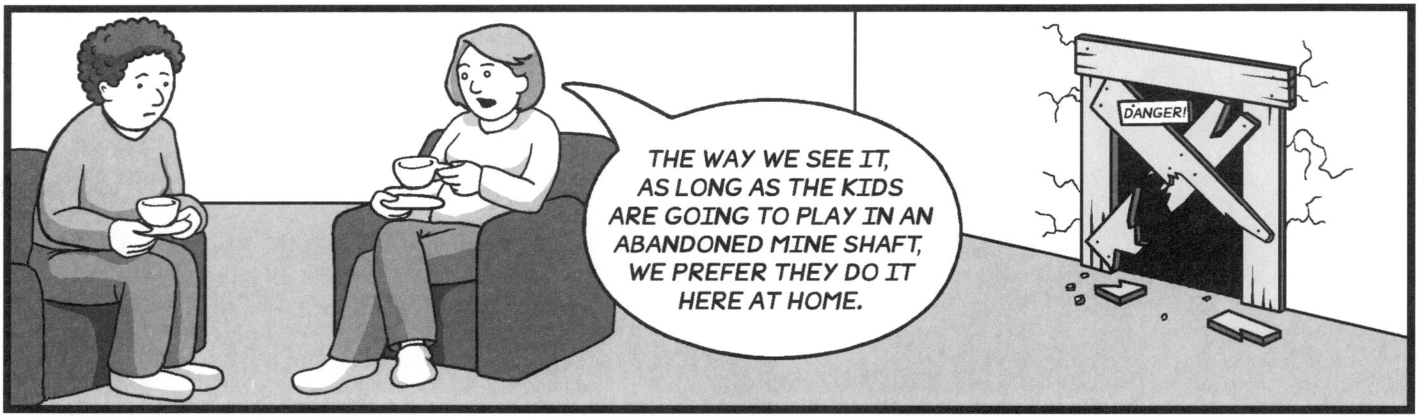
THE WAY WE SEE IT, AS LONG AS THE KIDS ARE GOING TO PLAY IN AN ABANDONED MINE SHAFT, WE PREFER THEY DO IT HERE AT HOME.
DANGER!

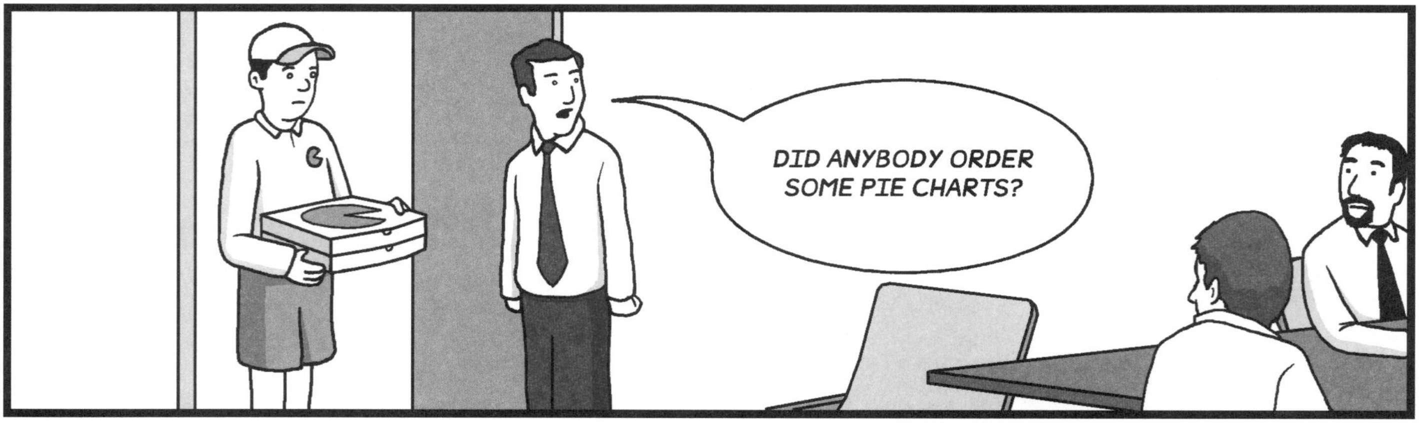
DID ANYBODY ORDER SOME PIE CHARTS?

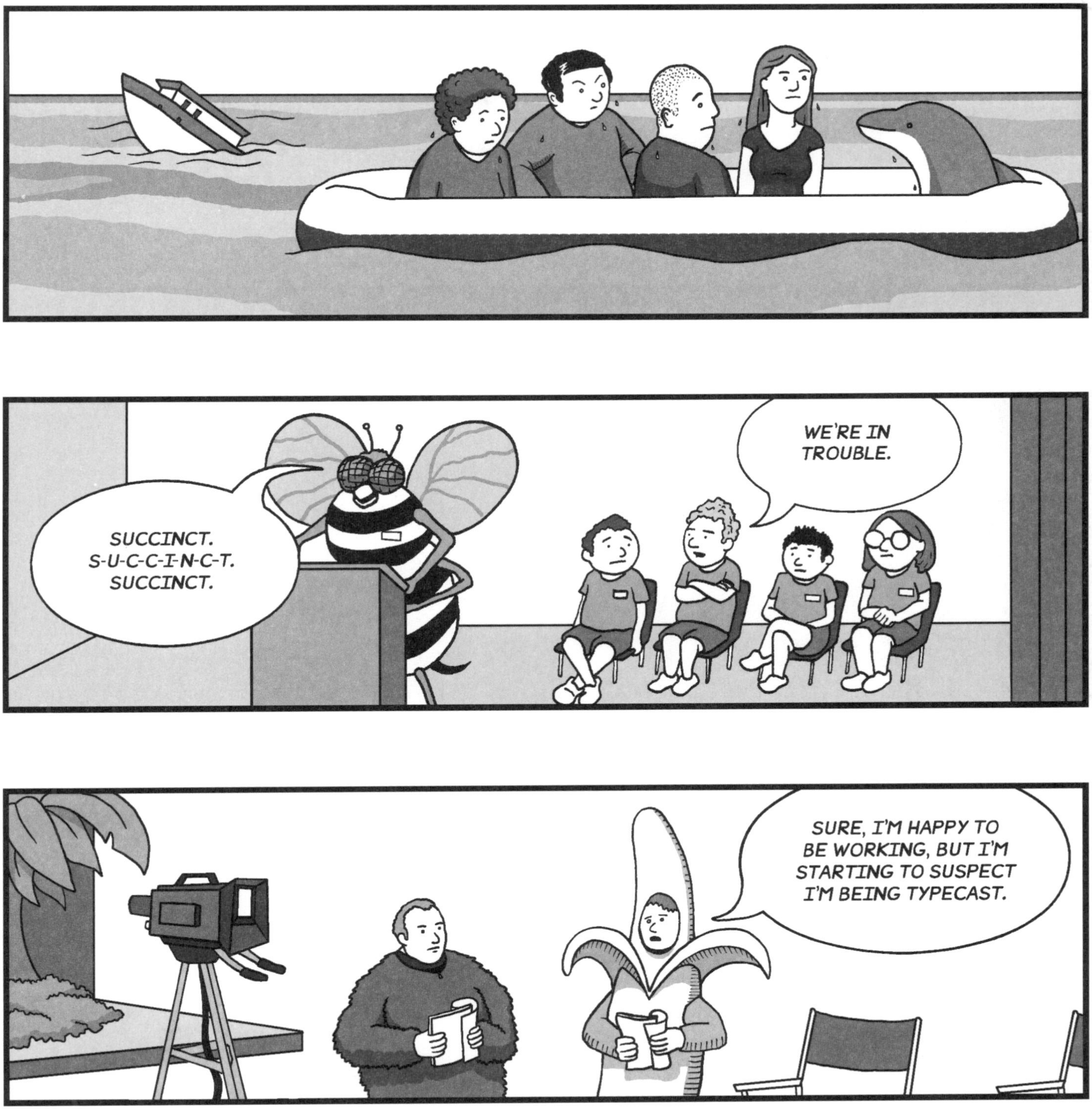
SUCCINCT. S-U-C-C-I-N-C-T. SUCCINCT.
WE'RE IN TROUBLE.
SURE, I'M HAPPY TO BE WORKING, BUT I'M STARTING TO SUSPECT I'M BEING TYPECAST.

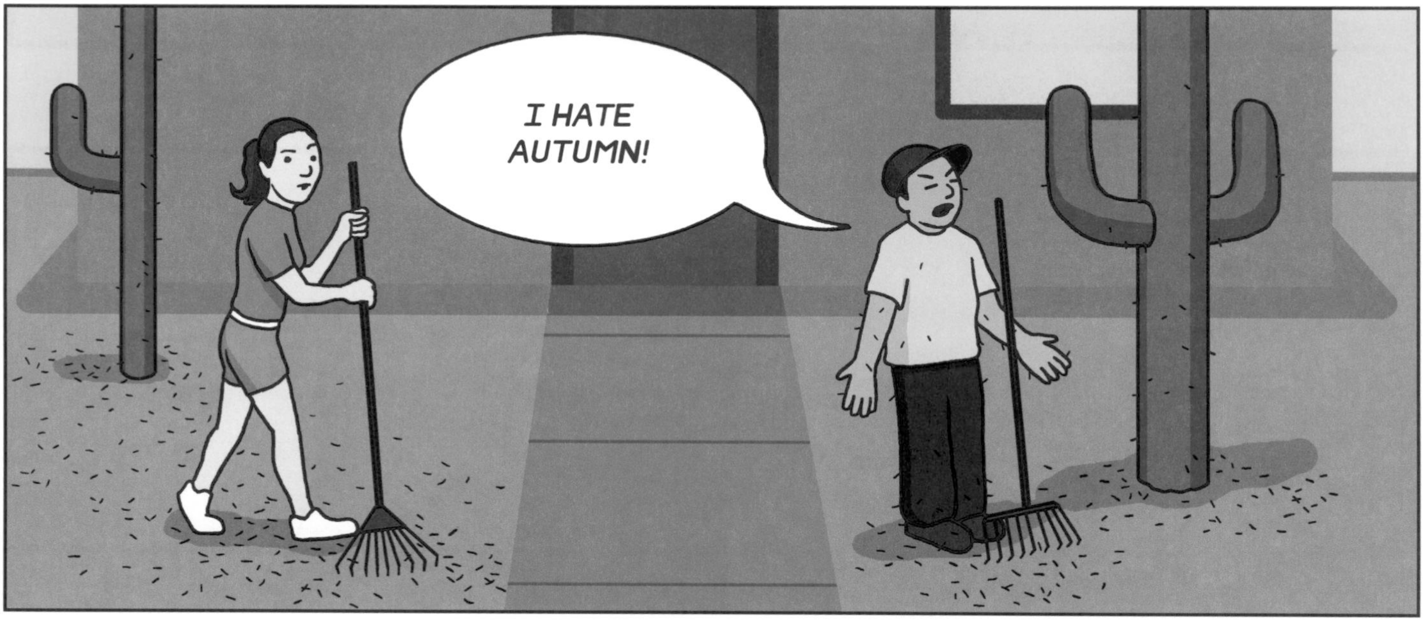
I HATE AUTUMN!

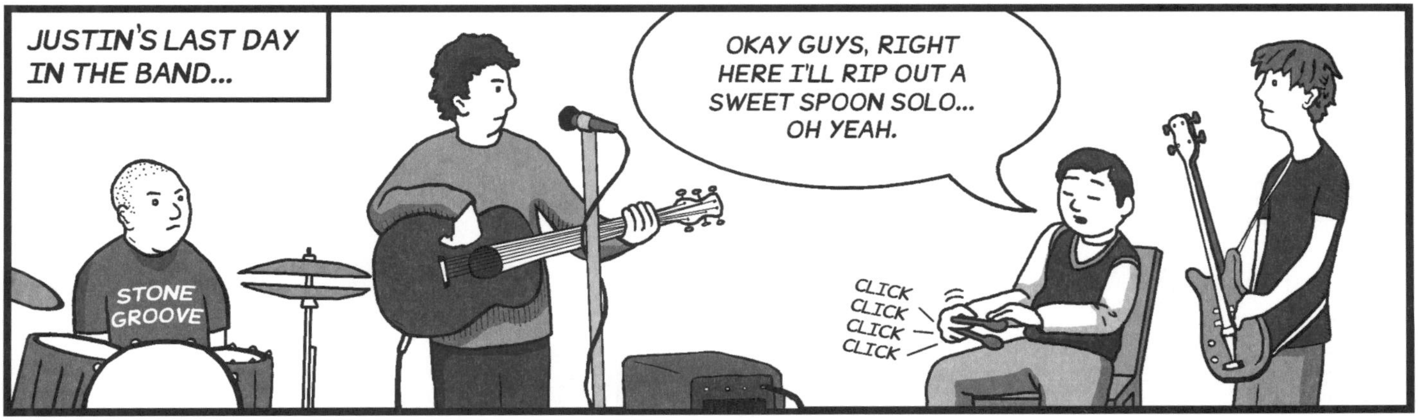
JUSTIN'S LAST DAY IN THE BAND...
OKAY GUYS, RIGHT HERE I'LL RIP OUT A SWEET SPOON SOLO... OH YEAH.
STONE GROOVE
CLICK CLICK CLICK CLICK

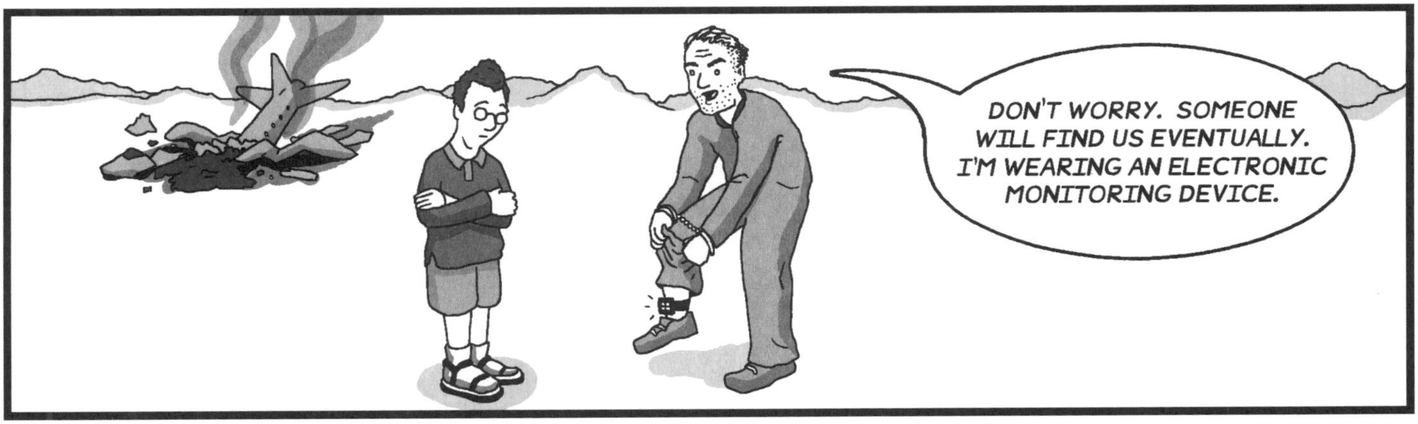
DON'T WORRY. SOMEONE WILL FIND US EVENTUALLY. I'M WEARING AN ELECTRONIC MONITORING DEVICE.

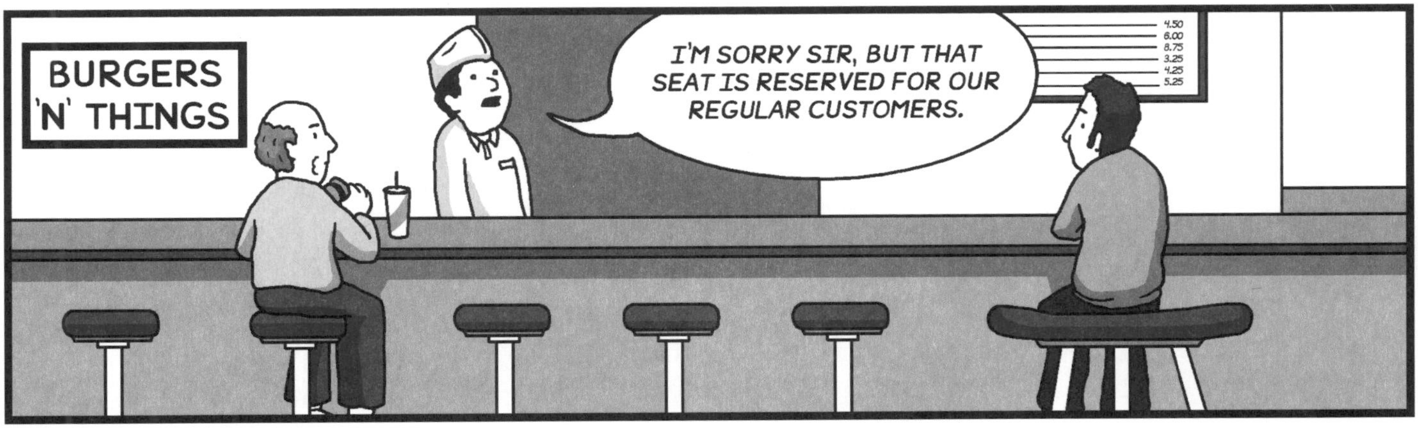
BURGERS 'N' THINGS
I'M SORRY SIR, BUT THAT SEAT IS RESERVED FOR OUR REGULAR CUSTOMERS.
4.50
6.00
8.75
3.25
4.25
5.25

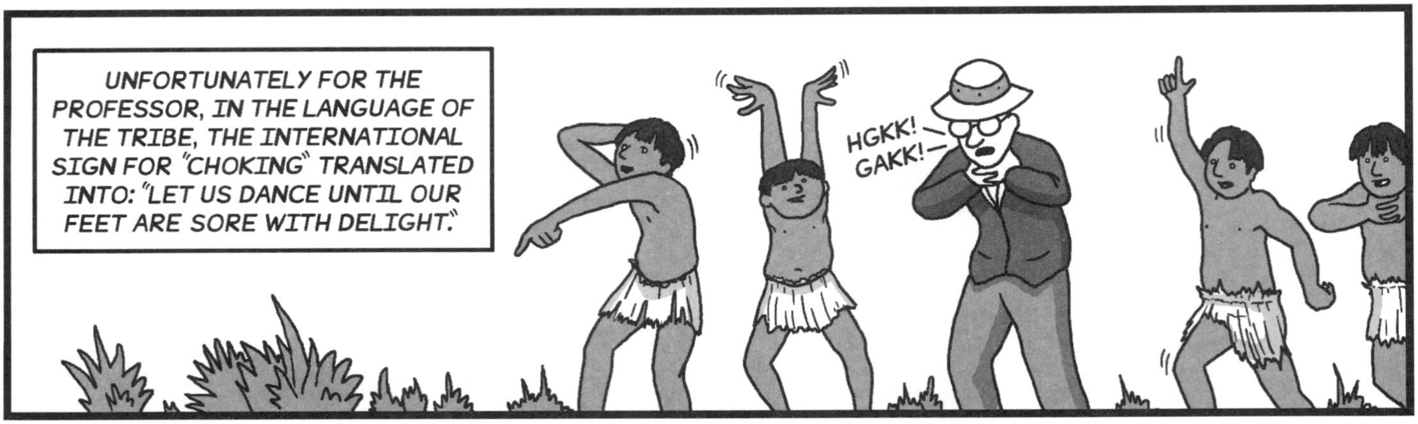
UNFORTUNATELY FOR THE PROFESSOR, IN THE LANGUAGE OF THE TRIBE, THE INTERNATIONAL SIGN FOR "CHOKING" TRANSLATED INTO: "LET US DANCE UNTIL OUR FEET ARE SORE WITH DELIGHT."
HGKK!
GAKK!

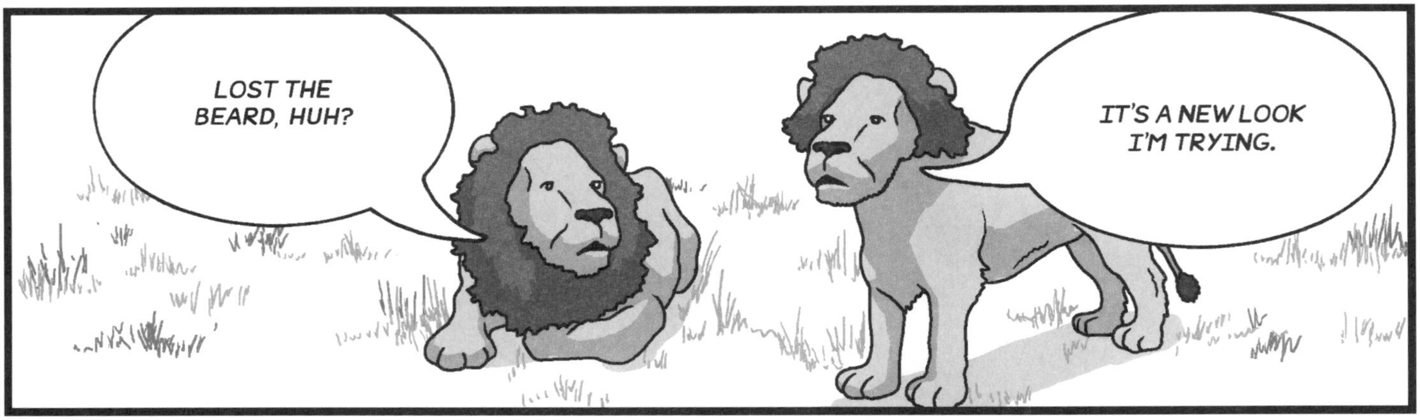
LOST THE BEARD, HUH?
IT'S A NEW LOOK I'M TRYING.

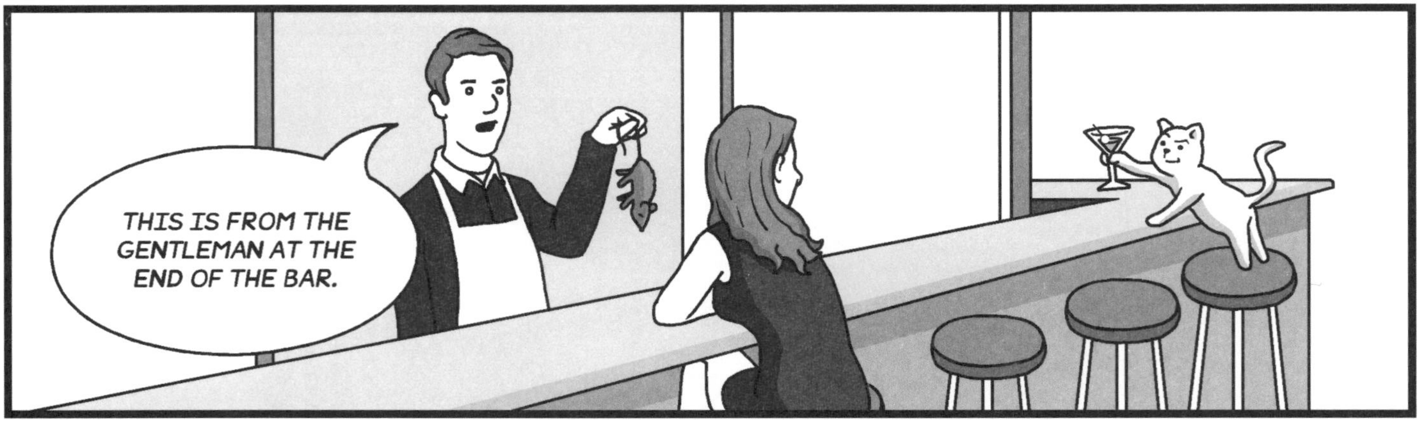
THIS IS FROM THE GENTLEMAN AT THE END OF THE BAR.

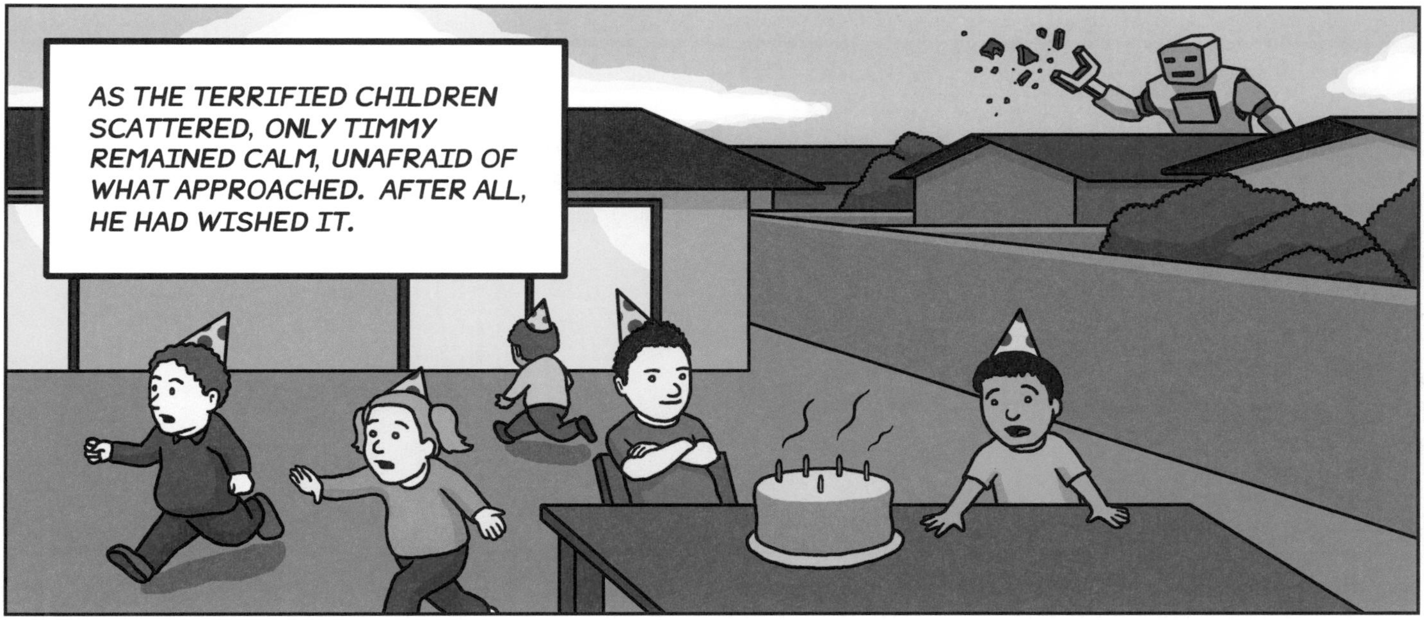
AS THE TERRIFIED CHILDREN SCATTERED, ONLY TIMMY REMAINED CALM, UNAFRAID OF WHAT APPROACHED. AFTER ALL, HE HAD WISHED IT.

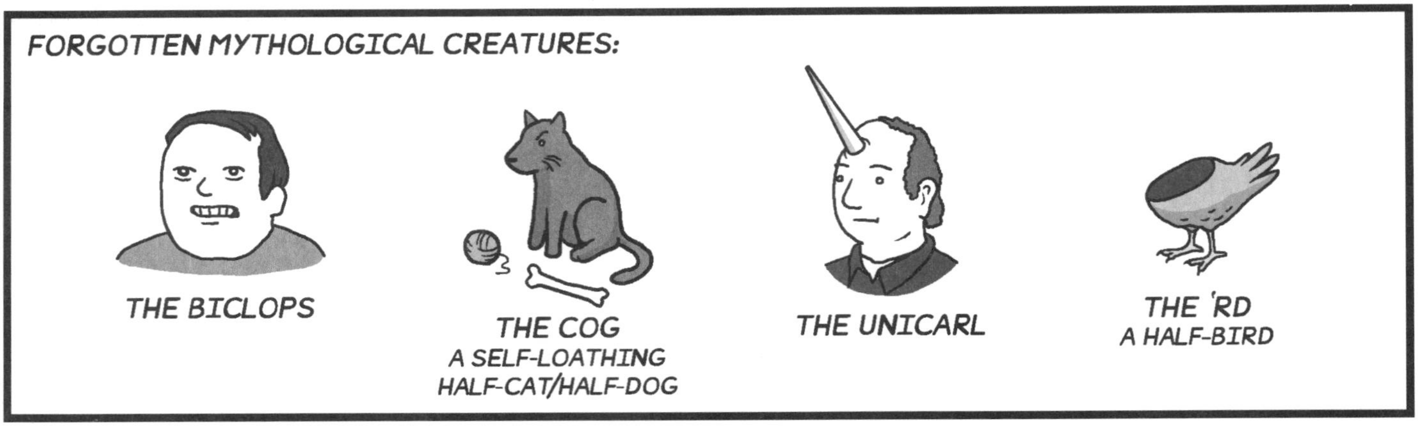
FORGOTTEN MYTHOLOGICAL CREATURES:
THE BICLOPS
THE COG
A SELF-LOATHING HALF-CAT/HALF-DOG
THE UNICARL
THE 'RD
A HALF-BIRD

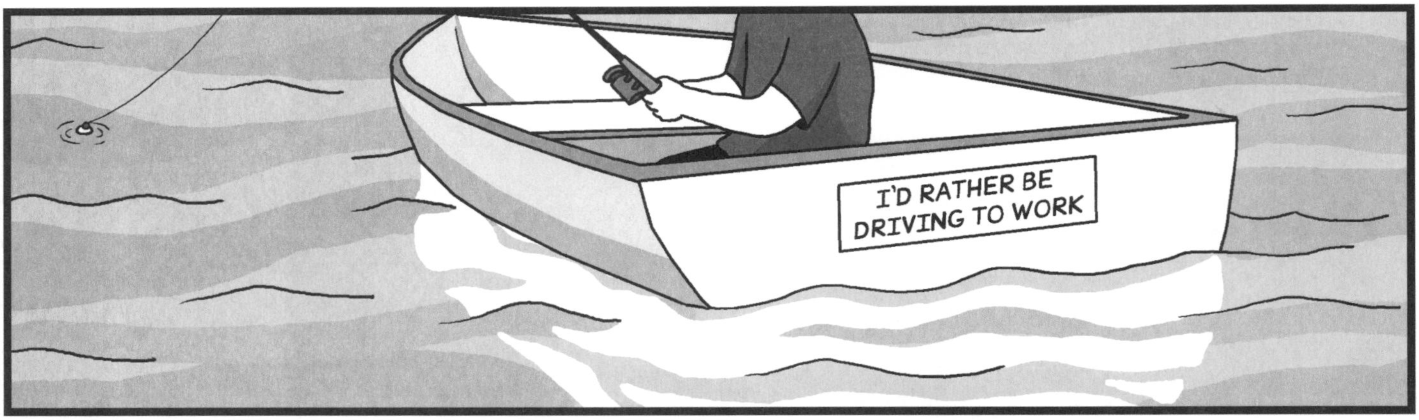
I'D RATHER BE DRIVING TO WORK

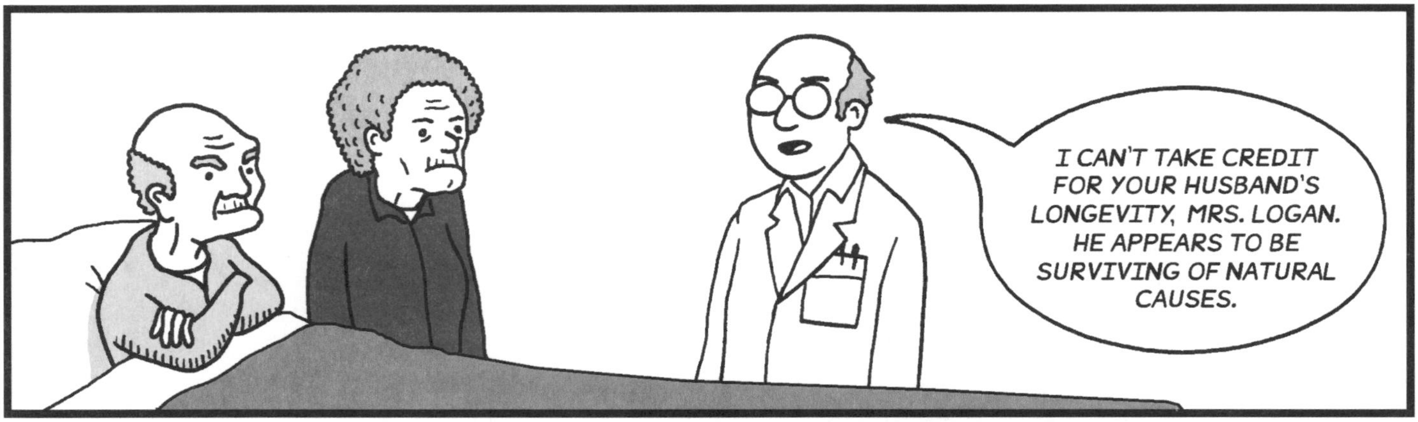
I CAN'T TAKE CREDIT FOR YOUR HUSBAND'S LONGEVITY, MRS. LOGAN. HE APPEARS TO BE SURVIVING OF NATURAL CAUSES.

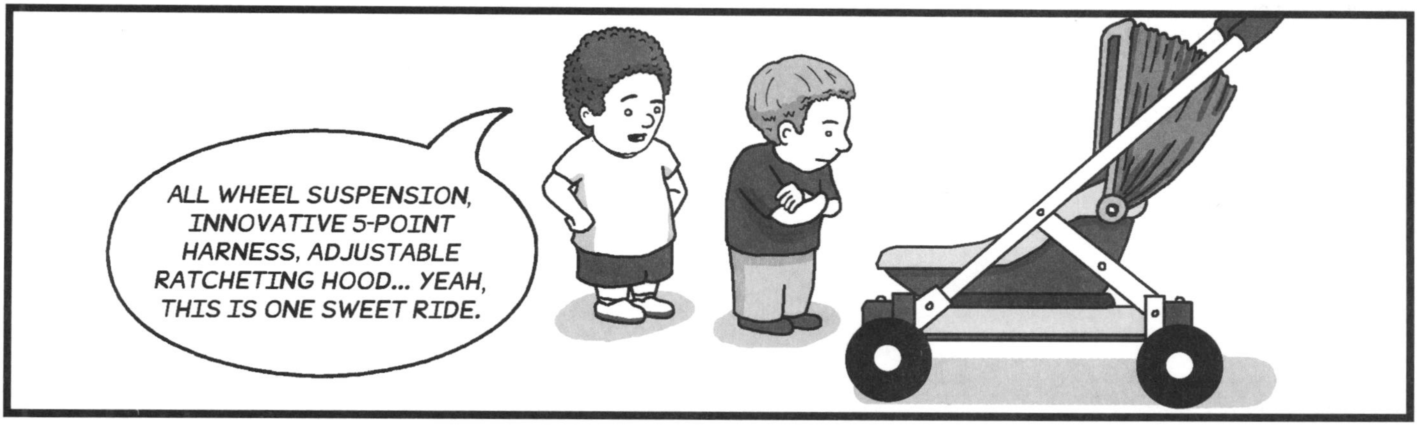
ALL WHEEL SUSPENSION, INNOVATIVE 5-POINT HARNESS, ADJUSTABLE RATCHETING HOOD... YEAH, THIS IS ONE SWEET RIDE.

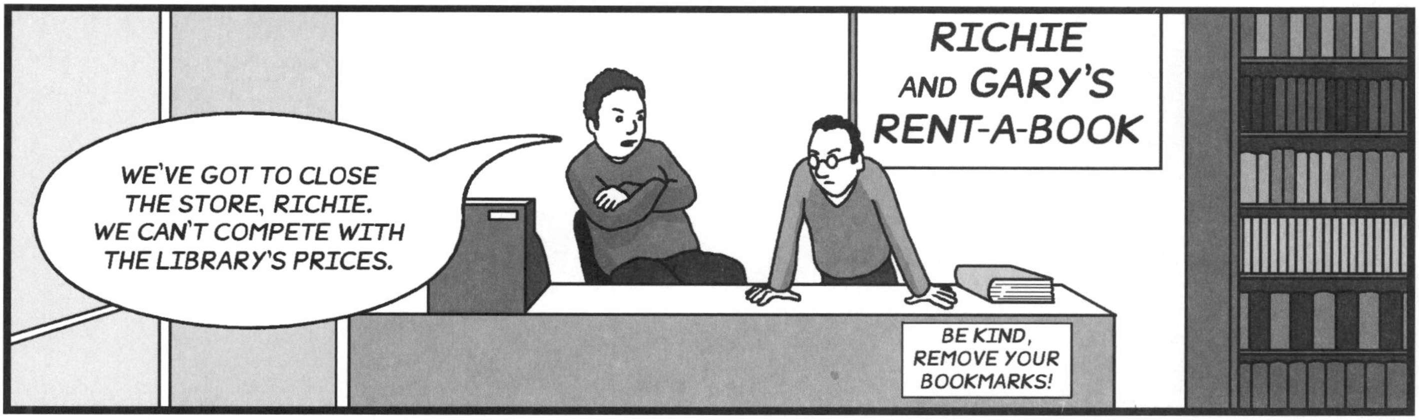
RICHIE AND GARY'S RENT-A-BOOK
WE'VE GOT TO CLOSE THE STORE, RICHIE. WE CAN'T COMPETE WITH THE LIBRARY'S PRICES.
BE KIND, REMOVE YOUR BOOKMARKS!

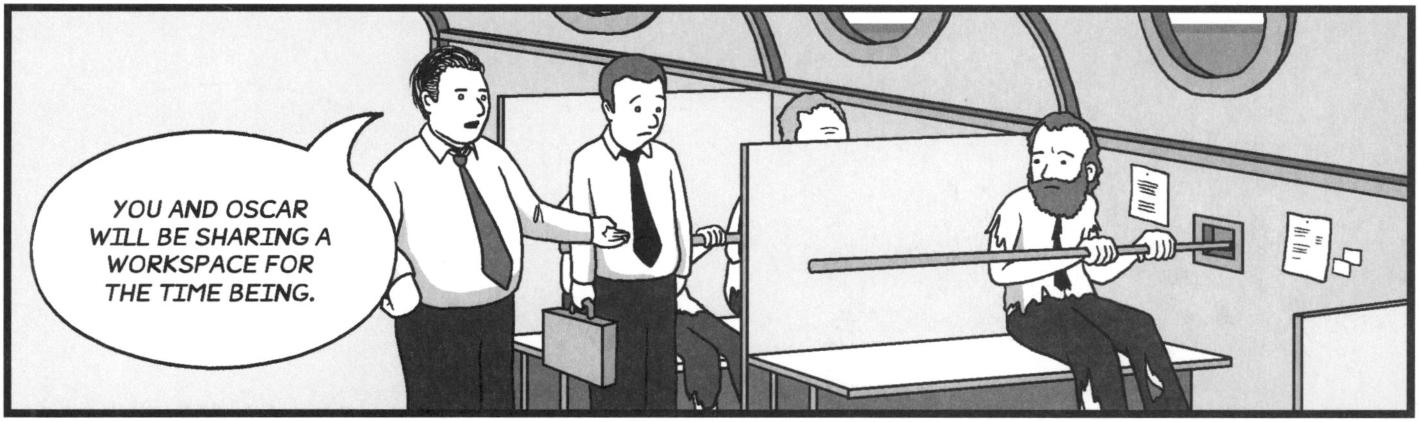
YOU AND OSCAR WILL BE SHARING A WORKSPACE FOR THE TIME BEING.

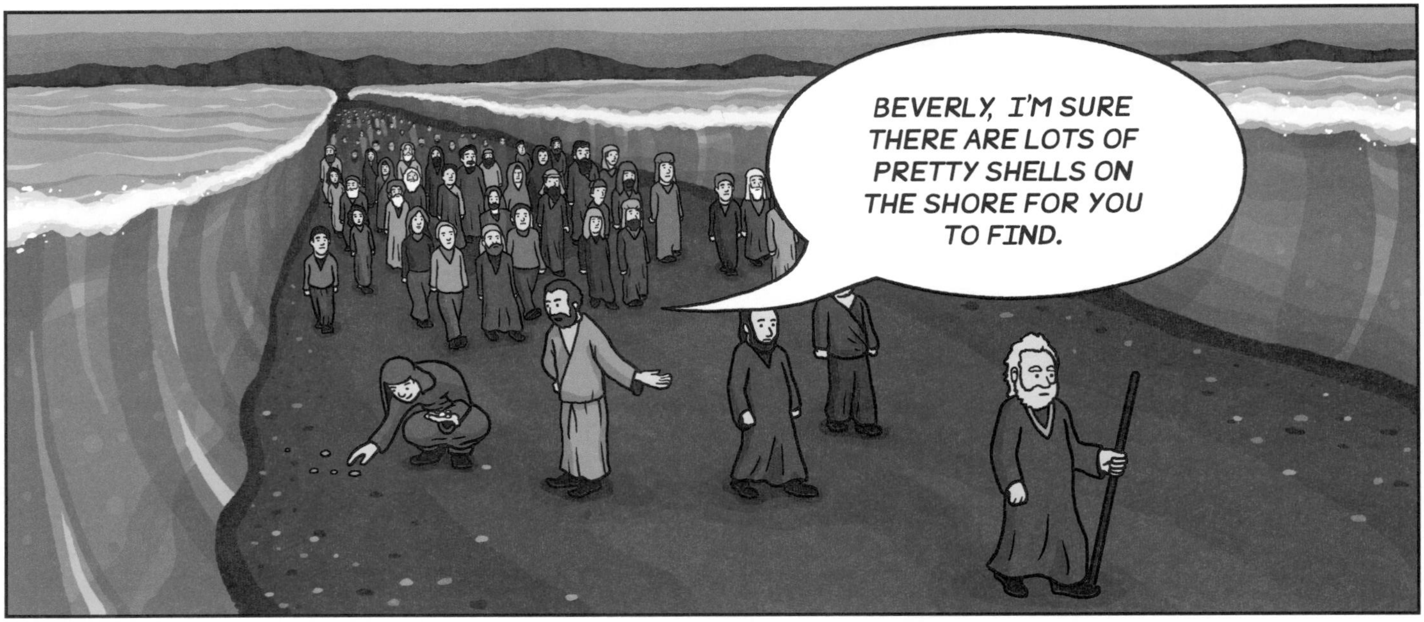
BEVERLY, I'M SURE THERE ARE LOTS OF PRETTY SHELLS ON THE SHORE FOR YOU TO FIND.

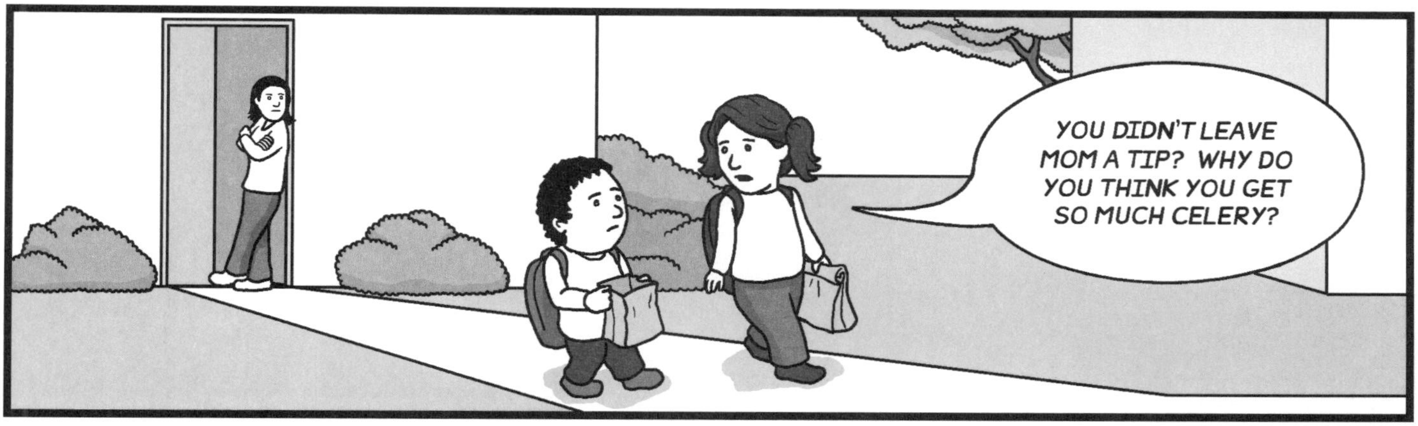
YOU DIDN'T LEAVE MOM A TIP? WHY DO YOU THINK YOU GET SO MUCH CELERY?

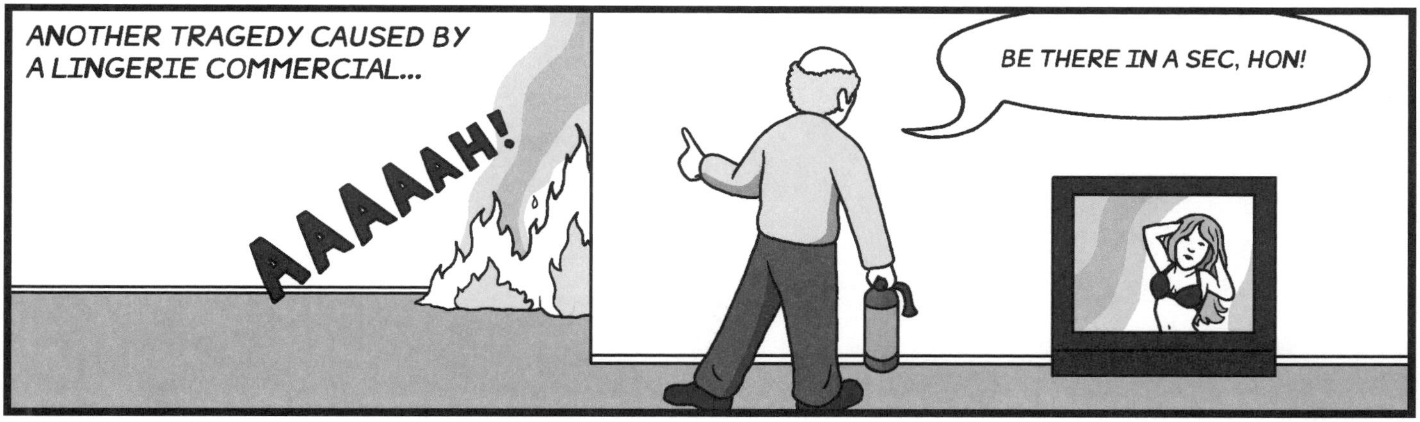
ANOTHER TRAGEDY CAUSED BY A LINGERIE COMMERCIAL...
AAAAAH!
BE THERE IN A SEC, HON!

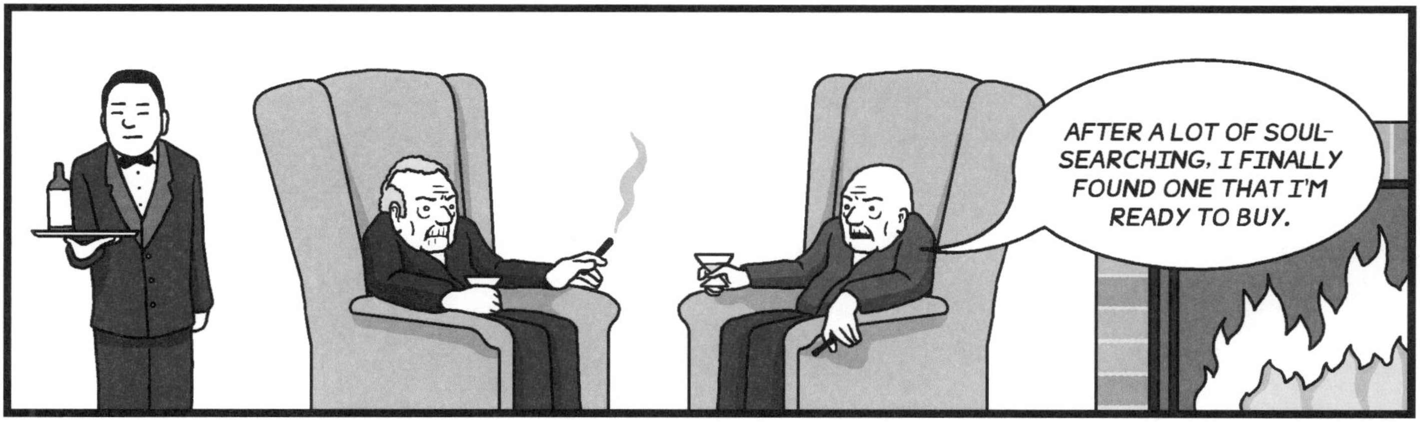
AFTER A LOT OF SOUL-SEARCHING, I FINALLY FOUND ONE THAT I'M READY TO BUY.

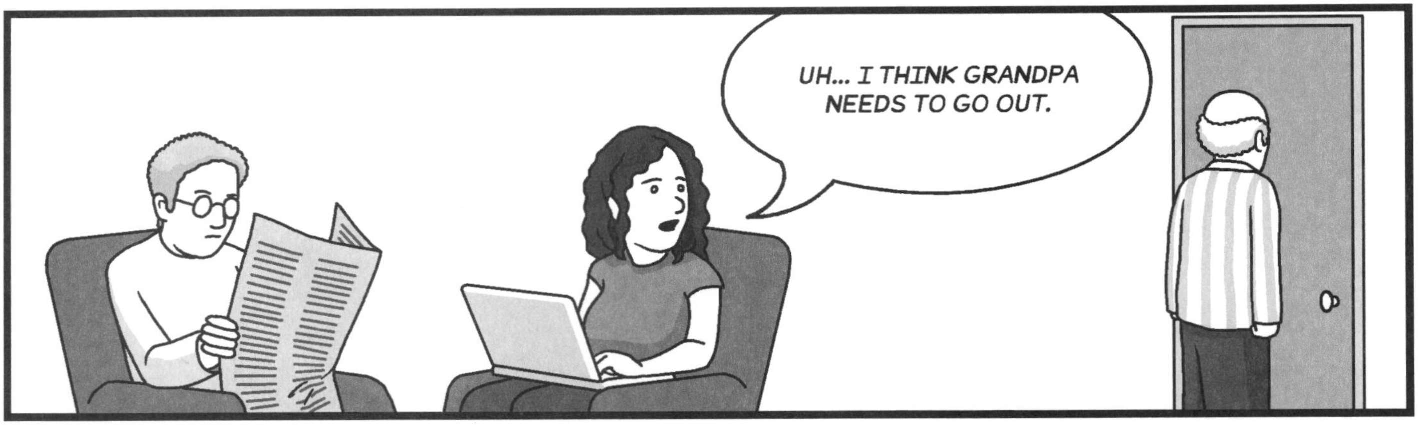
UH... I THINK GRANDPA NEEDS TO GO OUT.

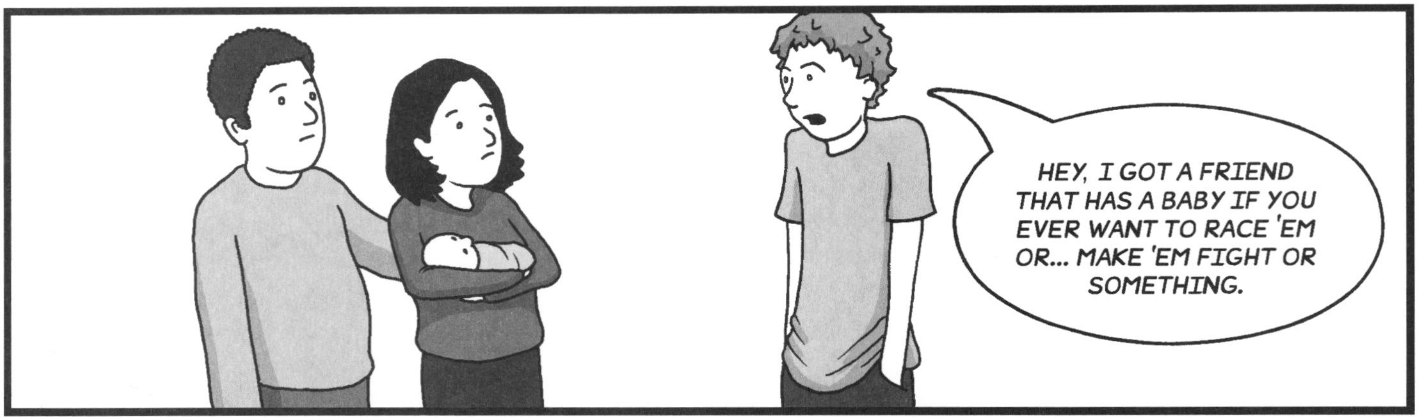
HEY, I GOT A FRIEND THAT HAS A BABY IF YOU EVER WANT TO RACE 'EM OR... MAKE 'EM FIGHT OR SOMETHING.

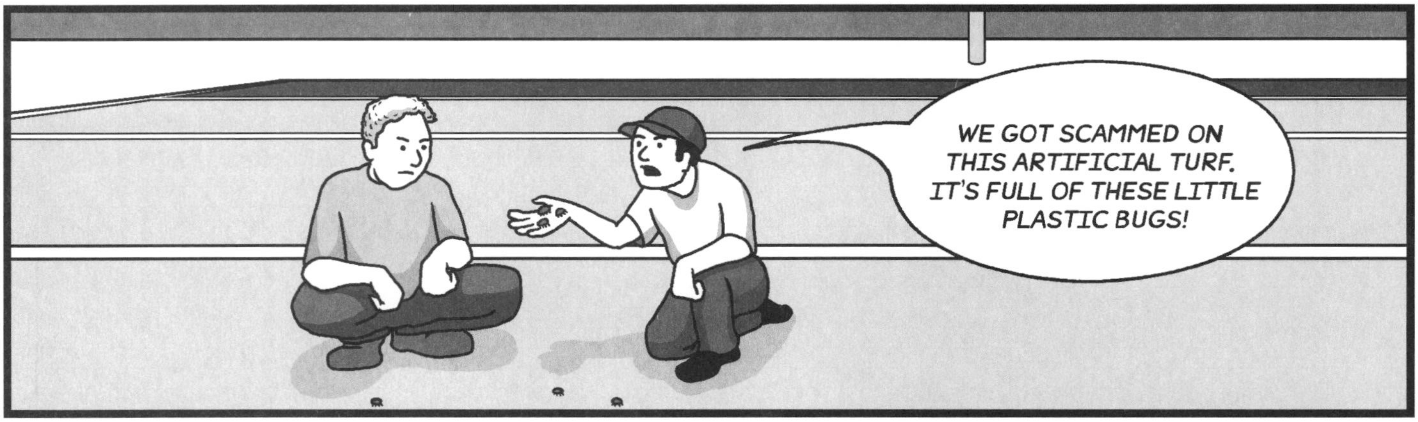
WE GOT SCAMMED ON THIS ARTIFICIAL TURF. IT'S FULL OF THESE LITTLE PLASTIC BUGS!

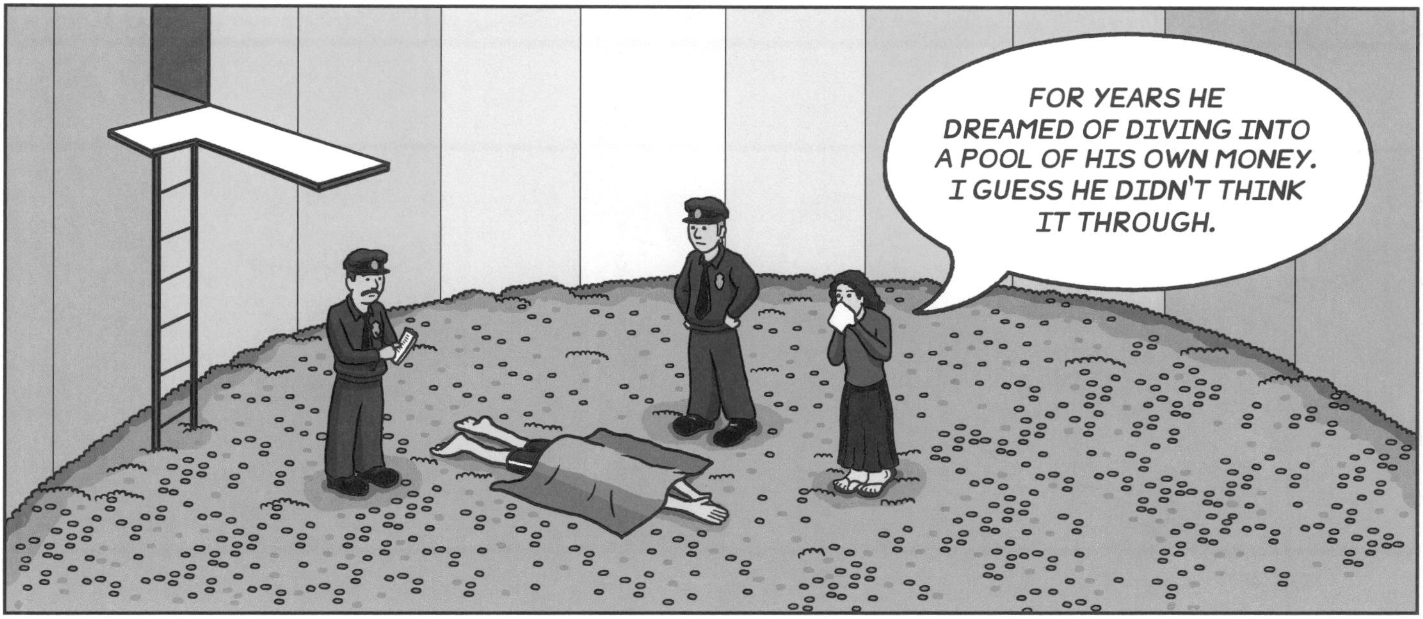
FOR YEARS HE DREAMED OF DIVING INTO A POOL OF HIS OWN MONEY. I GUESS HE DIDN'T THINK IT THROUGH.

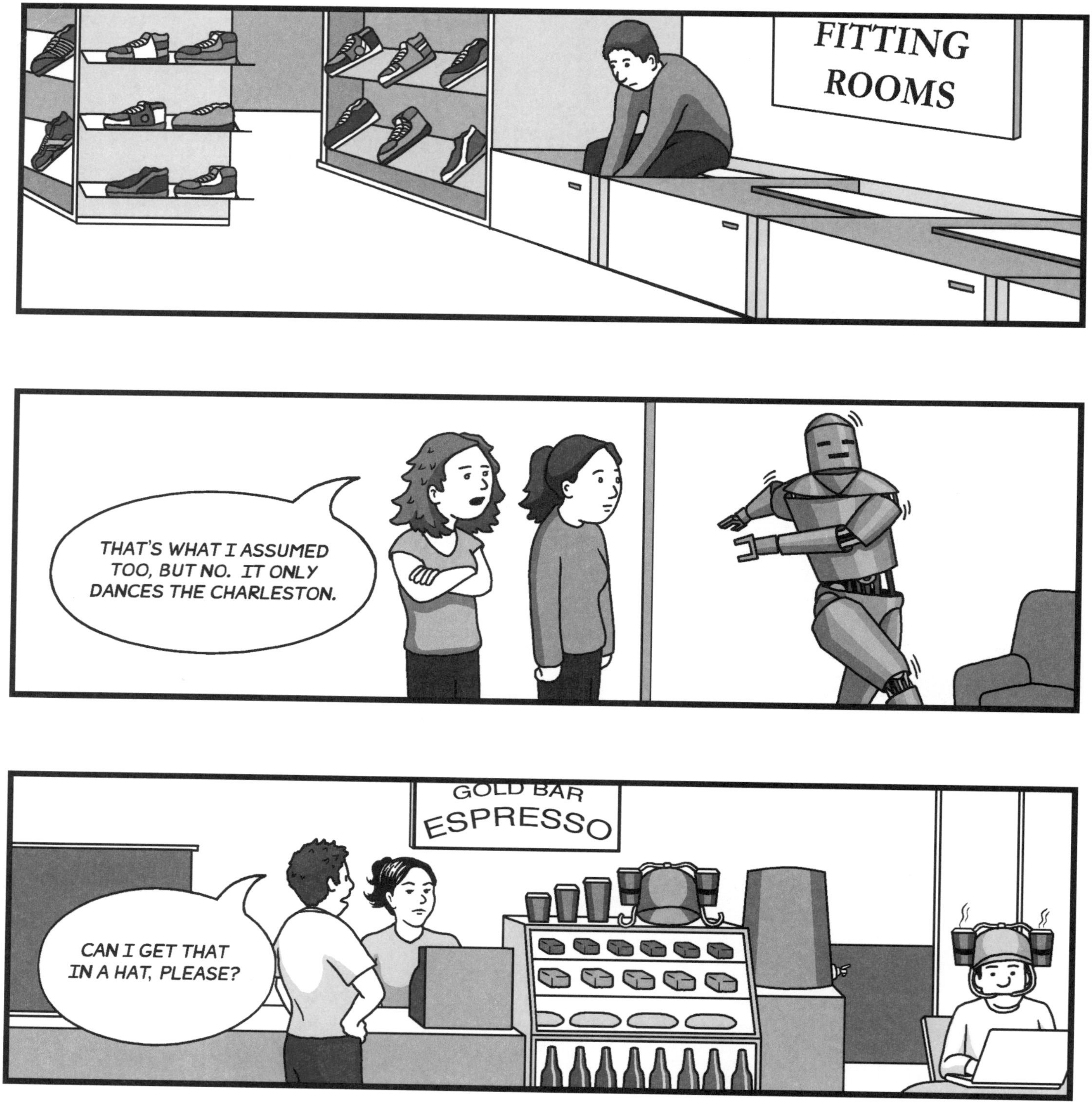
FITTING ROOMS
THAT'S WHAT I ASSUMED TOO, BUT NO. IT ONLY DANCES THE CHARLESTON.
GOLD BAR ESPRESSO
CAN I GET THAT IN A HAT, PLEASE?

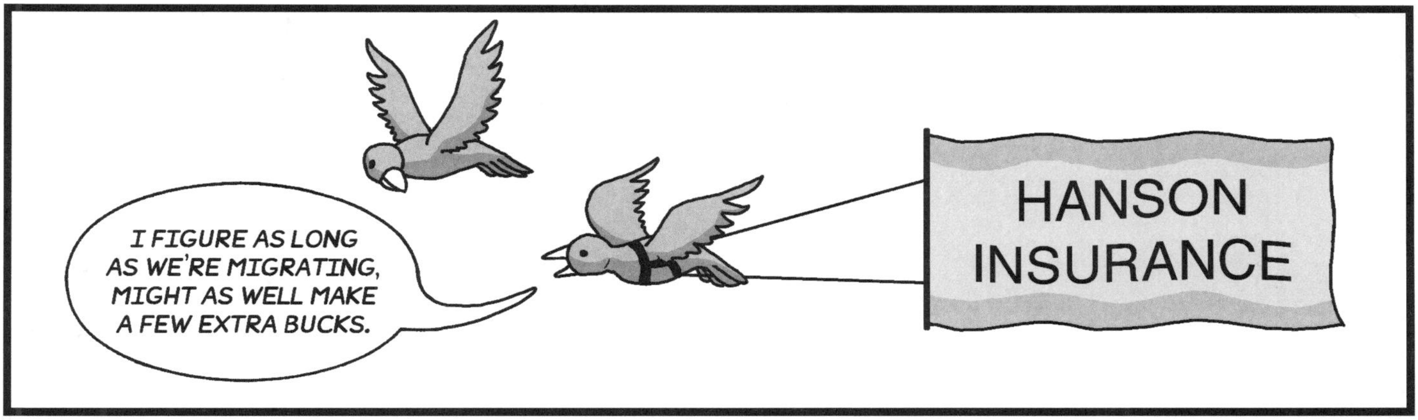
I FIGURE AS LONG AS WE'RE MIGRATING, MIGHT AS WELL MAKE A FEW EXTRA BUCKS.
HANSON INSURANCE

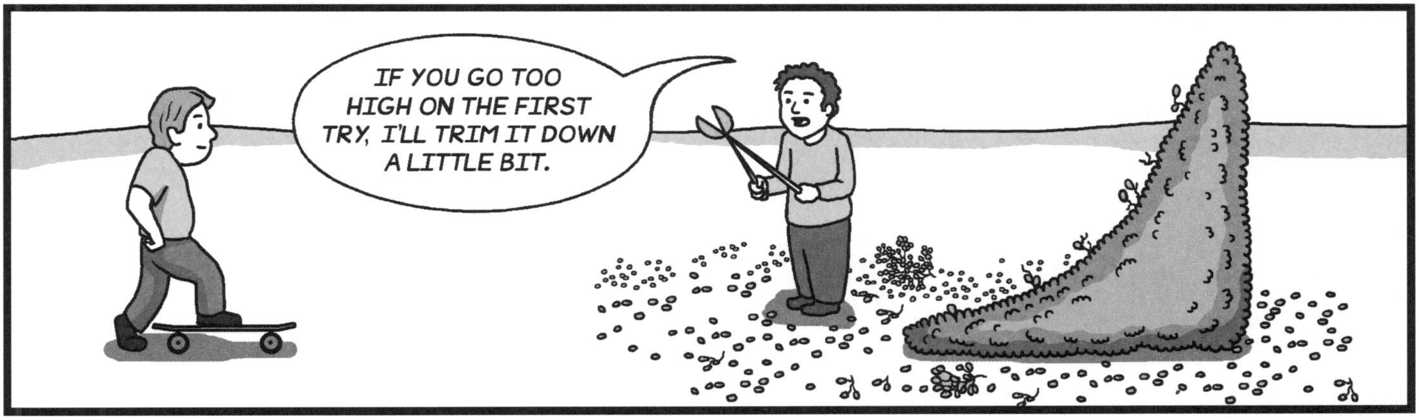
IF YOU GO TOO HIGH ON THE FIRST TRY, I'LL TRIM IT DOWN A LITTLE BIT.

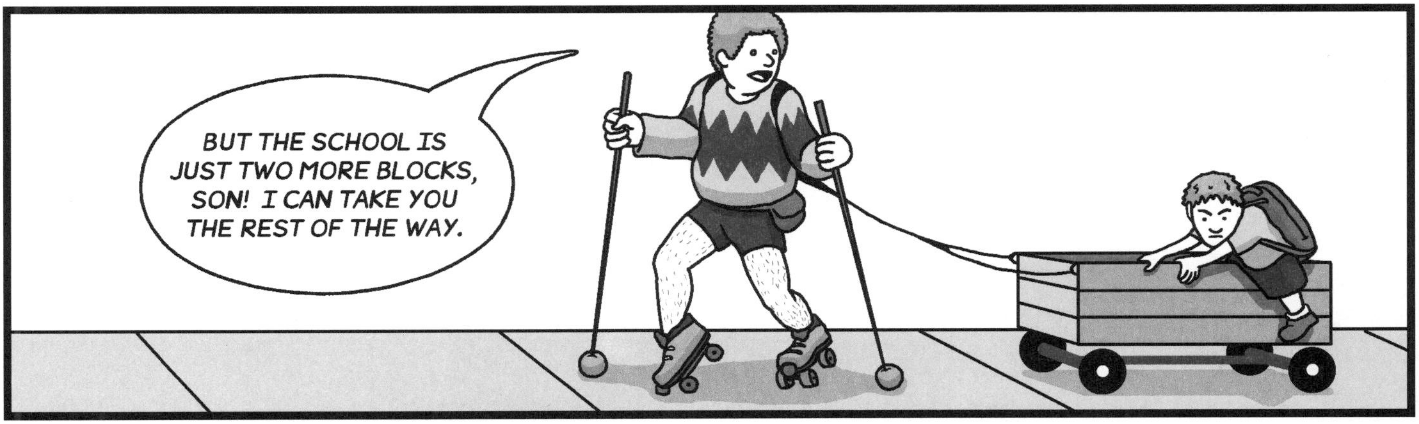
BUT THE SCHOOL IS JUST TWO MORE BLOCKS, SON! I CAN TAKE YOU THE REST OF THE WAY.

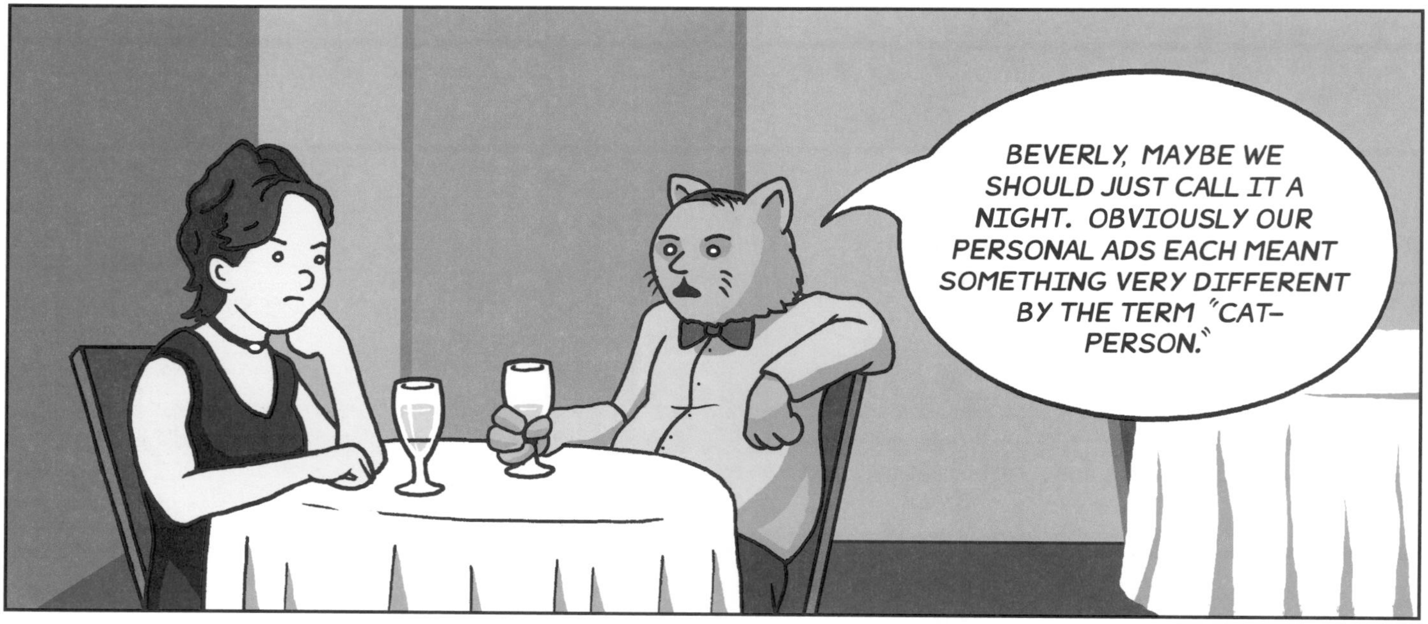
BEVERLY, MAYBE WE SHOULD JUST CALL IT A NIGHT. OBVIOUSLY OUR PERSONAL ADS EACH MEANT SOMETHING VERY DIFFERENT BY THE TERM "CAT-PERSON."

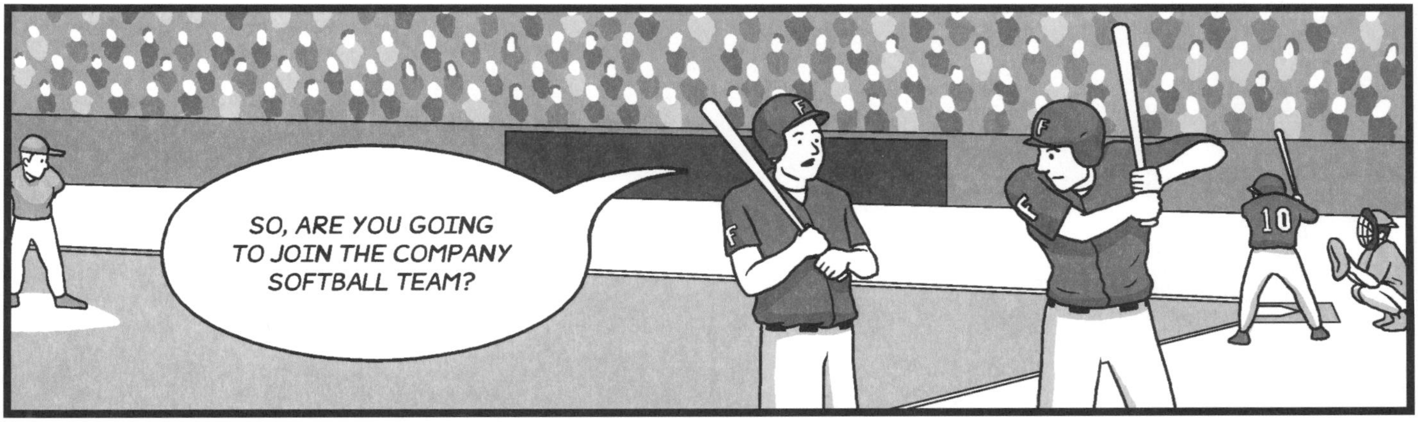
SO, ARE YOU GOING TO JOIN THE COMPANY SOFTBALL TEAM?

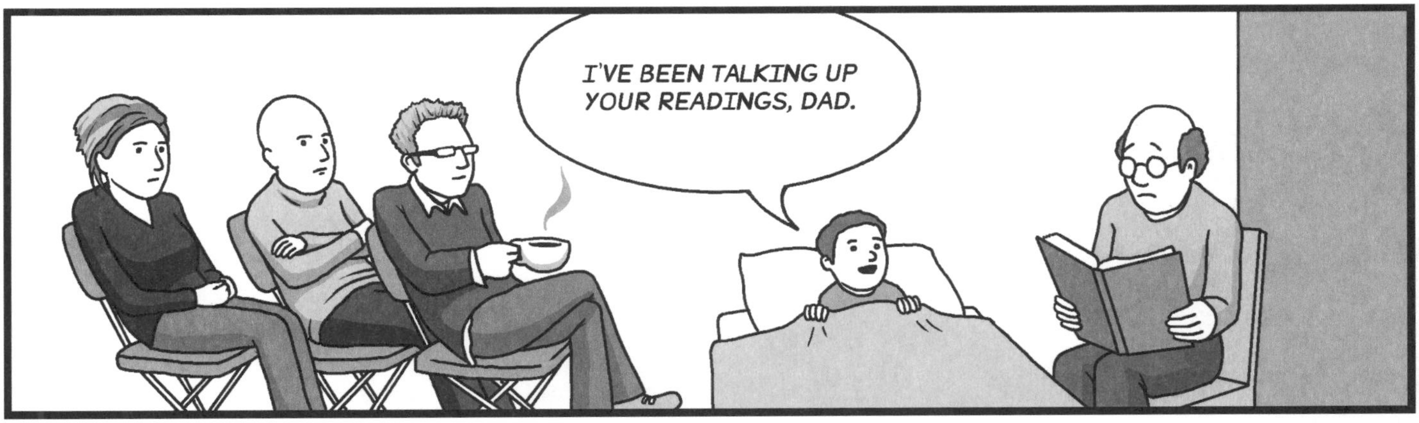
I'VE BEEN TALKING UP YOUR READINGS, DAD.

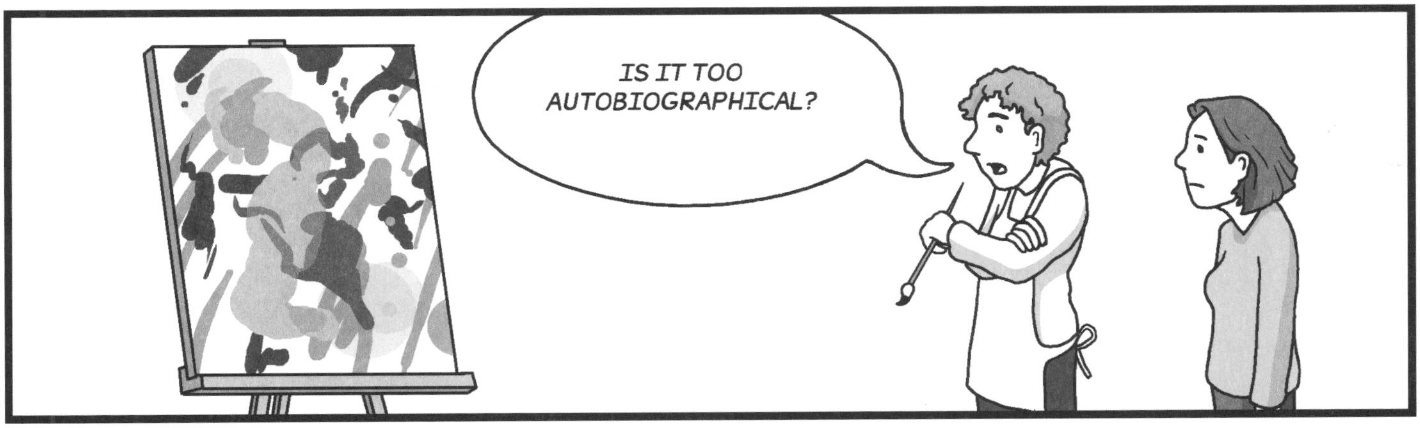
IS IT TOO AUTOBIOGRAPHICAL?

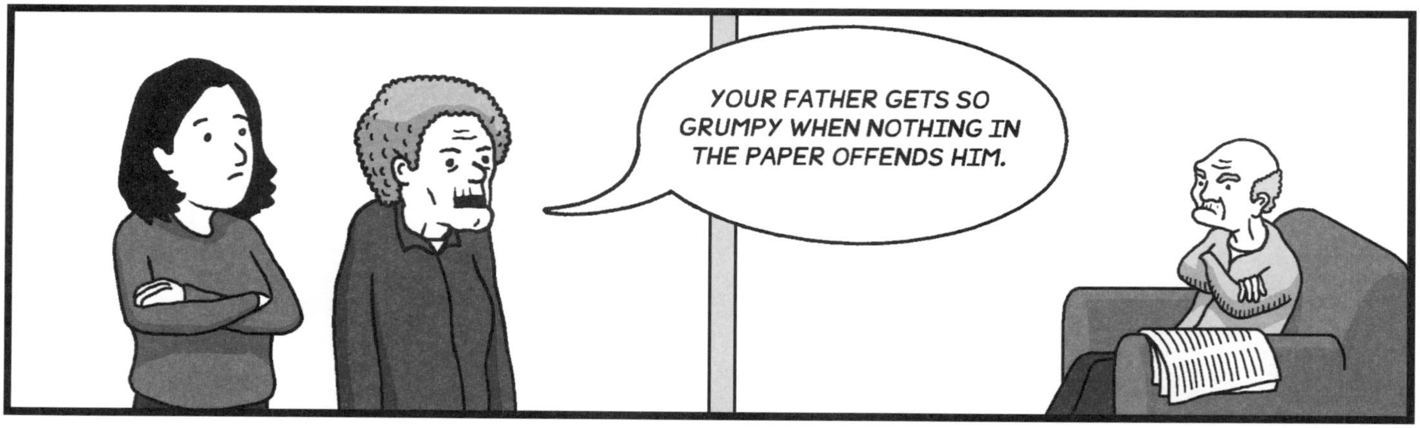
YOUR FATHER GETS SO GRUMPY WHEN NOTHING IN THE PAPER OFFENDS HIM.

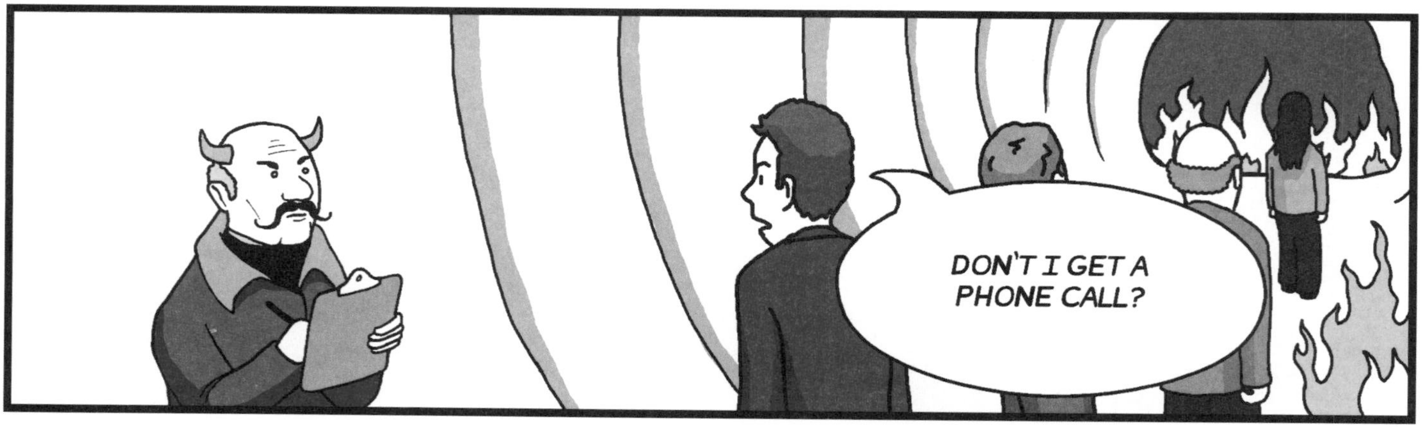
DON'T I GET A PHONE CALL?

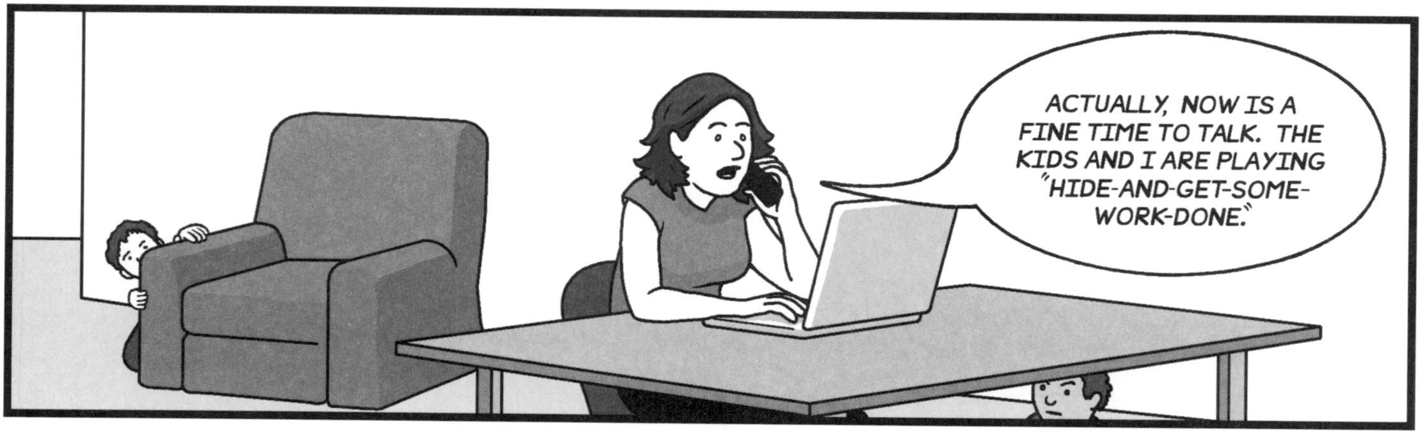
ACTUALLY, NOW IS A FINE TIME TO TALK. THE KIDS AND I ARE PLAYING "HIDE-AND-GET-SOME-WORK-DONE."

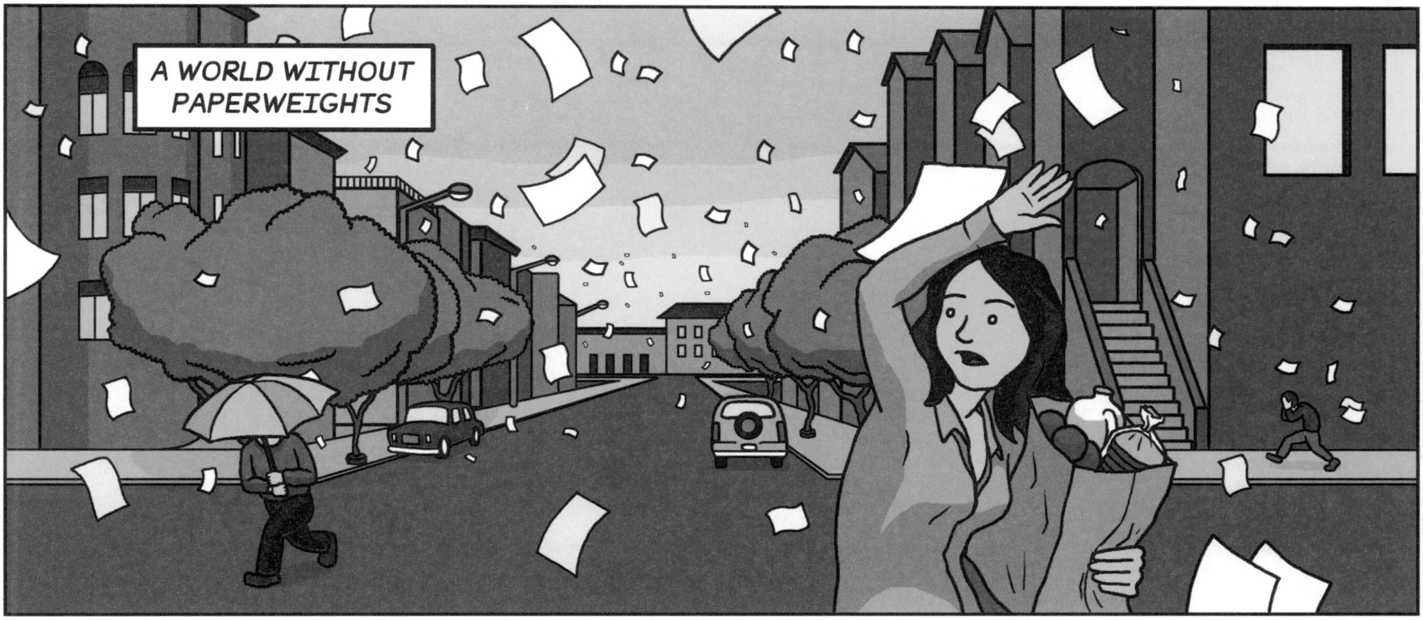
A WORLD WITHOUT PAPERWEIGHTS

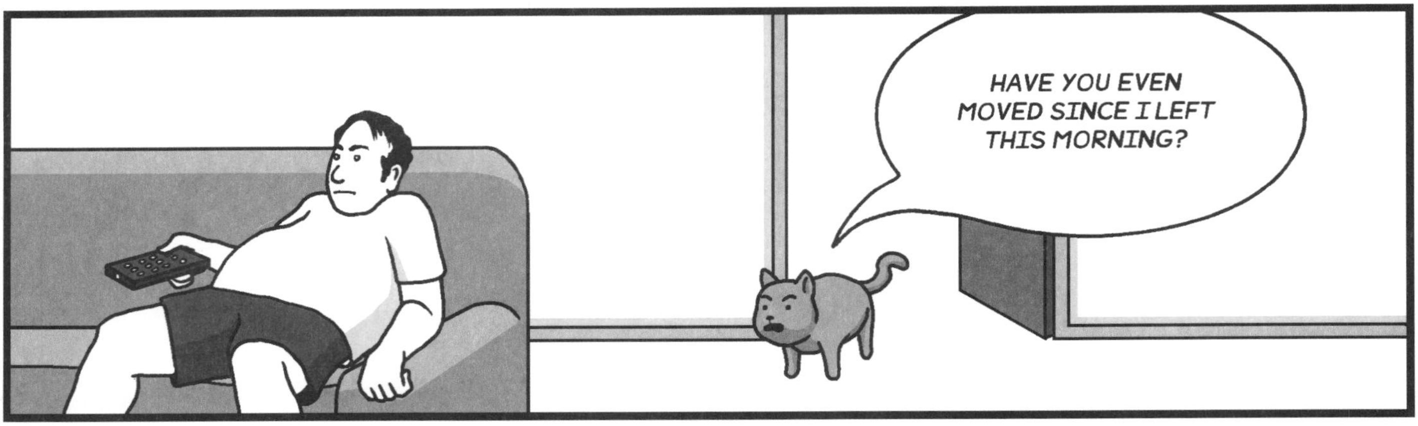
HAVE YOU EVEN MOVED SINCE I LEFT THIS MORNING?

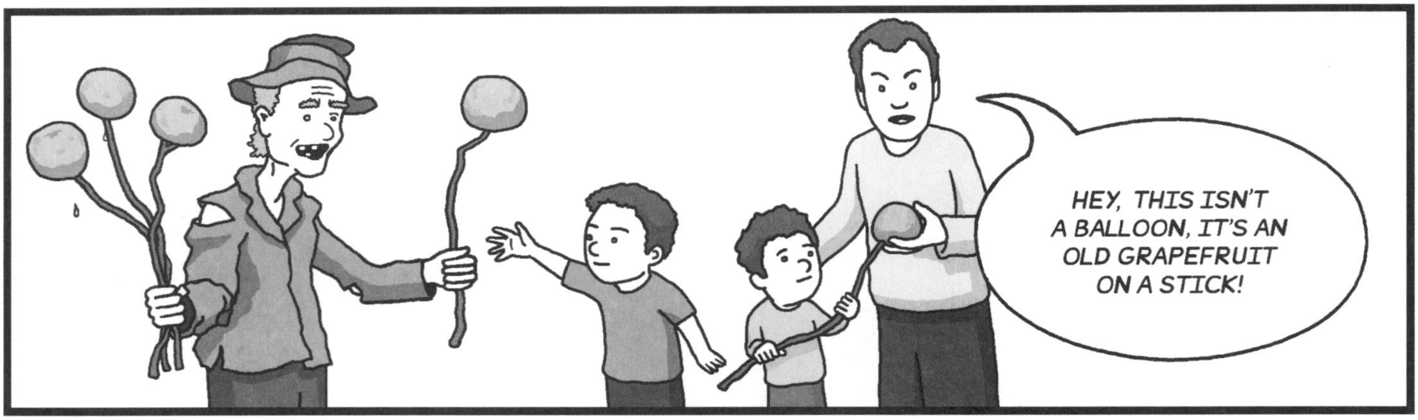
HEY, THIS ISN'T A BALLOON, IT'S AN OLD GRAPEFRUIT ON A STICK!

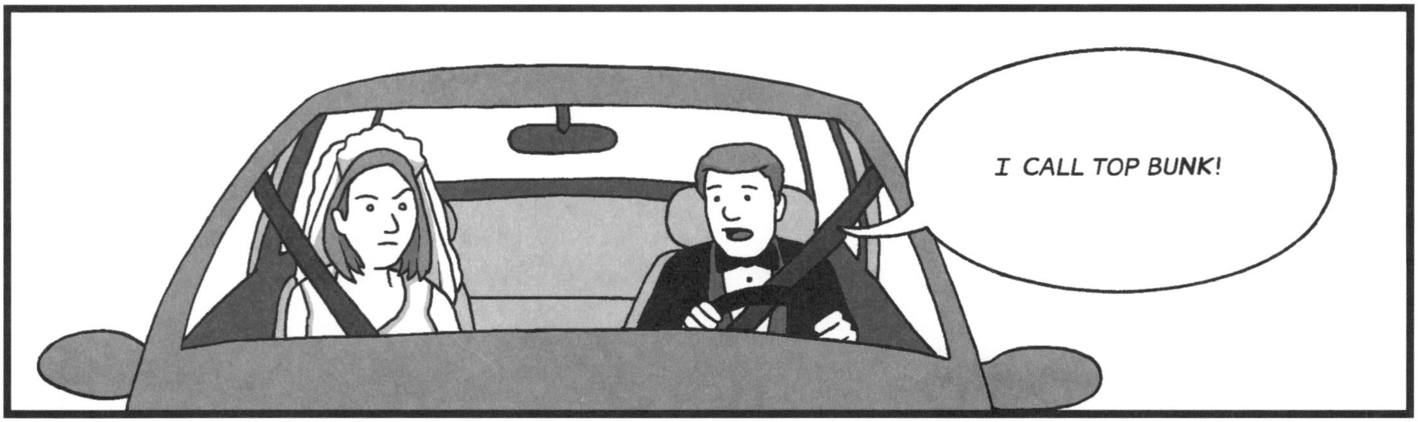
I CALL TOP BUNK!

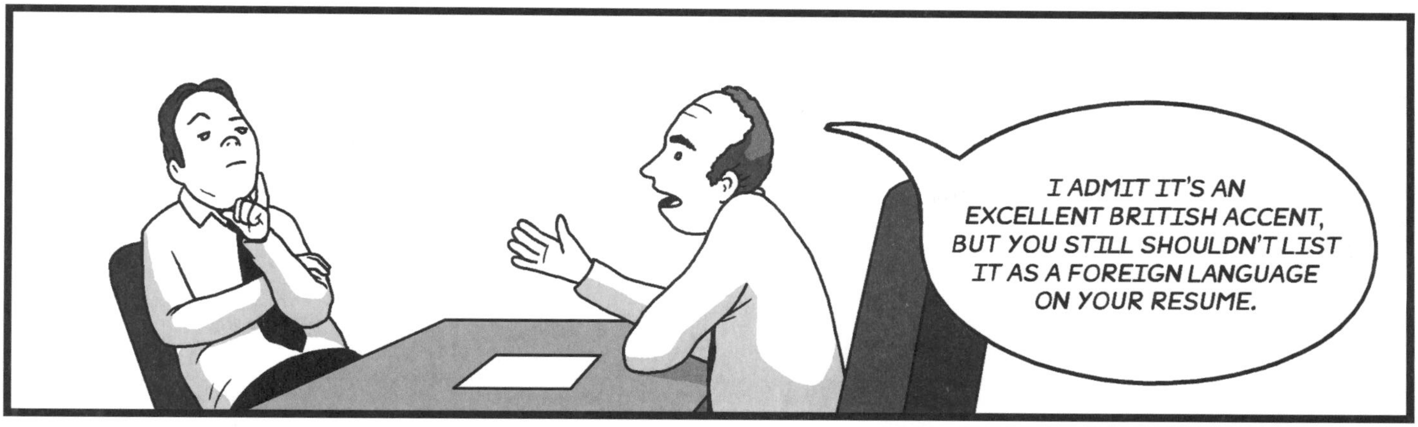
I ADMIT IT'S AN EXCELLENT BRITISH ACCENT, BUT YOU STILL SHOULDN'T LIST IT AS A FOREIGN LANGUAGE ON YOUR RESUME.

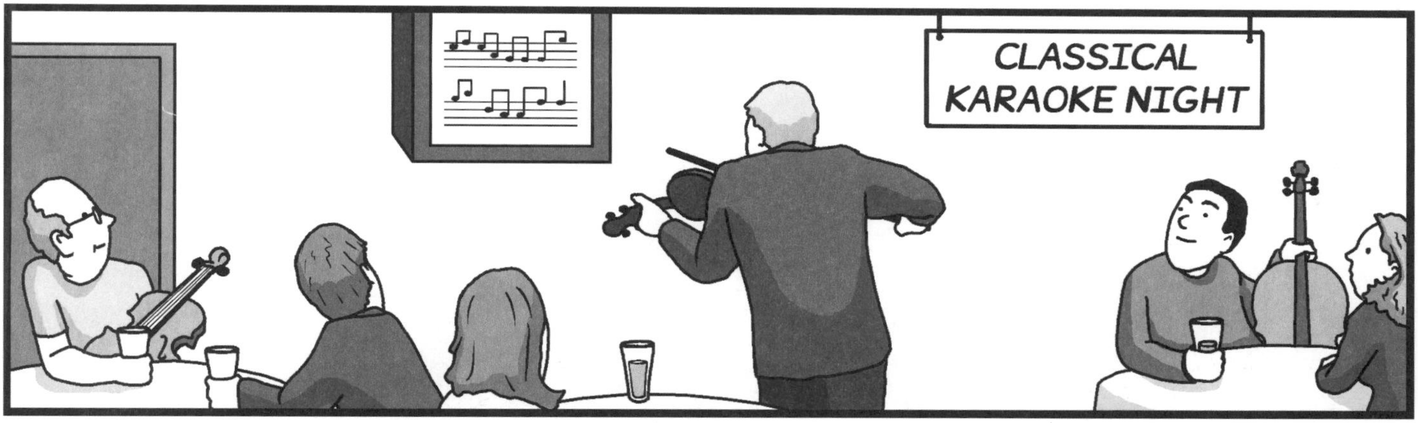
CLASSICAL KARAOKE NIGHT

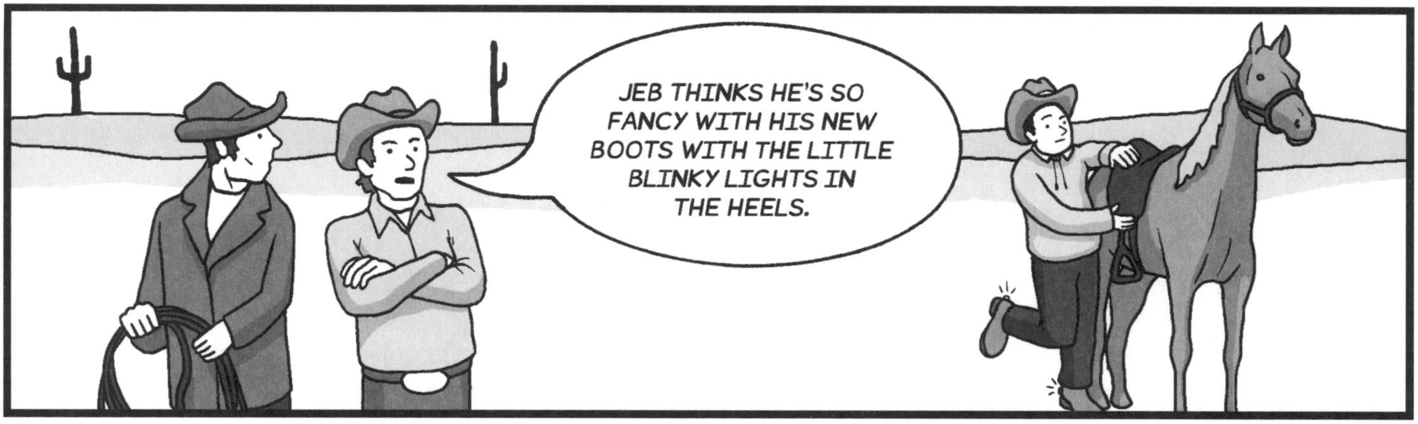
JEB THINKS HE'S SO FANCY WITH HIS NEW BOOTS WITH THE LITTLE BLINKY LIGHTS IN THE HEELS.

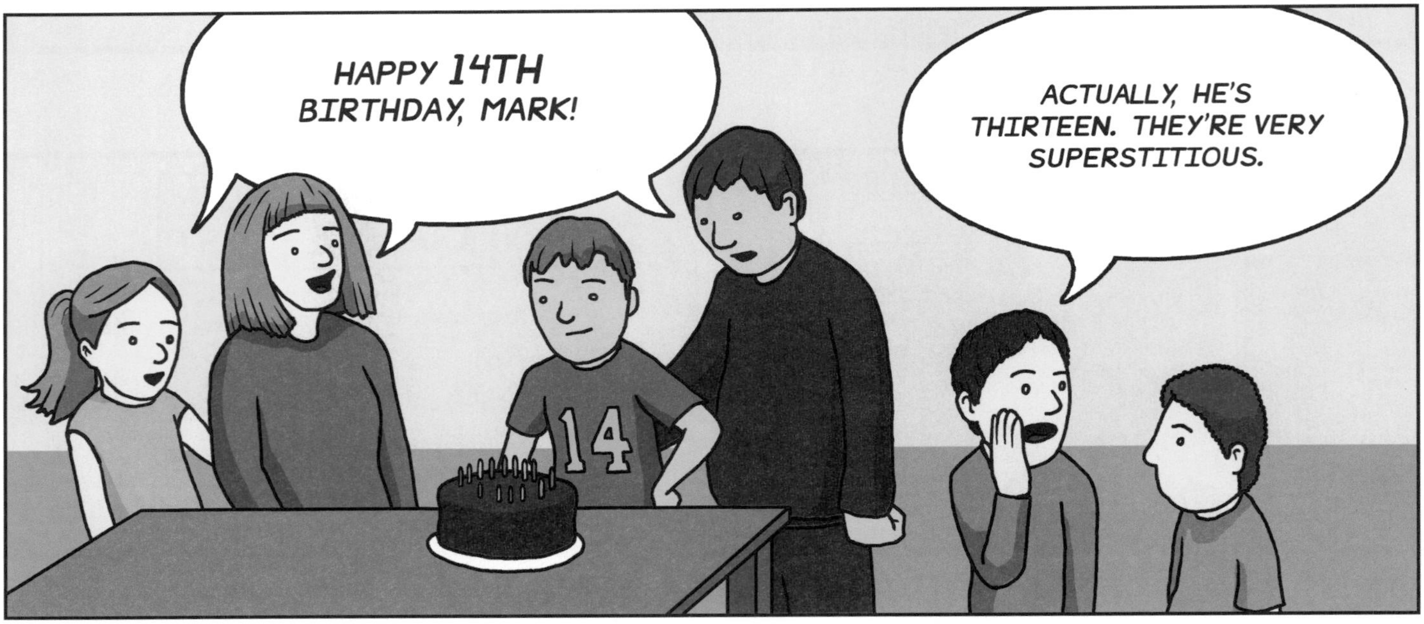
HAPPY 14TH BIRTHDAY, MARK!
14
ACTUALLY, HE'S THIRTEEN. THEY'RE VERY SUPERSTITIOUS.

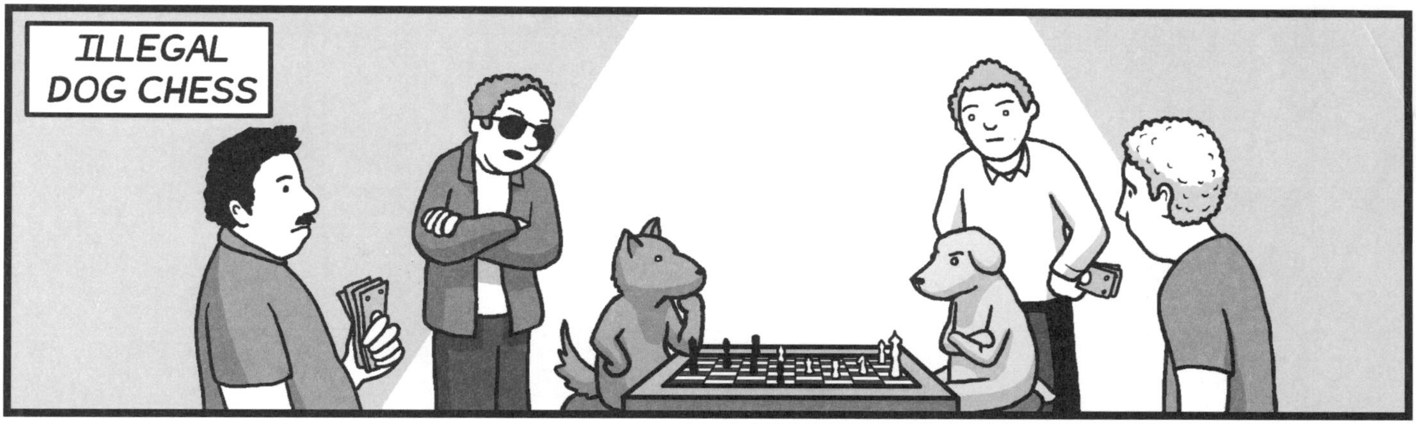
ILLEGAL DOG CHESS

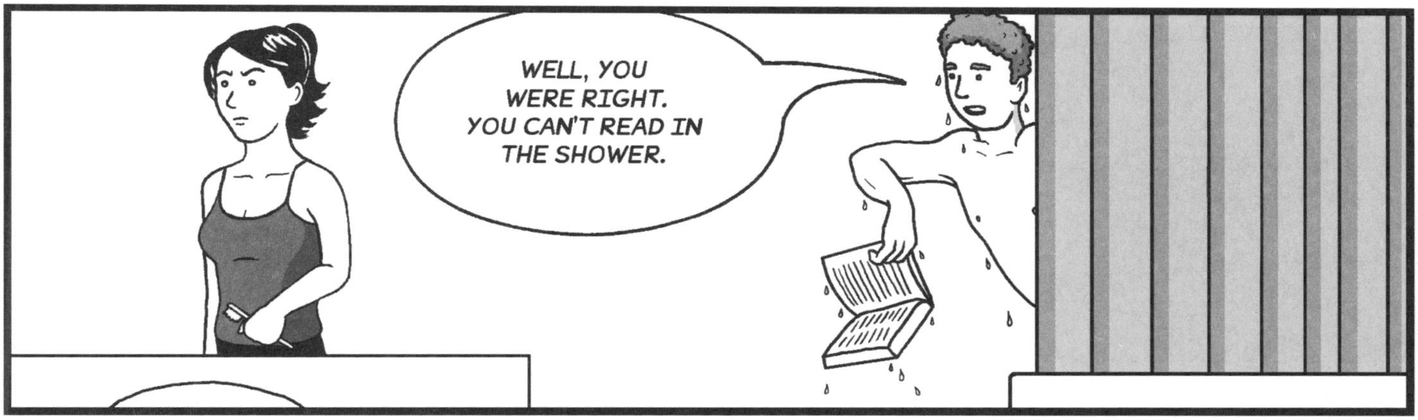
WELL, YOU WERE RIGHT. YOU CAN'T READ IN THE SHOWER.

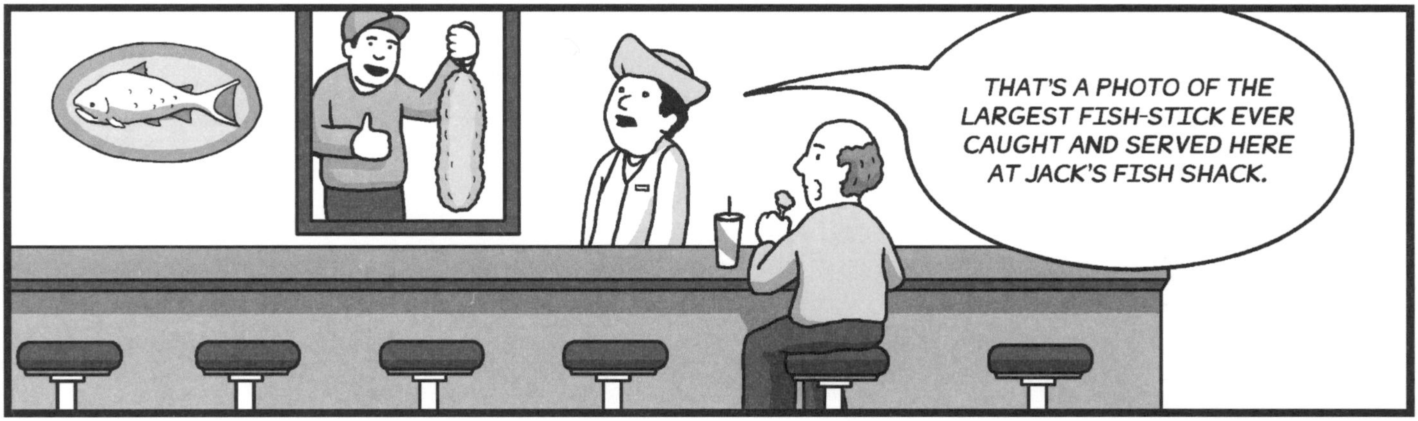
THAT'S A PHOTO OF THE LARGEST FISH-STICK EVER CAUGHT AND SERVED HERE AT JACK'S FISH SHACK.

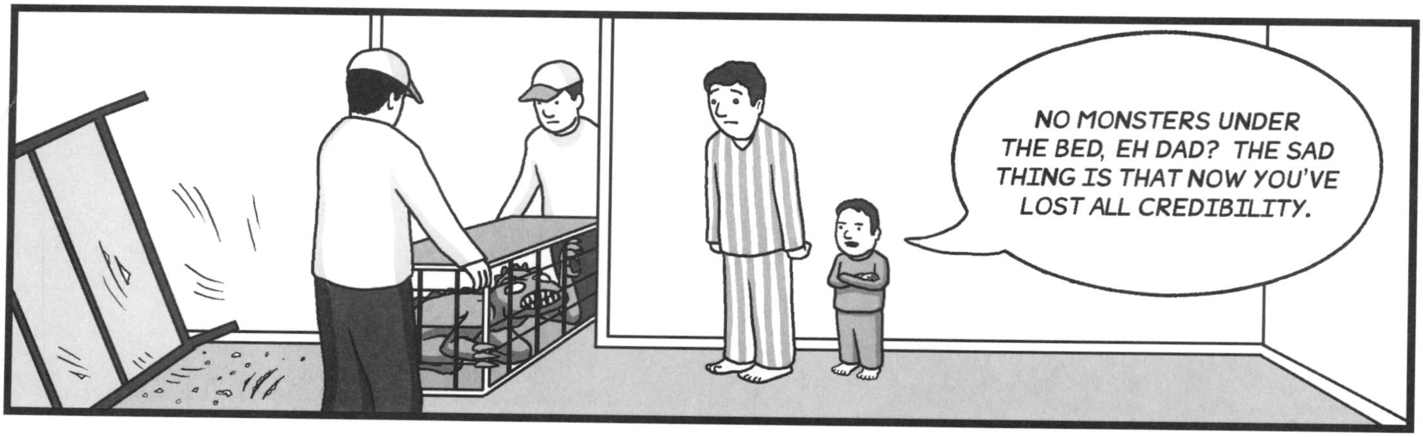
NO MONSTERS UNDER THE BED, EH DAD? THE SAD THING IS THAT NOW YOU'VE LOST ALL CREDIBILITY.

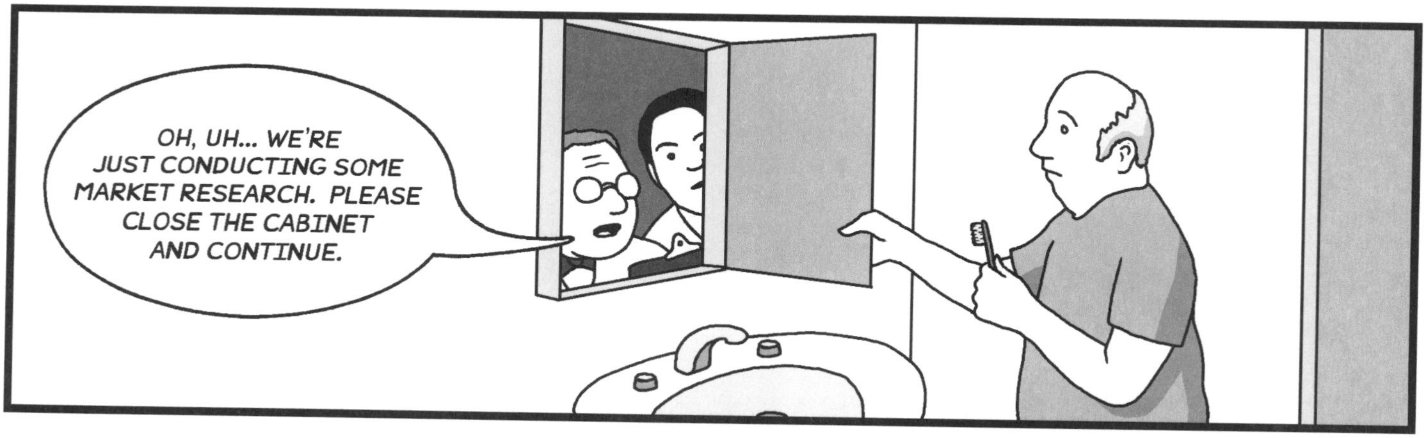
OH, UH... WE'RE JUST CONDUCTING SOME MARKET RESEARCH. PLEASE CLOSE THE CABINET AND CONTINUE.

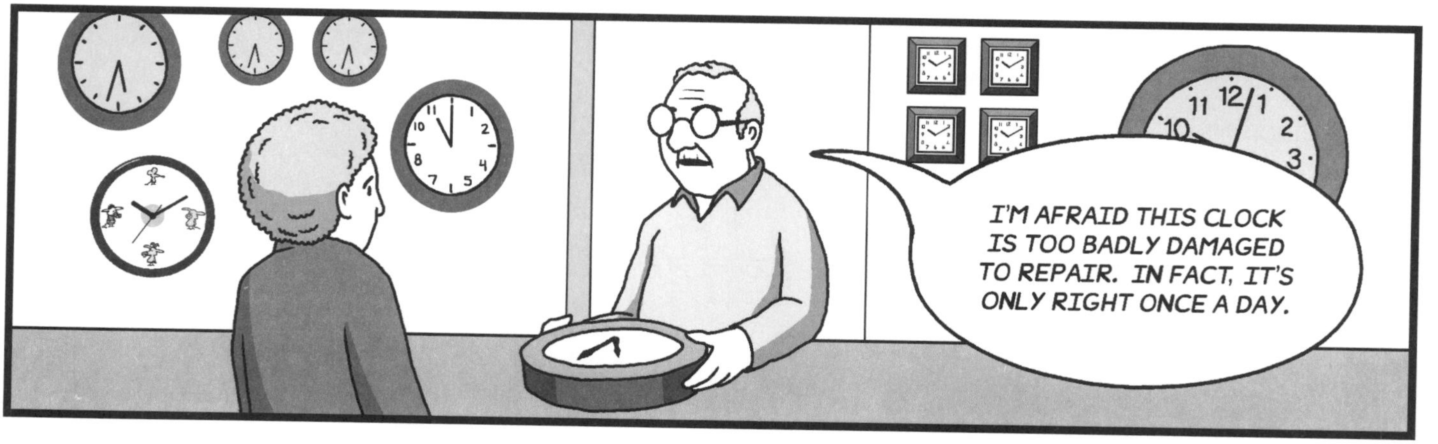
I'M AFRAID THIS CLOCK IS TOO BADLY DAMAGED TO REPAIR. IN FACT, IT'S ONLY RIGHT ONCE A DAY.

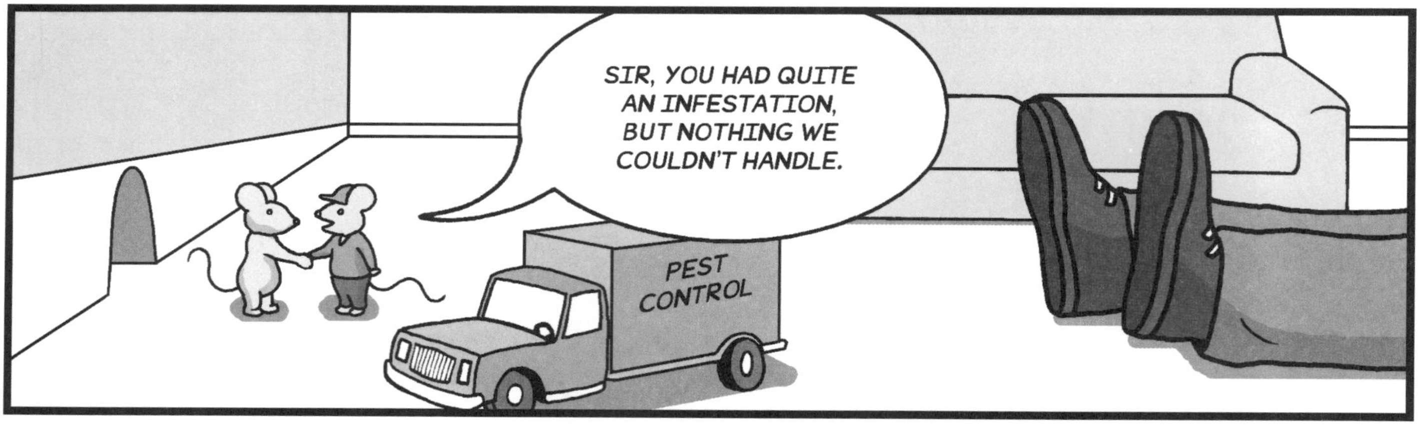
SIR, YOU HAD QUITE AN INFESTATION, BUT NOTHING WE COULDN'T HANDLE.
PEST CONTROL

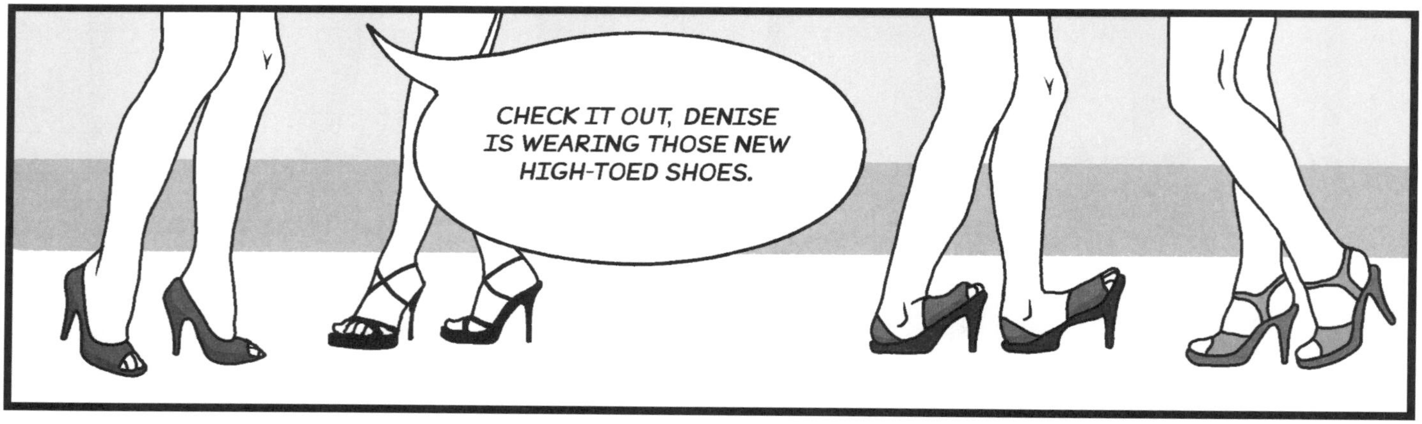
CHECK IT OUT, DENISE IS WEARING THOSE NEW HIGH-TOED SHOES.

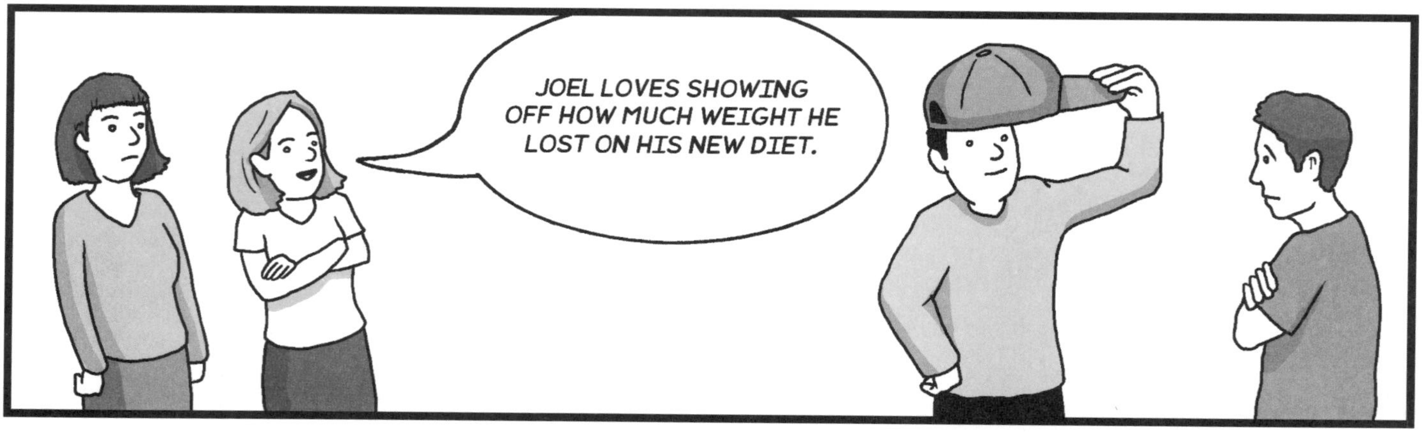
JOEL LOVES SHOWING OFF HOW MUCH WEIGHT HE LOST ON HIS NEW DIET.

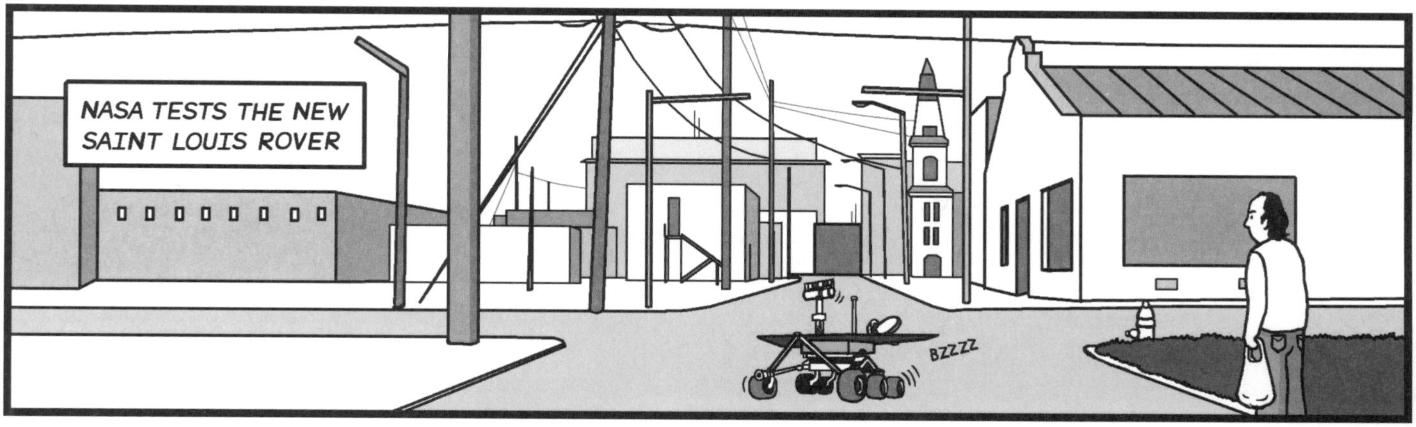
NASA TESTS THE NEW SAINT LOUIS ROVER
BZZZZ

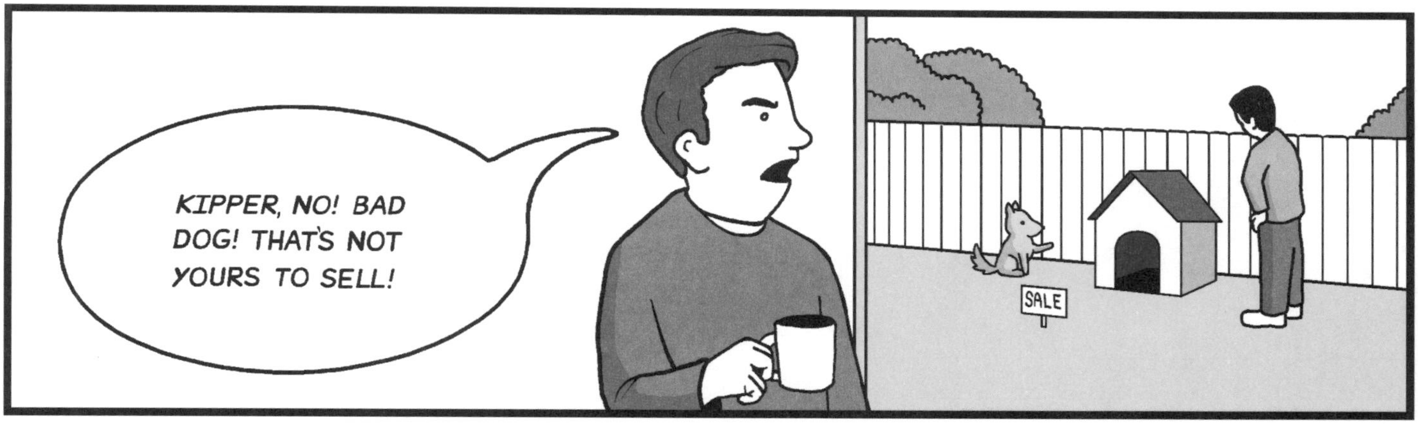
KIPPER, NO! BAD DOG! THAT'S NOT YOURS TO SELL!
SALE

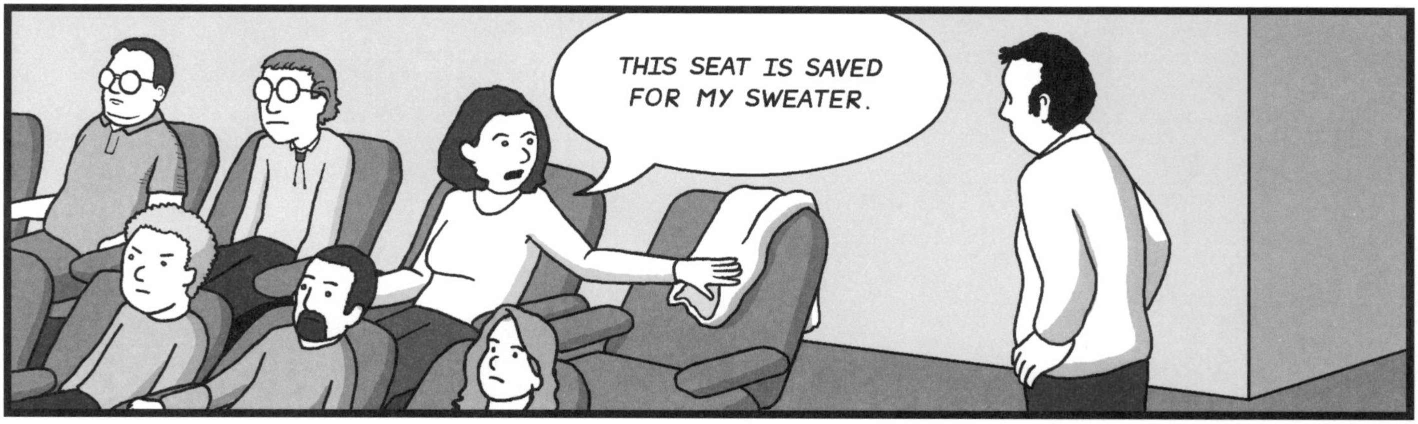
THIS SEAT IS SAVED FOR MY SWEATER.

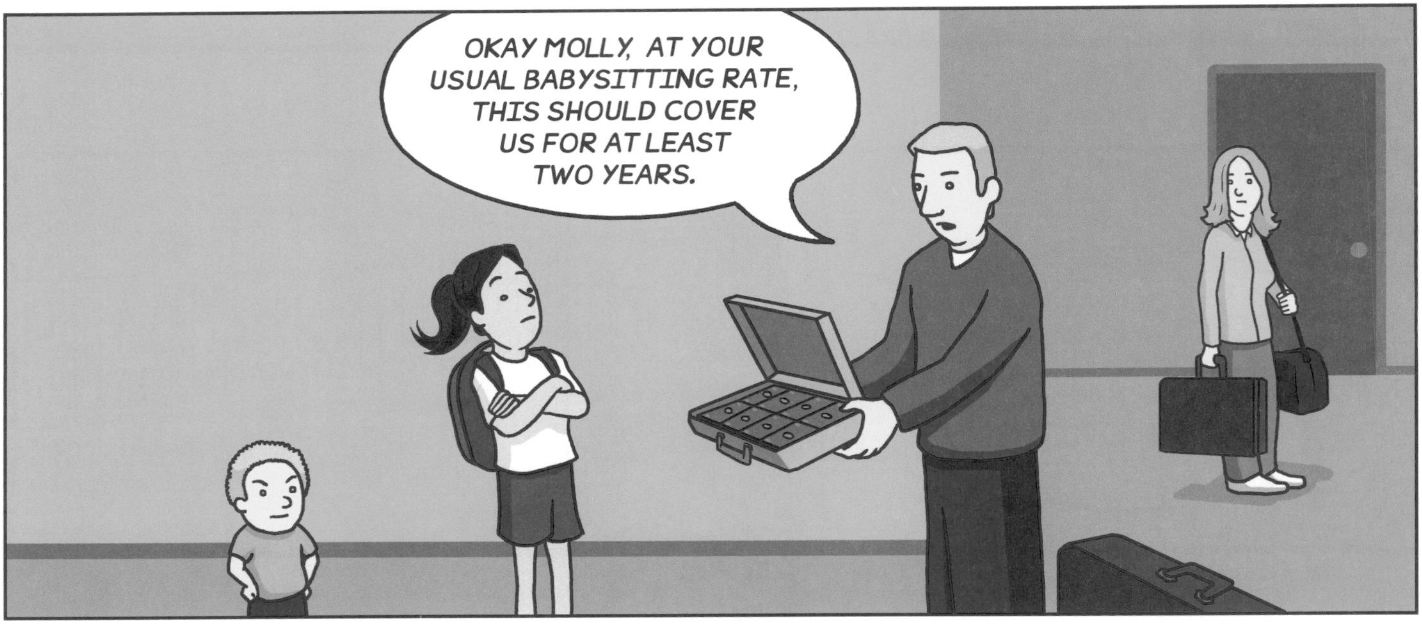
OKAY MOLLY, AT YOUR USUAL BABYSITTING RATE, THIS SHOULD COVER US FOR AT LEAST TWO YEARS.

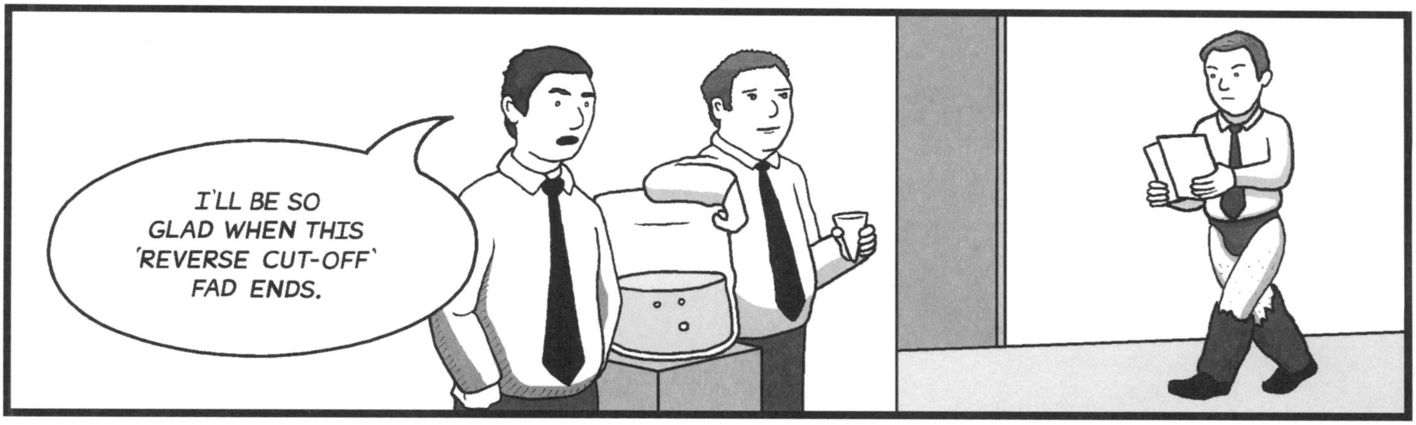
I'LL BE SO GLAD WHEN THIS 'REVERSE CUT-OFF' FAD ENDS.

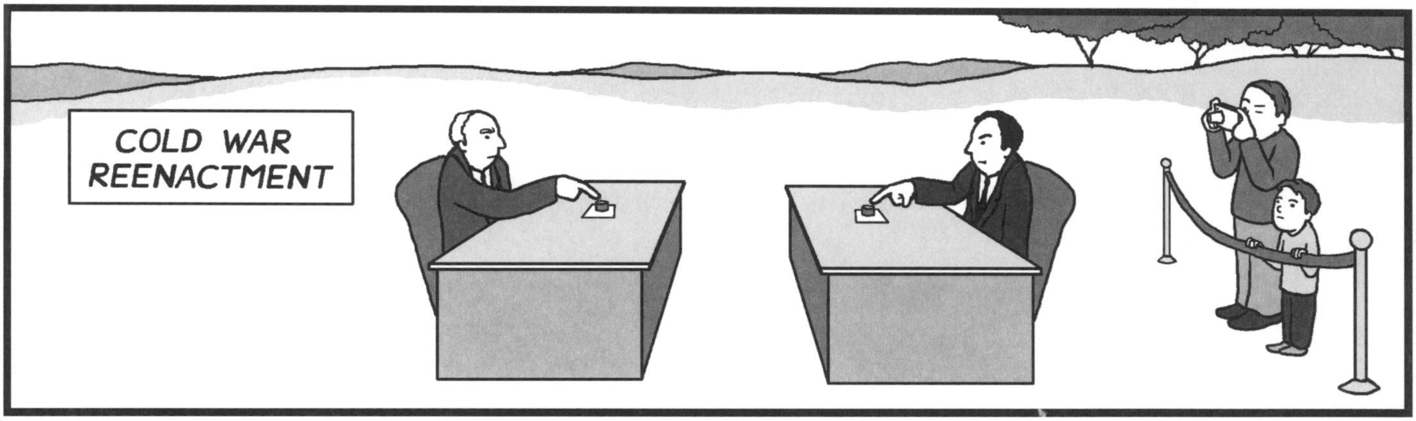
COLD WAR REENACTMENT

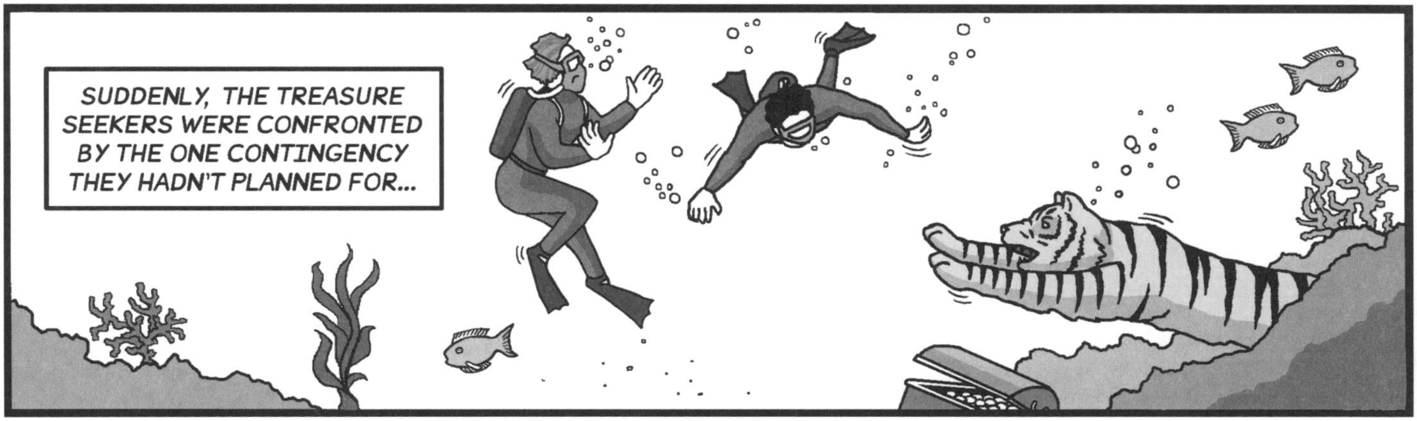
SUDDENLY, THE TREASURE SEEKERS WERE CONFRONTED BY THE ONE CONTINGENCY THEY HADN'T PLANNED FOR...

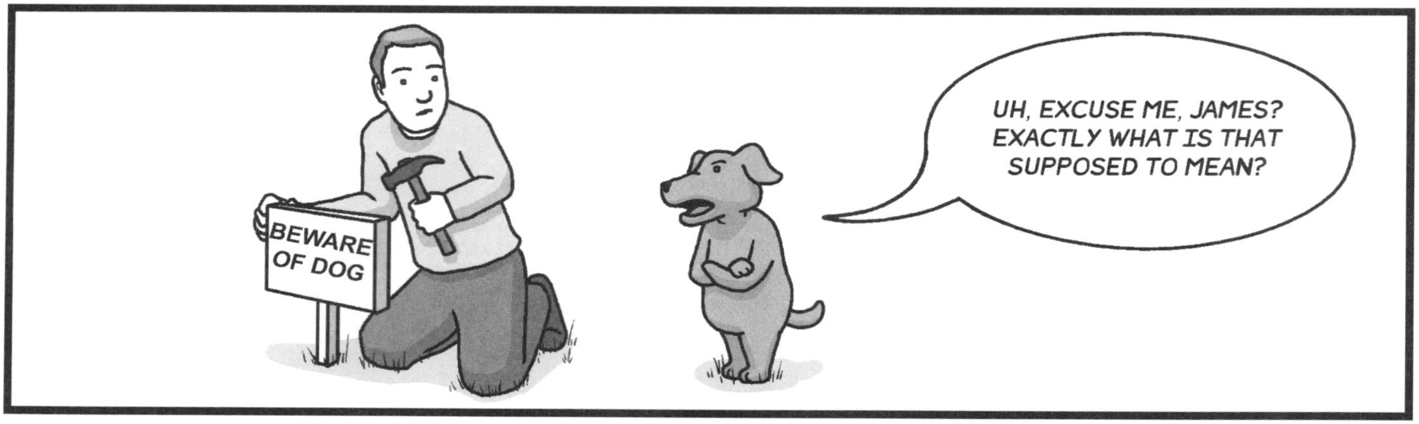
BEWARE OF DOG
UH, EXCUSE ME, JAMES? EXACTLY WHAT IS THAT SUPPOSED TO MEAN?

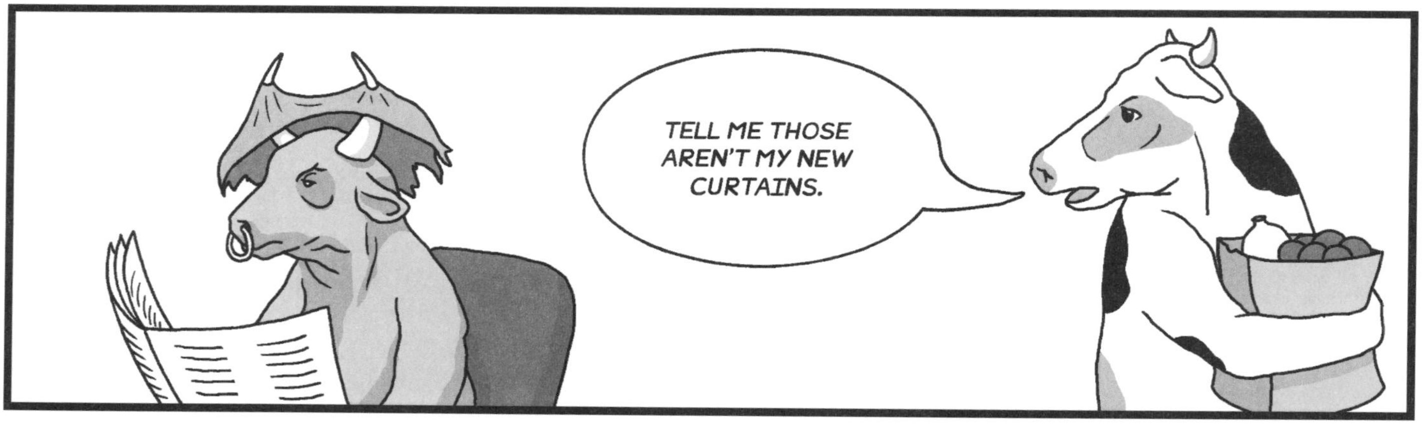
TELL ME THOSE AREN'T MY NEW CURTAINS.

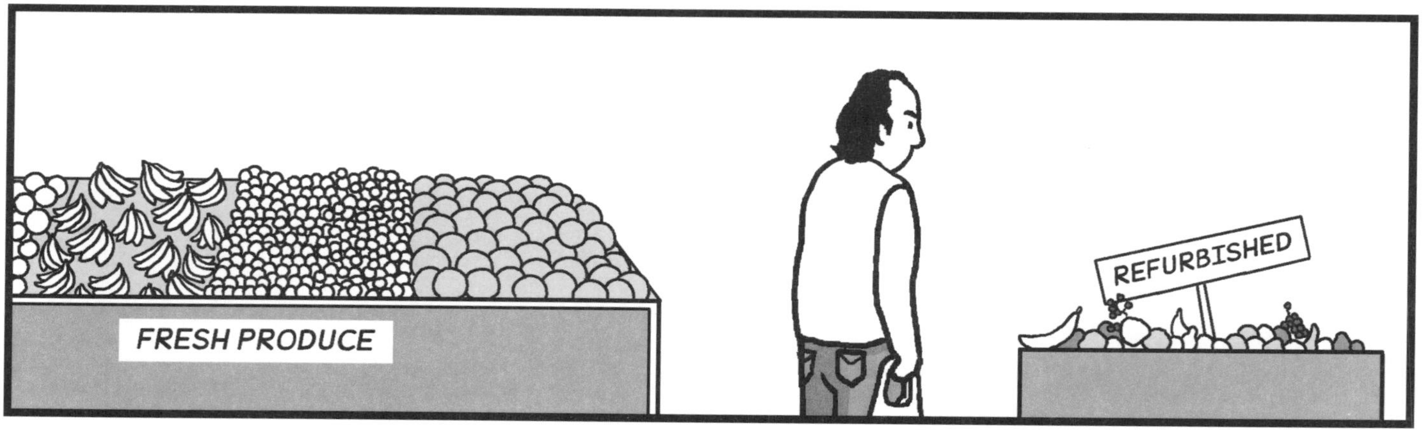
FRESH PRODUCE
REFURBISHED

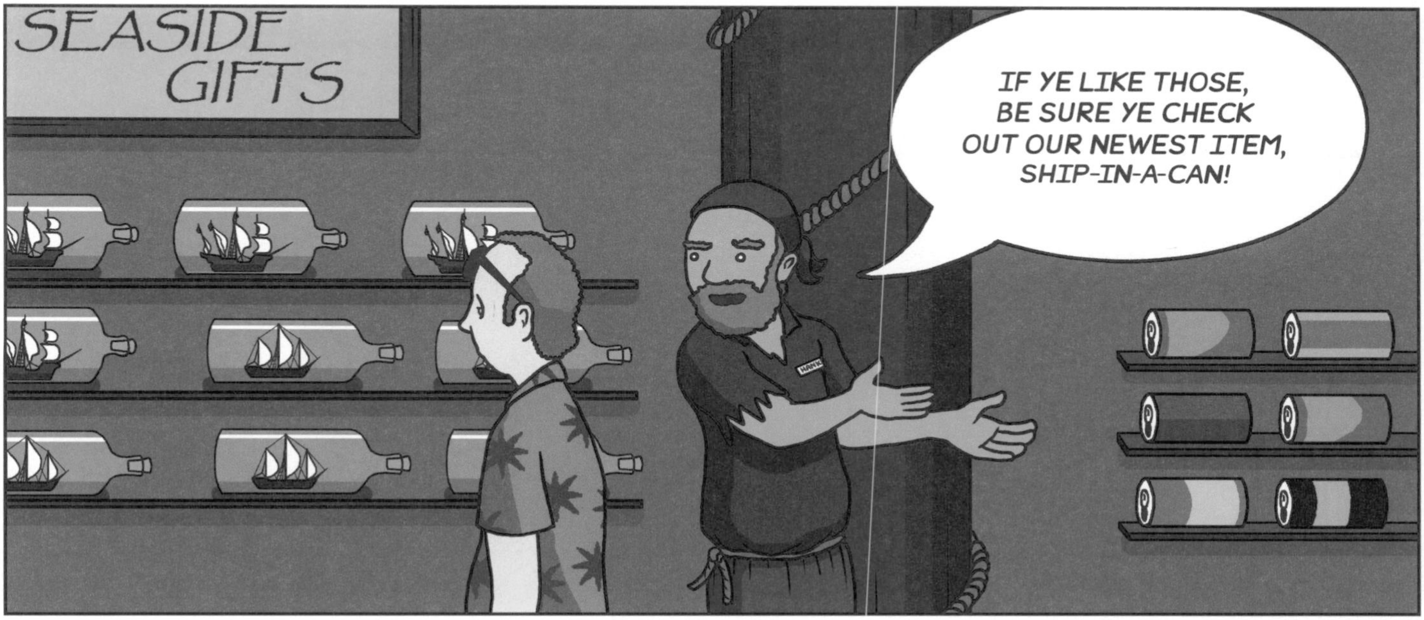
SEASIDE GIFTS
IF YE LIKE THOSE, BE SURE YE CHECK OUT OUR NEWEST ITEM, SHIP-IN-A-CAN!

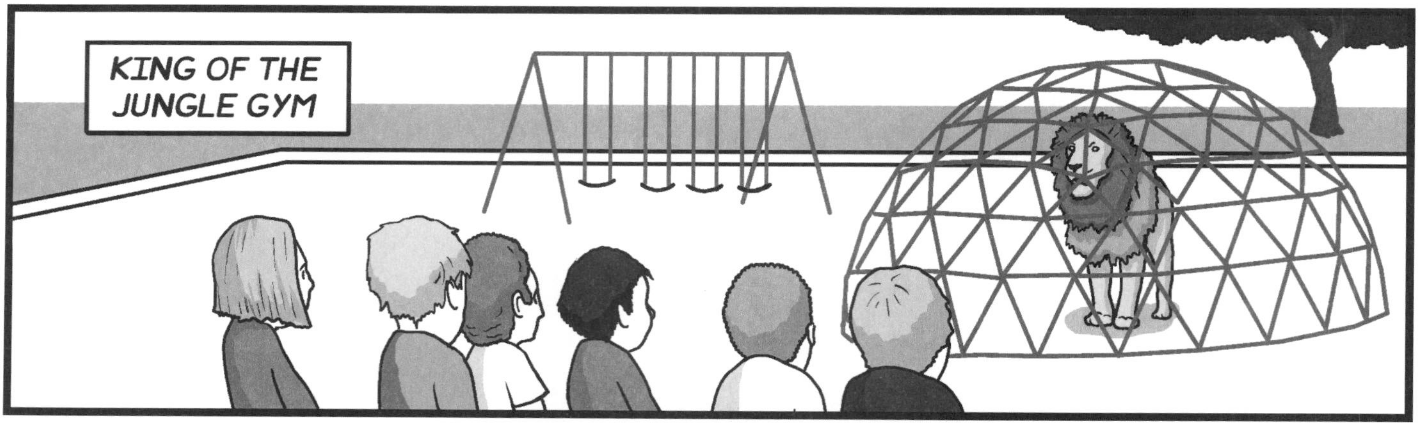
KING OF THE
JUNGLE GYM

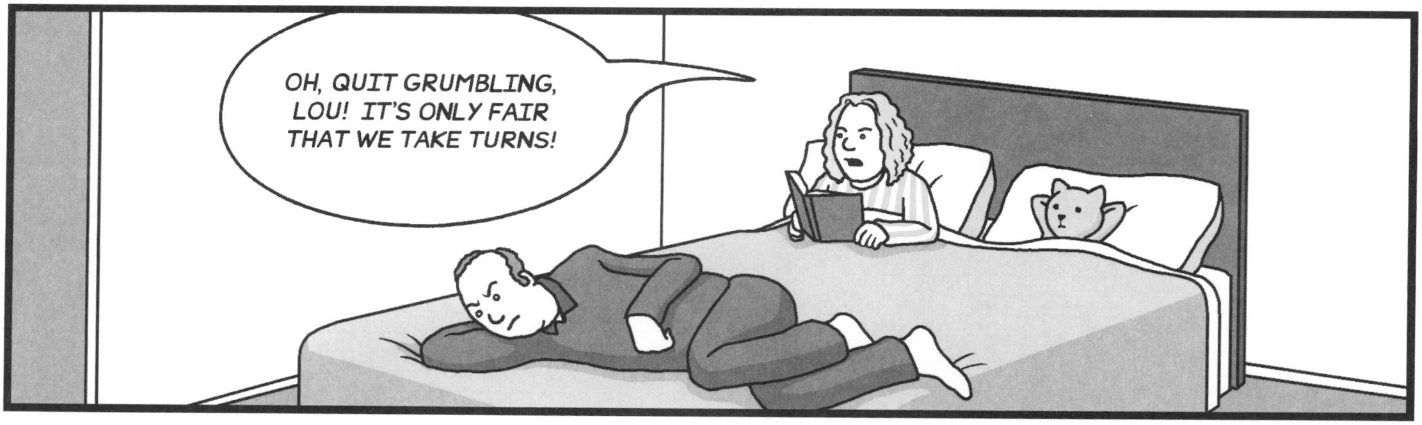
OH, QUIT GRUMBLING, LOU! IT'S ONLY FAIR THAT WE TAKE TURNS!

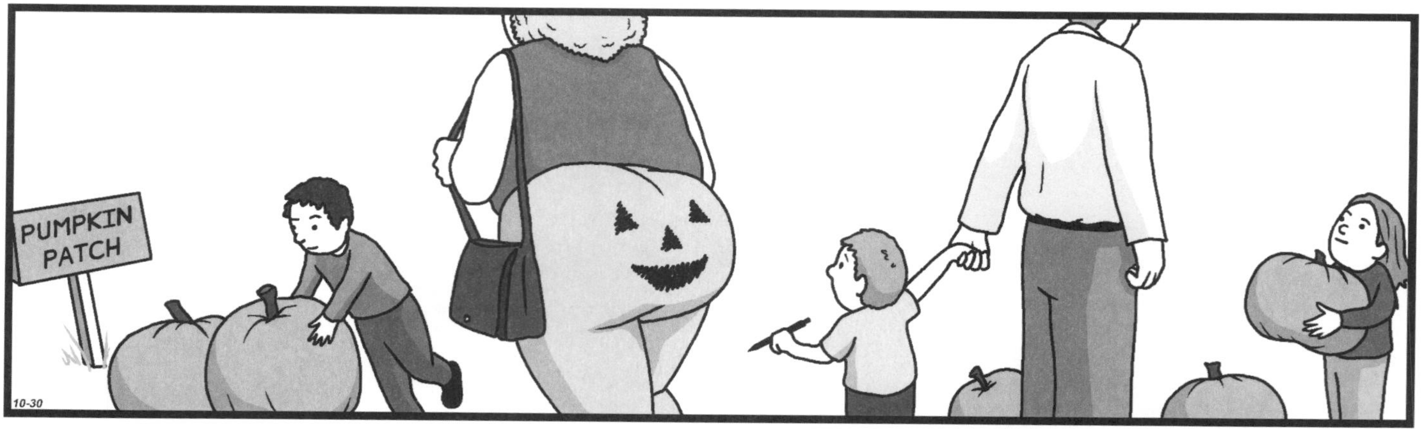
PUMPKIN
PATCH
10-30

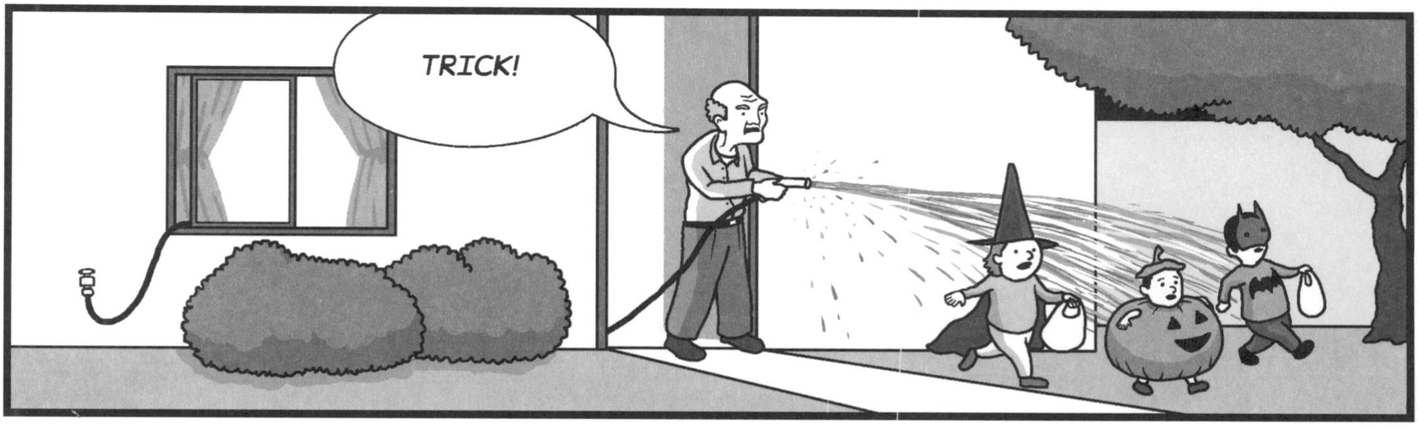
TRICK!

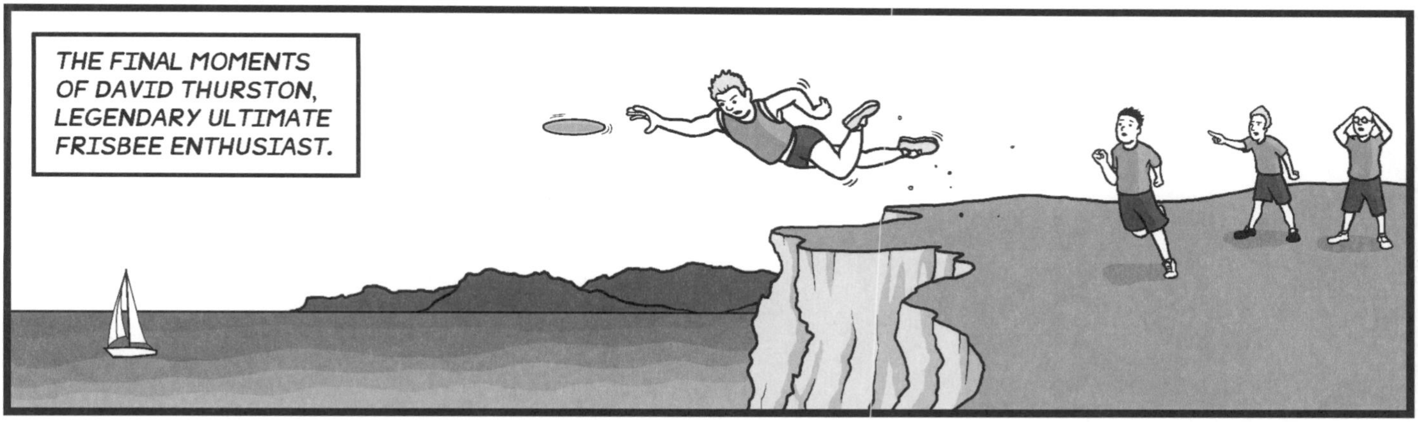
THE FINAL MOMENTS
OF DAVID THURSTON,
LEGENDARY ULTIMATE
FRISBEE ENTHUSIAST.

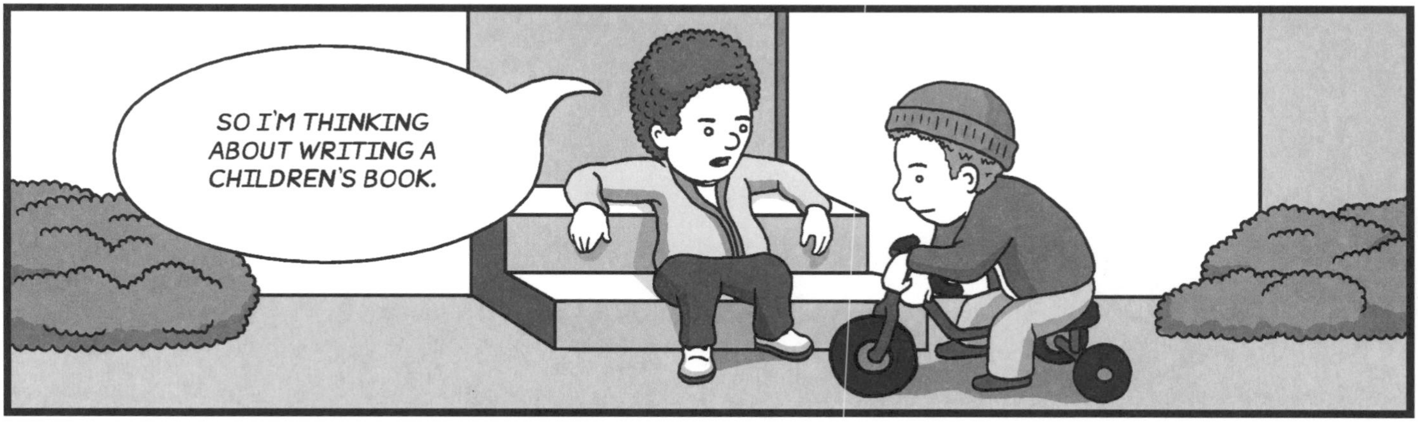
SO I'M THINKING
ABOUT WRITING A
CHILDREN'S BOOK.

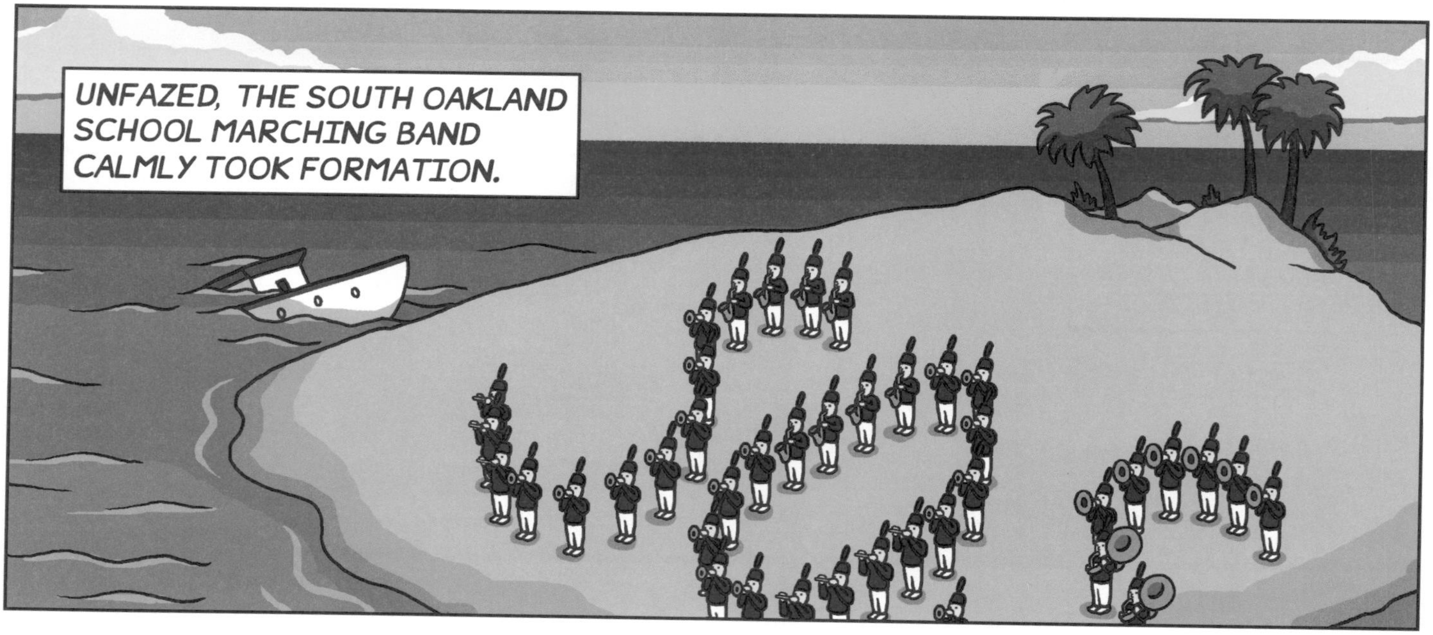
UNFAZED, THE SOUTH OAKLAND SCHOOL MARCHING BAND CALMLY TOOK FORMATION.

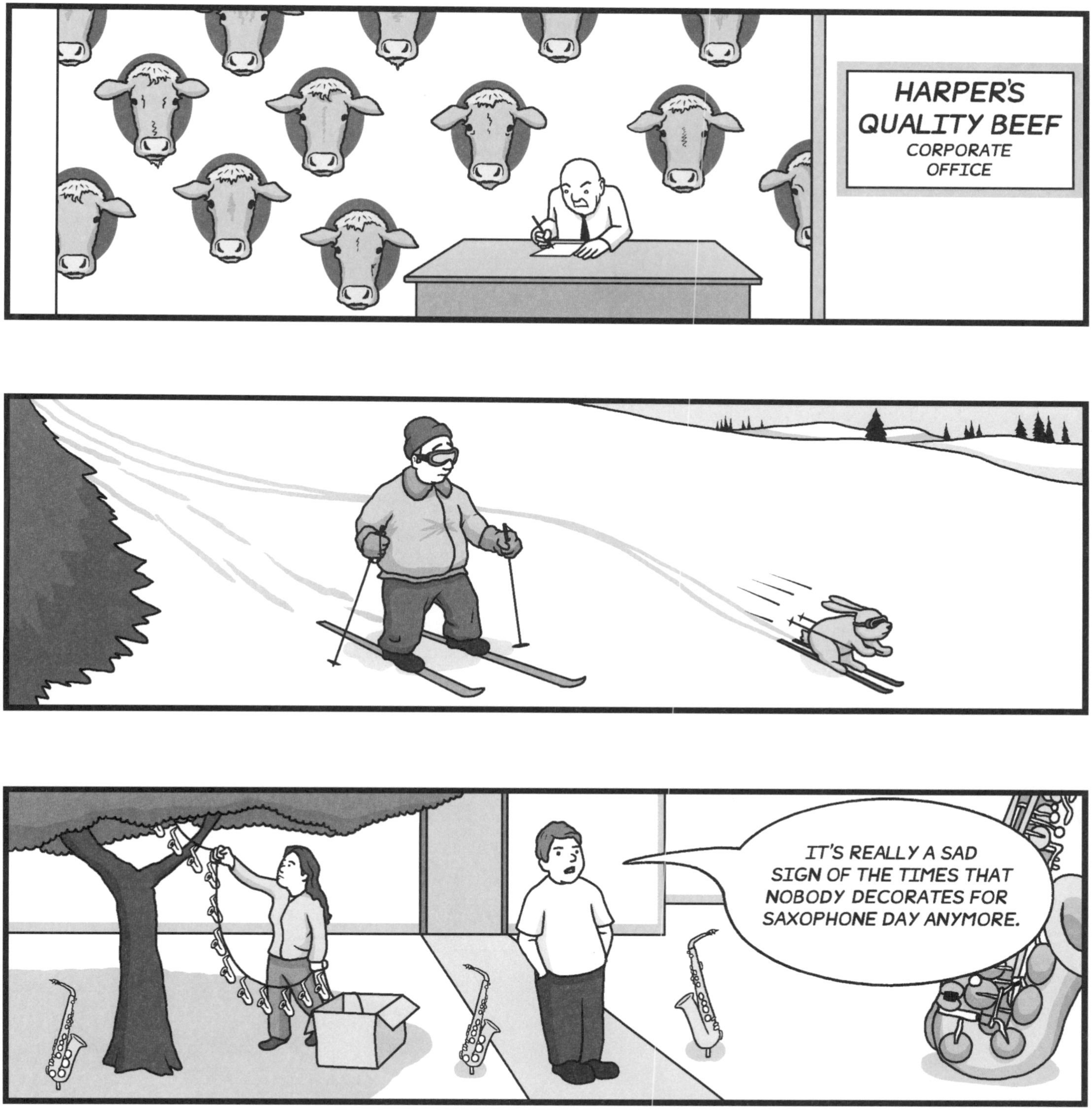
HARPER'S
QUALITY BEEF
CORPORATE
OFFICE
IT'S REALLY A SAD SIGN OF THE TIMES THAT NOBODY DECORATES FOR SAXOPHONE DAY ANYMORE.

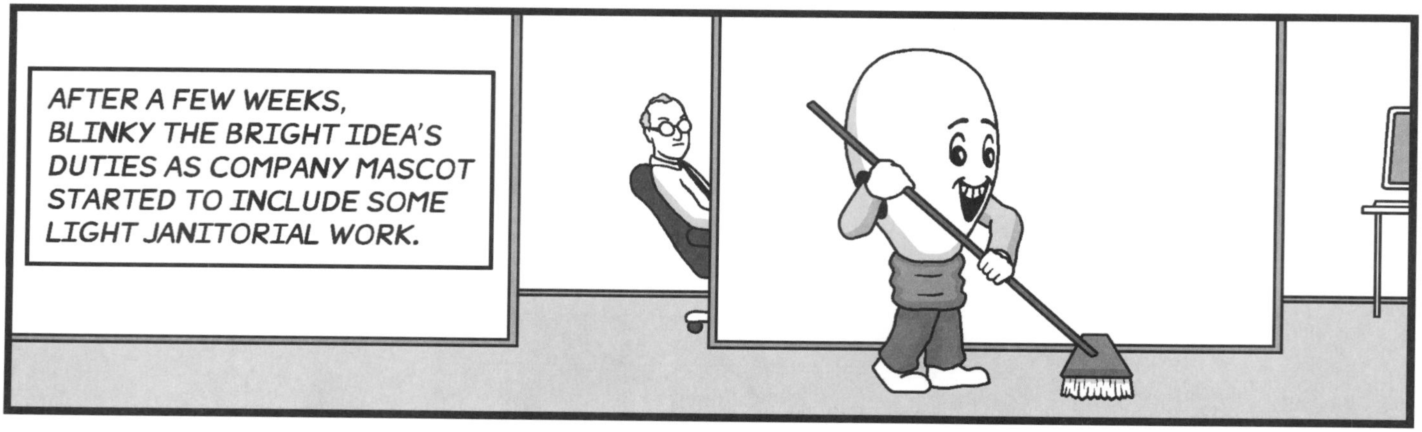
AFTER A FEW WEEKS, BLINKY THE BRIGHT IDEA'S DUTIES AS COMPANY MASCOT STARTED TO INCLUDE SOME LIGHT JANITORIAL WORK.

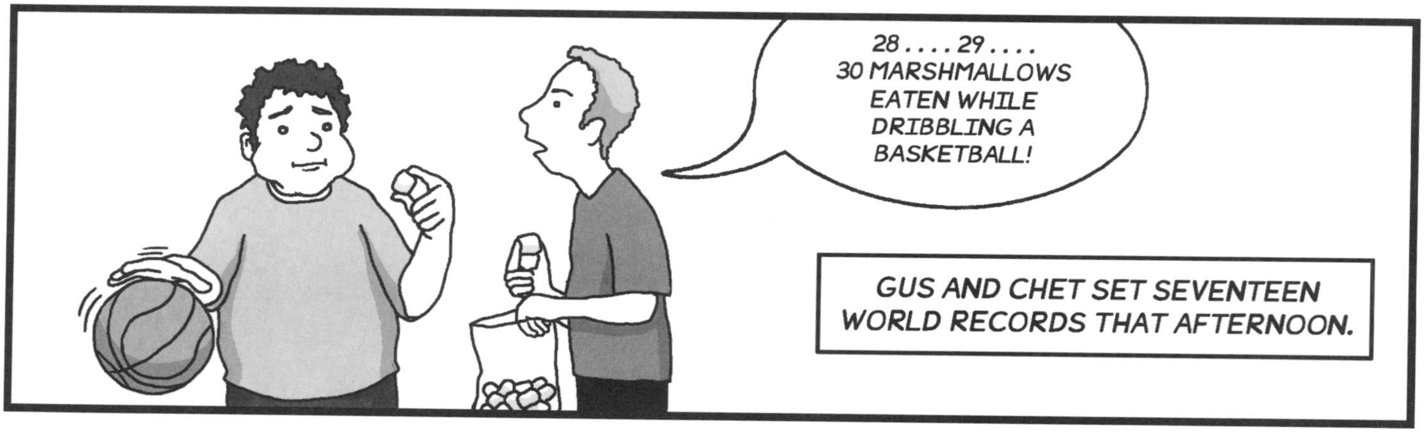
28 . . . . 29 . . . . 30 MARSHMALLOWS EATEN WHILE DRIBBLING A BASKETBALL!
GUS AND CHET SET SEVENTEEN WORLD RECORDS THAT AFTERNOON.

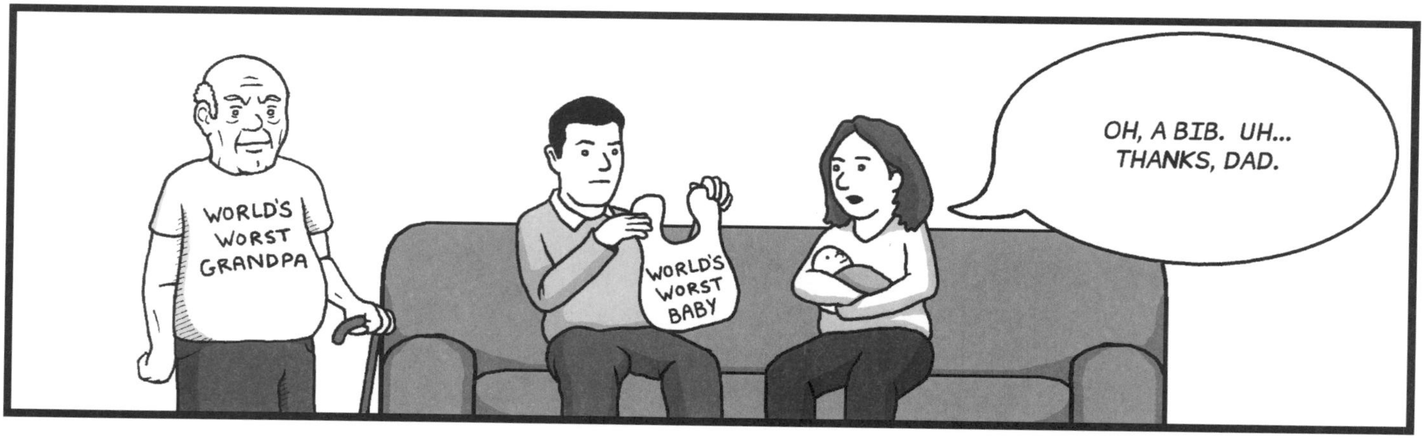
WORLD'S WORST GRANDPA
WORLD'S WORST BABY
OH, A BIB. UH... THANKS, DAD.

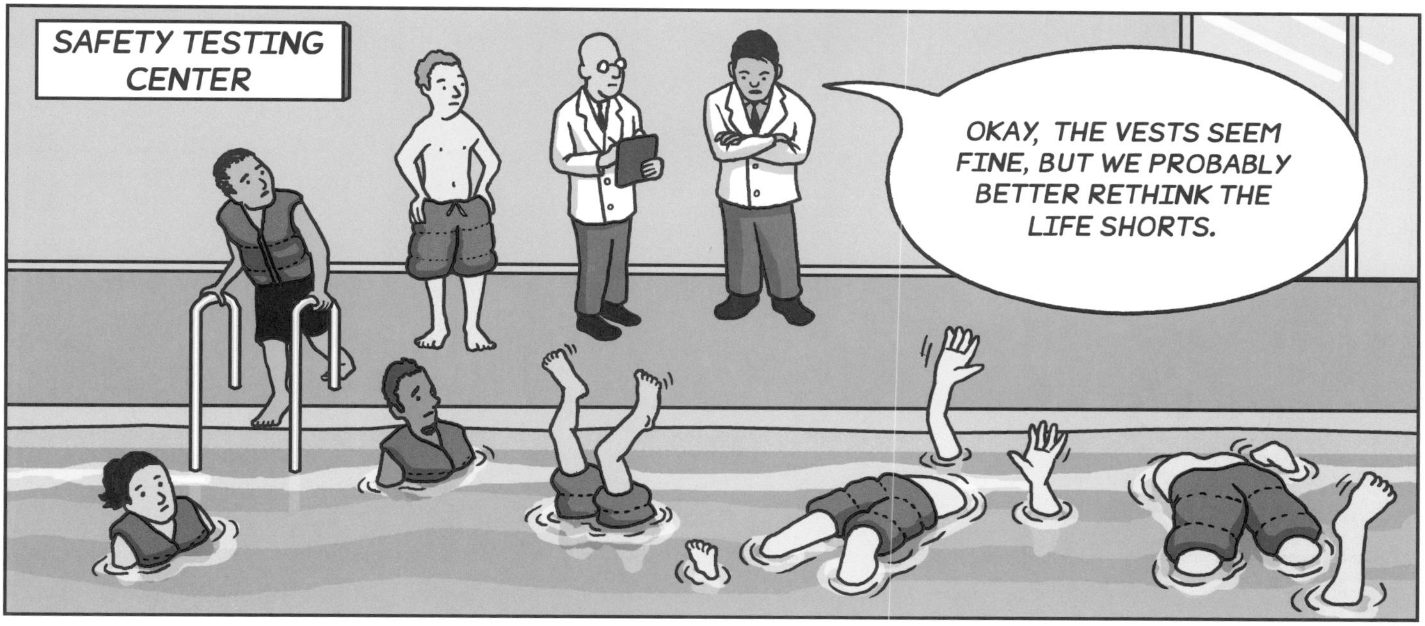
SAFETY TESTING CENTER
OKAY, THE VESTS SEEM FINE, BUT WE PROBABLY BETTER RETHINK THE LIFE SHORTS.